To M

Microsoft®
Windows® XP

SIMPLY VISUAL™

Faithe Wempen

SYBEX®

San Francisco ◆ London

Associate Publisher: Joel Fugazzotto

Acquisitions Editor: Elizabeth Peterson

Developmental Editor: Elizabeth Peterson

Production Editor: Rachel Gunn

Copyeditor: Anamary Ehlen

Compositor: Maureen Forys, Happenstance Type-O-Rama

Proofreader: Nancy Riddiough

Indexer: Nancy Guenther

Book Designer: Maureen Forys, Happenstance Type-O-Rama

Cover Designer: Caryl Gorska, Gorska Design

Cover Photograph: Randy Albritton, Photodisc

An earlier version of this book was published under the title Microsoft Windows
SYBEX Inc.

Library of Congress Card Number: 2004113396

ISBN: 0-7821-4394-6

SYBEX and the SYBEX logo are either registered trademarks or trademarks of S
countries.

Simply Visual is a trademark of SYBEX Inc.

Screen reproductions produced with FullShot 99. FullShot 99 © 1991-1999 Inbit
FullShot is a trademark of Inbit Incorporated.

Internet screen shot(s) using Microsoft Internet Explorer 6 reprinted by permiss

TRADEMARKS: SYBEX has attempted throughout this book to distinguish pro
by following the capitalization style used by the manufacturer.

The author and publisher have made their best efforts to prepare this book, and
ware whenever possible. Portions of the manuscript may be based upon pre-rel
turer(s). The author and the publisher make no representation or warranties of
accuracy of the contents herein and accept no liability of any kind including but
fitness for any particular purpose, or any losses or damages of any kind caused
from this book.

Manufactured in the United States of America

10 9 8 7 6 5 4 3 2 1

Acknowledgments

Thanks to the great folks at Sybex for their editorial and production work on this book, including Elizabeth Peterson, Rachel Gunn, and Anamary Ehlen. Thanks also to proofreader Nancy Riddiough and indexer Nancy Guenther. Great job, everyone!

Contents

Contents

Contents

Introduction

Welcome to *Windows XP Simply Visual,* the most effective tool for visual learners who want to become proficient in Windows XP.

This book is designed for visual learners—people who learn best by seeing something, rather than by reading a description of it. Traditionally, most computer books have been heavy on words and light on pictures, which is just the opposite of what works best for many people. More and more research studies these days are showing that many people learn most effectively when they can see pictures of each step of a process in addition to reading about it.

Don't let the many pictures in this book lead you to believe that it's light on coverage, however. You'll learn all the essential skills for managing files, running programs, using the Internet, and keeping your PC running smoothly, in this easy-to-follow book.

What Is Windows XP?

Windows XP is the latest version of Microsoft Windows, the most popular personal computer (PC) operating system in the world. Windows provides a graphical interface, through which you can run programs, manage files, connect to the Internet, and perform many other tasks as well. Windows serves as the mediator and translator between the human user (that's you!) and the computer's hardware components. Here is a basic Windows XP screen, for example:

Home Edition versus Professional

This book covers Windows XP Home Edition. The Home Edition of Windows XP is just what it sounds like: a version designed for use on PCs in homes, home offices, and small businesses. It has fewer features than the Professional version, and it costs less, making it more affordable for the average person who doesn't have a large company paying the bills.

The Home Edition is the right choice for the vast majority of individual PC owners. Consider Windows XP Professional instead if any of these situations apply to you:

- The computer will be a part of a large corporate network. In that case, you could benefit from the increased networking capabilities and flexibility.

- A complex security system is required. The Home Edition provides only basic password and user account security, with few fine-tuning options. If you want very specific permissions at the file or folder level, you'll want Windows XP Professional.

- You need support for multiple monitors. The Home Edition doesn't support more than one monitor at a time; Professional supports many.

- You need to connect remotely to a PC at another location. The Remote Desktop feature is available only in Professional.

- You need to use Microsoft Backup, a utility for backing up and restoring data. This program is available only in Professional. It's not the only way to back up data, however; a variety of backup programs are available from other companies.

- You want to take advantage of file system features such as disk quotas and file encryption. These are typically handled by a network administrator, and individual users will seldom have a use for them.

If you are using the computer at home, or as part of a small office containing only a few computers to be networked together, there is little reason to spend the extra money for Windows XP Professional. The Home Edition is ideal for your needs.

System Requirements for the Home Edition

If you have a very old computer, you might not be able to upgrade to Windows XP Home Edition. Check your system against the following requirements if you are not sure:

- ◆ Processor: 300MHz or higher recommended; 233MHz required
- ◆ Memory: 128MB recommended; 64MB required
- ◆ Hard disk: 1.5GB available
- ◆ Video: support for at least 800 × 600 resolution, 256 colors
- ◆ CD-ROM or DVD drive

You will need additional hardware in order to use certain features. For example, to connect to the Internet, you will need either a modem or a network, cable, or DSL connection; and to listen to music and hear sounds, you will need a sound card.

What's New in Windows XP?

There are lots of great new features in Windows XP compared to Windows 98 or Windows Me, which were the preferred home versions of Windows prior to Windows XP. Here's a quick rundown of the top new features:

Search Companion   Searching for files and folders is now easier with the user-friendly Search Companion feature. See Chapter 3.

Start menu   The Start menu has been redesigned for greater usability and faster access to the programs you use most often. See Chapter 5.

Scanners and cameras   Built-in support for many models of scanners and digital cameras means that you can transfer pictures directly to your hard disk without any special software required. See Chapter 8.

Media Player   The Media Player program has been revamped and updated for the latest audio and video formats, including MP3, WAV, MOV, and AVI. See Chapter 9.

Fast user switching   Now you don't have to log off in order for someone else to log on to the computer. You can switch freely between users while programs and documents remain open. See Chapter 14.

Online print ordering Windows XP can help you transmit digital images to an online photo processing center for hard-copy prints. See Chapter 8.

Remote Assistance A user needing help with his or her PC can send an assistance request to another Windows XP user, who can then take control of the sender's PC via the Internet and fix the problem. See Chapter 21.

These are just a few of the many enhancements and improvements you'll find in Windows XP Home Edition.

What's New in This Book?

Windows XP first came on the scene in 2001, and in the several years since then, two major updates have been released: Service Pack 1 (SP1) and Service Pack 2 (SP2). These service packs have made Windows XP more stable, secure, and feature-rich.

This book has been updated to reflect the new features in both of these service packs, so you'll have the most recent help available. Some of the new features include:

- ◆ Windows Update improvements. See Chapter 6.

- ◆ Better management of photographs. See Chapter 8.

- ◆ A whole new Windows Media Player application. See Chapter 9.

- ◆ A new version of Windows Movie Maker. See Chapter 10.

- ◆ Better home networking capabilities, including a wireless networking setup wizard. See Chapter 15.

- ◆ Several security, privacy, and usability improvements to Internet Explorer. See Chapters 17 and 19.

- ◆ Protection in Outlook Express from attachments that might potentially contain viruses. See Chapter 18.

- ◆ Enhanced security settings and a more customizable Windows Firewall. See Chapter 21.

If you don't yet have Service Pack 2, make sure that Automatic Updates is turned on (covered in Chapter 6) and let the Windows Update feature download and install the update for you.

Special Helps in This Book

In addition to the clear, step-by-step, illustrated instructions in this book, you'll also find a number of special helps:

| NOTE | Notes provide additional information or options related to the procedure being described. |

| TIP | Tips offer suggestions for improving productivity or ease-of-use. |

| WARNING | Warnings point out possible pitfalls. |

Margin notes provide information that is tangential to the main discussion or that might be useful to pursue on your own.

Glossary terms
Important vocabulary words that you should know appear in the margin, along with easy-to-understand definitions.

Chapter on the Web

If you have a disability that limits your vision, hearing, or mobility, you might be interested in the accessibility features in Windows XP. These features are covered in a bonus chapter, "Using the Accessibility Tools," which is available online. Go to Sybex's Web site, www.sybex.com. On the Home page, type the book's ISBN code, **4394**, in the Search box and then click Go. On the search results page, click the book's title to go to the page for the book.

Part 1

Navigating and Managing Files and Folders in Windows XP

In the first part of this book, you'll become familiar with the Windows XP Home Edition interface and learn how to view and manage files, folders, and disks. File management is an important basic skill that you'll use often in working with Windows, so studying this first will give you an advantage in everything else you learn about later in the book.

Navigating and Managing Files and Folders in Windows XP

1

Getting Started with Windows XP Home Edition

Microsoft Windows XP Home Edition is the latest version of the Windows operating system for personal computers. It provides an easy-to-use graphical interface for managing files, running programs, and connecting with the Internet. This chapter explains how to start and exit from Windows and the purpose of some of the items you see on-screen. You'll also learn how to open the built-in Help and Support system and how to look up information in it.

Starting Windows

Windows XP Home Edition starts automatically when you turn on your computer—you don't need to do anything special to start it. Windows takes from 1 to 3 minutes to load when you turn on the computer, and while it loads, you see messages and introductory graphics on the screen.

When Windows finishes loading, you see the Windows desktop, which is discussed more in the next section.

If the PC happens to be set up for multiple users, a screen appears before you get to the desktop, asking which user you are. Just click your username to continue, or click Guest if you don't have a username. Chapter 14 covers the setup and maintenance of usernames on a multiuser system.

Learning the Parts of the Screen

If you are brand-new to the Windows **operating system**, this section will help you get up to speed on basic navigation and terminology.

The **desktop** is the background you see on-screen. When you first install Windows XP, the picture on the background shows a green-meadow landscape, but you can change that picture (as you'll learn in Chapter 11) or remove the

Operating system

The software that creates the interface between you and your PC, so that you can issue commands. The operating system also makes the computer aware of its devices (such as disk drives and printers) and manages any connections to other computers or to the Internet.

Desktop

The background area in Windows, on which everything else sits.

picture entirely, leaving a solid-color background. Everything that happens in Windows starts from the desktop, and most of the other parts of the screen are connected to it.

Start Button and Start Menu

The Start button, in the lower-left corner, is your gateway to the **programs** you can run and the settings you can adjust. When you click the Start button, a two-column menu opens.

In the left column are frequently used programs, along with an All Programs option. Click All Programs to see a complete list of programs you can run. To run one of the programs on the All Programs list or in the left column, simply click it. You'll learn more about running programs in Chapter 5.

At the top of the right column are shortcuts to various special-purpose folders:

> **My Documents** is a storage folder for data files you create in **applications** such as Microsoft Word and Microsoft Excel. Chapter 5 covers working with programs.

> **My Pictures** is a storage folder for photographs you have scanned or transferred from a digital camera. See Chapter 8.

Program

At the most basic level, a program is nothing more than executable computer code—that is, code that causes something to happen. For example, you might run a program that sets your computer's clock to the correct date and time, or that provides an on-screen calculator for your use.

If you've used earlier versions of Windows, the Windows XP Start menu might seem strange to you. If you prefer, you can go back to the look-and-feel of the classic Start menu. To do so, right-click the Start button and choose Properties. Then click Classic Start Menu and click OK. You'll learn how to do more of this type of customization in Part IV.

Application

A program that performs a useful task, other than simply keeping the computer up and running. For example, the Microsoft Word application is a word processor. Most applications these days are complex, consisting of multiple subprograms and many interrelated files. Many people use the terms *program* and *application* interchangeably.

My Music is a storage folder for music and video clips used in Windows Media Player. See Chapter 9.

My Computer opens a file management window in which you can browse all the drives on your computer. See Chapter 3.

TIP   Earlier versions of Windows included a My Computer icon on the desktop. If you miss that, you can create a My Computer shortcut on the desktop, as explained in Chapter 7.

Local area network (LAN)

A group of computers that are physically located in the same building and are connected to one another with cables, infrared signals, or some other networking scheme, in order to share files and printers.

My Network Places helps you find and view files and folders on other computers in your **local area network (LAN)** if you have one. See Chapter 15. This shortcut doesn't appear if you don't have a network.

Farther down in the right column is an assortment of useful commands, each of which is covered later in the book:

Control Panel enables you to customize how Windows looks and performs. It's covered in Chapters 11 through 13.

Help and Support opens the Help and Support Services window, where you can get information about Windows functionality. It's covered later in this chapter.

Search helps you locate a file or folder stored on one of your PC's drives. See Chapter 3.

Run opens a text box in which you can type a command that you want to run. This is an advanced feature that beginners will seldom use.

At the bottom of the Start menu are buttons for logging off and for turning off, or shutting down, the computer. Shutting down is covered later in this chapter. Logging off is applicable only if you have multiple users set up; see Chapter 14.

Icons

Icons are the small pictures that sit on the desktop. They represent files, folders, or applications to which you might want quick access. Windows XP comes with a Recycle Bin icon on the desktop, and you can add your own favorite items there, too (see Chapter 7).

Some icons represent the actual file or folder, such that deleting the icon on the desktop will delete the original item. Other icons are merely **shortcuts**, or pointers, to the original item. Shortcut icons can be distinguished from regular icons by the small, curved arrow in the corner. Deleting a shortcut icon does nothing to the original item.

Taskbar

The taskbar is the horizontal bar at the bottom of the screen. The Start button is at the left end, and a clock is at the right end. In the middle are rectangular bars for any open applications or other windows. (If you don't have anything open, this area will be empty.)

You can switch between windows by clicking the bar for the window you want to work with. Chapter 5 goes into that in more detail.

Other programs you install may also add icons to the desktop; for example, if you have Microsoft Office installed, a Microsoft Outlook icon appears on the desktop.

Shortcut
An icon that points to an object, such as a file or folder, stored on one of the computer's drives. Shortcuts provide quick, easy access to frequently needed files without your having to place the files themselves on the desktop.

In earlier Windows versions, a Quick Launch toolbar appeared by default to the right of the Start button. See Chapter 2 if you want to enable it in Windows XP.

System tray

The area to the left of the clock in the taskbar, which displays icons for any programs that are running behind the scenes in Windows. Examples of such programs might include a virus protection utility, a fax program, or an instant messaging program such as MSN Messenger.

The area to the immediate left of the clock is the **system tray**, displaying the icons for any programs that are running in the background. Chapter 7 explains how to work with system tray programs.

> **NOTE** If you see a left-arrow (<) button there, it means that some of the system tray icons are hidden; you can click that button to display them. When the system tray is open, the button changes to >.

Using Help and Support

Windows XP doesn't come with a printed manual, but all the information that would have gone into a manual (and more) is available through the Help and Support utility.

To open Help and Support:

1. Click the Start button, then click Help and Support.

2. The Help and Support Center window opens.

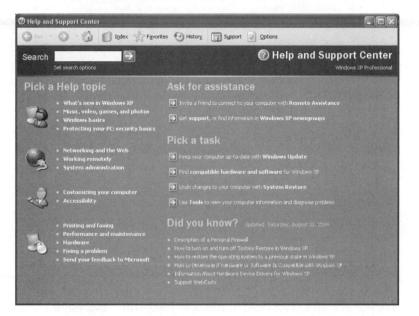

TIP   You can press the F1 key as a shortcut to performing these steps.

There are several ways to locate information in the Help and Support Center window, as the following sections explain.

Browsing Help Topics

From the main Help and Support Center window, you can browse some popular **topics** much as you might skim a book to look for a subject of interest. Just follow these steps:

1. In the left column, click a topic to browse, such as Windows Basics, for example. This opens a two-pane window.

2. In the left pane, click the subject area you want. A list of help articles appears in the right pane. Click the name of the help article you want to read, such as Start a Program.

Topic
The Windows help system uses the term *topic* rather broadly. It can refer to a subject category that contains multiple help articles or to an individual article.

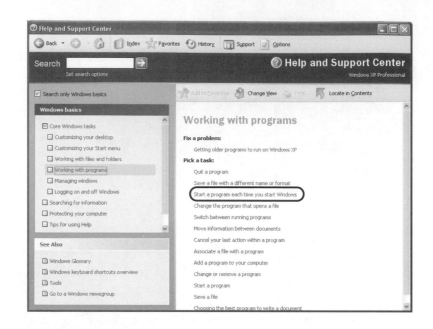

3. The article you clicked appears in the right-hand pane.

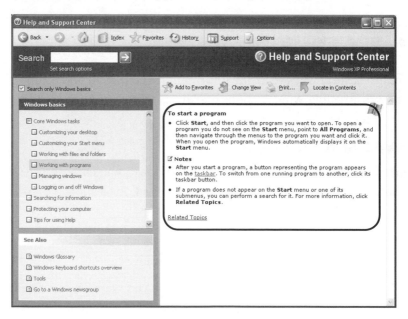

When you point to a title, the mouse pointer turns into a hand, just as when you're working with hyperlinks on a Web page. Chapter 17 talks more about Web pages.

See "Working with Help Topics" later in this chapter to learn about the features of the help articles themselves, including what the various colors of underlined text signify.

4. (Optional) If you want to return to the preceding screen, click the Back button in the top toolbar. You can return to the opening screen at any time by clicking the Home button.

Using the Help Index

If you know the name of the feature you want to learn about, you can look it up in the index. Just as in a book, the index is an alphabetical listing of terms.

1. In the Help and Support Center window, click Index. The left pane displays an index list. (If there was anything in the right pane from a previous activity, it remains there for the time being.)

2. Begin typing the word or phrase you want in the text box above the list. The index list will automatically scroll to that word's portion of the list. When you see the word you want, double-click it; or if it's a topic heading (such as "passwords" in the following figure), double-click an article beneath it. That article appears in the right pane, as though you had browsed for it.

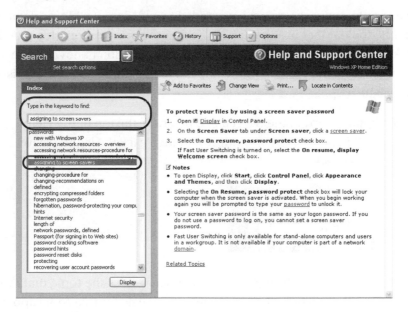

3. Some topics display a Topics Found **dialog box** when you double-click them, listing multiple topics that feature the word you chose. If that happens, click the article you want to read (in this case, "Change a user's password") and then click Display.

Dialog box

A mini-window that appears on-screen asking for more information about what you want to do. It gives you the opportunity to make choices about the way a particular command will execute, such as printing or saving your work. A dialog box can be distinguished from a regular window because it contains at least one command button, such as Display, OK, Cancel, Yes, or Close.

Topics Found

Click a topic, then click Display.

Title

Change a user's password

Password hints

Display   Cancel

Searching for a Help Topic

If you aren't sure of the official name for what you want to know, try the Search feature. It does a full-text search for a particular word and brings up a list of every topic that contains that word.

For example, suppose you have upgraded from Windows Me, and you miss that little toolbar that used to appear next to the Start button. (It's called the Quick Launch toolbar, by the way, but let's say you don't know that.) You could search for the word *toolbar,* in the hope that something about that missing item will turn up.

> There is also a search feature in Windows itself that lets you search the complete text of all files on your entire computer. You'll learn about it in Chapter 3.

1. Type a word in the Search text box near the top of the Help and Support Center window and then click the right-arrow button 🡒.

2. In the Search Results pane that appears, click the topic that most closely matches what you want. The article for that topic appears in the right pane, with all instances of the searched-for word highlighted.

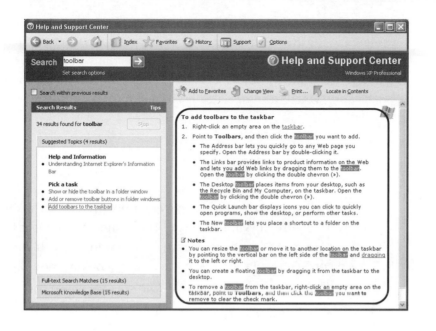

Working with Help Topics

Regardless of how you arrive at a particular help topic, you work with it the same way. The following sections explain what you can do with a help topic after locating it.

Working with Underlined Text

Depending on the article, you might see red-, green-, and/or blue-underlined text in it.

> **Green-underlined text** indicates that a definition of the underlined word(s) is available. To see the definition in a pop-up box, click the word. In the figure that follows, the green-underlined word *drag* has been clicked, and, as you can see, its definition has popped up.

Blue-underlined "Related Topics" text indicates that there are topics related to the article that you're currently viewing. Click Related Topics to see a list of topics you can jump to. In the following figure, the blue-underlined Related Topics has been clicked. Notice that the underlining goes away when the associated list appears.

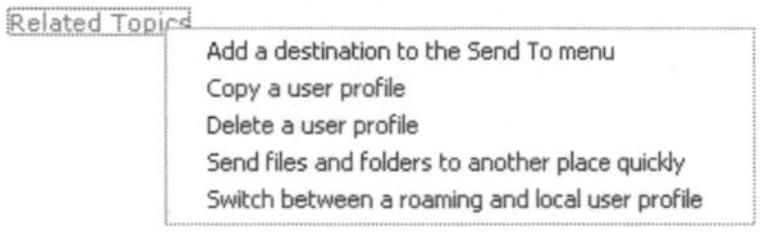

Related Topics

Add a destination to the Send To menu
Copy a user profile
Delete a user profile
Send files and folders to another place quickly
Switch between a roaming and local user profile

Blue-underlined text with an arrow symbol indicates a link to a window or feature in Windows itself. These shortcuts appear in some help topics to give you a head start in performing a task. If you were to click Add or Remove Programs in the example below, the Add or Remove Programs dialog box would appear.

1. Open Add or Remove Programs in Control Panel.

Blue-underlined Related Topics text turns red when you move the mouse over it.

A blue-underlined link to a program feature turns red after you click the link to open that feature. It remains red even after you close the feature's window.

Changing the Help Window View

By default, the Help and Support Center window takes up the whole screen. If you would like a smaller window, click the Change View button Change View. This hides the left pane, leaving only the right one (the one containing the help article).

Printing a Help Topic

We'll get into printing in more detail in Chapters 5 and 13, but here's a quick preview—enough to get you started printing the information you find in the help system.

1. Display the help topic you want to print, then click the Print button Print... .

2. The Print dialog box opens. Change any of the print settings if needed, then click Print.

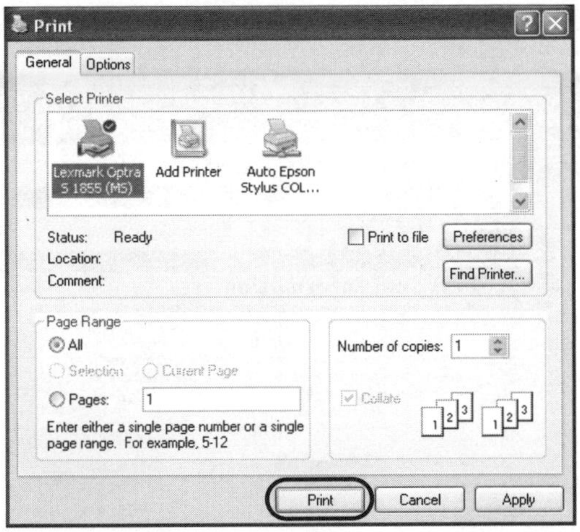

To close the Print dialog box without printing, click Cancel. See Chapter 2 for more information about dialog boxes.

Browsing Support Options

In Windows XP, Microsoft has changed the name of the help system to Help *and Support,* and there's a reason for that. You can click Support to display a selection of topics that detail how you can get more help if you still have a question or problem after reviewing the help system's offerings.

To check out the support features:

1. Click the Support button .

2. Several categories of support options appear in the left pane. Click the one you want. For example, you might click Get Help from Microsoft. In the following figure, I have clicked that, and it has connected me to a Web page that's now asking for my contact information so that help can be provided.

> **NOTE**   If you choose Ask a Friend to Help, you'll be guided through the Remote Assistance feature, which is covered in detail in Chapter 21.

[screenshot of Help and Support Center window showing Support panel and Personal Information form]

3. Work through the prompts to ask a question, look up information, or whatever you need to do.

Closing the Help System

When you are finished using the Help and Support Center window, click the red Close button ☒ to close it.

Using What's This?

Besides the formal help system that you've just seen, you can also get informal, on-the-spot help in many dialog boxes. Whenever you see a question mark in the top-right corner of a window, you can do the following:

1. Click the question-mark button ⏹. The mouse pointer changes to an arrow with a question mark.

If you have changed your desktop appearance or scheme, the Close button may not be red. Chapter 11 explains desktop appearance options.

2. Click the part of the dialog box that you would like help with. If help is available for that object, it appears. For example, here the Name box was clicked, and then, as you can see, a help box popped up.

Shutting Down Windows

When you are finished using your PC, you shouldn't just turn off the power, because that could cause later problems in Windows. Instead, you should use the Shut Down command on the Start menu to ensure that Windows shuts down in an orderly way that closes all open files and saves your work in any open programs.

When shutting down, you have two options: Turn Off and Restart. If you are going to be away from the PC, you will probably want to turn it off. If the computer is acting strangely and you want to start fresh, you will want to restart.

Turning Off or Restarting the PC

To turn off or restart the PC:

1. Click the Start button. The Start menu opens.

2. Click Turn Off Computer.

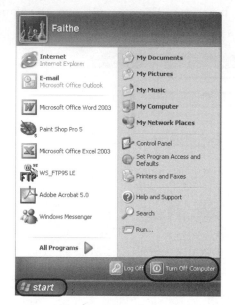

3. A box appears, asking what you want to do. Click Turn Off or Restart, depending on which you want to do.

   The third option, Stand By (or Hibernate), puts the PC in a low-power-usage mode but leaves it turned on. See the following section.

   If you chose Turn Off, Windows shuts down; and, if your computer will allow it, Windows turns off the computer's power switch. If not, a message appears on-screen instructing you to turn off the power yourself. (Don't forget that the monitor has a separate power switch.) If you chose Restart, the PC resets itself and reloads Windows. (It takes about 1 minute.)

Using Standby or Hibernate

Some computers have power management features that enable you to put them in a low-power, "sleeping" state when you aren't using them, rather than shut them down entirely. Some people prefer this to shutting down the computer—it helps them save electricity but they don't have to wait for Windows to reload when they return to the computer.

While the computer is in this state, any programs you were using remain open, along with any data files. When you want to start working again, you just press a button and everything springs awake again, just as you left it. The computer still uses a tiny bit of power to maintain its memory of the system's status, but the big energy-burning components shut down, such as the display and the hard disks.

Follow these steps to put the computer to sleep:

1. Click the Start button. The Start menu opens.

2. Click Turn Off Computer.

3. Click Stand By.

Then, when you are ready to wake the computer up, simply press its power button. (Don't hold it down; just press and release.) The computer springs back to life.

WARNING In earlier versions of Windows, some computers occasionally had trouble waking up from standby. The computer would appear to be "dead" because it wouldn't come out of its sleep state. If you experience this, try holding down the computer's power button for 5 seconds to force it to restart. Then contact your PC manufacturer to see if a fix is available.

Hibernate has the same end result as standby, but works differently. Hibernate uses a small amount of hard-disk space to store the contents of the computer's memory before shutting down completely. Then, when it wakes up from hibernation, it reads that data from the hard disk and rewrites it back to memory, and suddenly you are exactly where you left off.

Because hibernate stores memory content to the hard disk, the computer doesn't use any power at all while it is hibernating. This is great for laptops because of the limited battery power, but it isn't very useful for desktop PCs because they are always plugged in. Unless you have a laptop, the hibernate option does not appear by default.

TIP You can enable or disable hibernate and set automatic standby and hibernate thresholds using Power Options in Control Panel. You'll learn more about these power settings in Chapter 20.

2 Navigating in a Window

A lmost everything in Microsoft Windows—
programs you run, lists of files you work with,
and so on—appears in a window. Learning how to
work with a window is one of the most important
Windows skills you can master. In this chapter,
you'll learn about the parts of a window and how
to open, close, resize, and reposition a window on
your screen. You'll also learn how to work with
menus and toolbars in a window, and how to make
selections in dialog boxes that open as a result of
selecting a menu command or clicking a toolbar
button.

Parts of a Window

Window
A defined rectangular area on-screen in which a program runs or a file listing appears.

All **windows** have some common features, no matter what program you are using or activity you are performing in Microsoft Windows:

Title bar   The colored bar across the top of the window.

Window controls   The three buttons at the right end of the title bar, which you can use to change the size of the window. See the "Minimizing and Maximizing" section later in this chapter.

Menu bar   The row of words directly below the title bar. Each word represents a menu that drops down when you click on it, displaying commands you can issue. See "Working with Menus" later in the chapter.

In addition, some windows have these additional elements:

Toolbars   One or more rows of graphical buttons that provide shortcuts to common activities in the program you are working with.

Status bar   A thin bar at the bottom of the window, in which status messages appear. This bar's exact content changes depending on the program or activity.

The status bar doesn't appear by default. See Chapter 4 to learn how to turn it on.

Explorer bar   A pane that shows details about the selected file(s) or folder(s) in a **file management window**.

File management window
A term used in this book to refer generically to any window that lists files and folders on a disk.

Scroll bar A bar that appears to the right of (or sometimes below) the window content when there is more content than can fit in the window at once. It enables you to scroll the undisplayed content into view. For details, see "Scrolling a Window's Content" later in this chapter.

Toolbar

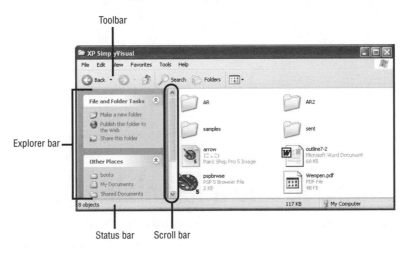

Explorer bar

Status bar   Scroll bar

Opening and Closing a Window

Nearly every activity in Windows XP causes a window to open. You can open a window containing a program by starting the program from the Start menu, as you will learn in Chapter 5. You can open a file management window by opening My Computer, covered in Chapter 3. In addition, most of the icons on the desktop represent files or utilities you can open in a window by double-clicking them.

Regardless of how you opened the window, you can close it by clicking the Close button (the big red X) in the top-right corner.

For practice, do the following to open and then close the **Recycle Bin** window:

1. Double-click the Recycle Bin icon on the desktop.

The Close button may not be red if you're not using the default desktop appearance settings. See Chapter 11 to learn about changes you can make that will cause windows and other on-screen objects to have a different look.

Recycle Bin

When you delete files, they are placed in the Recycle Bin rather than destroyed immediately. Later, after a specified period of time or when the Recycle Bin becomes too full, the files are deleted. This provides some safety from accidental deletion of important items. You'll learn more about it in Chapter 3.

2. You should now see the Recycle Bin window. Click the Close button ☒ to close it.

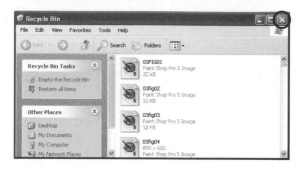

Minimizing and Maximizing

Most windows have two other buttons besides the Close button at the right end of the title bar: Minimize and Maximize. These buttons hide the window and enlarge it to its maximum size, respectively.

Minimizing a Window

Minimizing a window hides it so that it doesn't take up space on-screen, but doesn't close it. If you have many windows open at once, you might want to minimize some of them to reduce the clutter on your Windows desktop.

The minimized window appears in the taskbar at the bottom of the screen, and you can **restore** it by clicking its name there.

To try minimizing a window, do the following:

1. Double-click the Recycle Bin icon to reopen the Recycle Bin window.

2. Click the Minimize button 🗕 in the top-right corner of the Recycle Bin window.

3. The Recycle Bin window disappears, but its name still appears in the taskbar. To restore the window, click it there.

Many beginners get confused about closing versus minimizing. Closing clears the window and its contents from the computer's memory completely. If you were working on a document, for example, and you closed its window, you would need to restart your word processing program and reopen that document if you wanted to make more changes to it. Minimizing hides the window, but the window remains open and its content remains active; you can redisplay it by simply clicking its name in the taskbar.

Restore

To bring a window back to the size and position it had before you minimized or maximized it.

Maximizing a Window

Maximizing a window enlarges it so that it fills the entire screen. You might want to maximize a window containing a word processing document you are working on, for example, so that you can see more of the document on-screen at once.

When you maximize a window, the Maximize button is replaced with a Restore button. You can use this button to return the window to its normal size when you are finished working with it in maximized form.

To maximize and then restore the Recycle Bin window you've been practicing with, for example:

1. Click the Maximize button 🔲. The window enlarges to fill the entire screen.

2. Click the Restore button 🗗. The window returns to its original size.

Moving and Resizing a Window

A nonmaximized window (that is, one that doesn't fill the entire screen) can be moved and resized to fit your needs. For example, you might want to move a window out of the way so you can access an icon on the desktop, or to make a window larger or smaller to accommodate the content in it.

Moving a Window

To move a window, **drag** it by its title bar. The title bar functions as a "handle" for repositioning the window anywhere you want it.

Resizing a Window

You can resize a window by dragging the left, right, or bottom border. When you position the mouse pointer over a border, the pointer changes to a double-headed arrow, indicating that you can hold down the mouse button and move the mouse to change the window's size.

In the next section, you'll learn how to change the window's nonmaximized size and position. Those settings aren't applicable for a maximized window because it has only one size—full-screen—and only one position.

Drag
With the mouse pointer, point to the object to be dragged, and then press and hold the left mouse button while you move the mouse. The object moves along with the mouse pointer, until you release the button.

If you point to a corner of the window, the pointer changes to a diagonal two-headed arrow, and you can change both the height and the width of the window at the same time by dragging.

Scrolling a Window's Content

When a window contains more content than can fit at once in the window at its current size, a scroll bar appears. It can appear to the right of the window, at the bottom, or in both places, depending on the program, the amount of undisplayed content, and the arrangement of the content.

To scroll through the window's content, drag the scroll box up or down (or to the right or left on a horizontal scroll bar). You can also click the arrows at the ends of the scroll bar to scroll in the indicated direction.

Scroll bars appear only when there is extra content that won't fit in the window. Therefore, the scroll bar may appear or disappear when you resize a window.

The window shown here has two panes, and each pane has its own scroll bar.

If there is a lot of undisplayed content, you might find it helpful to scroll through it one "windowful" at a time. To do so, click below the scroll box to scroll down or click above the scroll box to scroll up.

Switching among Open Windows

Active window
The window that Windows is currently paying attention to. It's "on top" of the stack if the windows overlap, and it's the one affected by any commands you issue.

Part of Microsoft Windows's appeal is that you can have many windows open at once, each doing its own thing. Only one window is **active** at a time, however. In the following illustration, the active window is the Calculator; all other windows are inactive. Notice also that in the taskbar, Calculator appears different from the other window names.

If any part of the window you want is visible on-screen, you can simply click on any visible portion of it to bring it to the front and make it active. For example, to make the My Computer window active in the preceding illustration, you could click on its title bar or on any other part of it.

If, however, the active window is maximized or sized so that it completely obscures the window you want, you must resort to some other way of making the desired window active. One way is to use the taskbar. For example, if I wanted to make the My Computer window active, I'd click its name on the taskbar.

The active window's title bar looks different from that of the other windows. In Windows XP's default appearance theme, the difference is subtle; the title bar is simply a little brighter and more vibrant. In other desktop themes, the difference may be more obvious. See Chapter 11 for more on desktop themes.

Another way is to use the "Alt+Tab" method. People who are more comfortable using the keyboard than the mouse often prefer this method:

1. Press and hold down the Alt key.

2. Press and release the Tab key. A box appears with an icon for each open window.

3. While holding down the Alt key, press the Tab key to move the selector from one icon to the next. The window's title appears beneath the selected icon.

4. When the desired window's icon is selected, release the Alt key. That window becomes active.

Working with Menus

Menus are great because they help you avoid having to memorize commands that you want to issue. Back in the olden days of MS-DOS, users needed to memorize commands to type, as well as the optional parameters for each command. In a menu-based environment like Windows XP, you can simply open the menu, peruse your options, and make your selection from the list.

You'll find several kinds of menus in Windows XP. The following sections detail each type.

Drop-Down Menus

Almost every window has a menu bar directly beneath its title bar. Each word on the menu bar is the name of a menu.

To open a menu and select a command:

1. Click the menu name to open its menu.

2. Click the command you want. Depending on which command you choose, any of several things could happen:

◆ A command could execute.

◆ A feature could be selected from a group of features. Commands with a round dot next to them are selected from a group. When you make another selection in that group, the original selection becomes deselected.

◆ A dialog box could open, requesting additional information about what you want to do. Most commands that open dialog boxes have an ellipsis (…) next to them. You will learn more about dialog boxes later in the chapter.

◆ A submenu with additional commands could pop out. Commands that open submenus have a right-pointing arrow next to them.

◆ A feature could be turned on or off. Commands with check marks beside them are currently on; each time you select one of these commands, the check mark toggles on or off.

If a command on the menu appears gray or dimmed, that command is not currently available. Usually this is because the command requires you to select something before you issue it.

Notice that each menu name and each command has an underlined letter. This is its selection letter. If you prefer using the keyboard, you can hold down the Alt key and press the selection letter to make your selection.

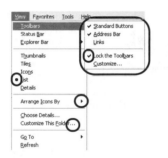

Start Menu

The Start menu is not part of a particular window; it is a Windows XP feature in itself. Clicking the Start button (in the bottom-left corner of the screen) opens the Start menu, from which you can select programs you want to run or activities you want to perform (such as searching for a certain file or changing system settings).

1. Click the Start button. The Start menu opens.

2. If you see what you want on the initial menu, click it. Otherwise, go on to step 3.

3. Point to All Programs. A menu of the programs installed on the PC appears. Some of the items on the menu represent submenus; others represent the programs themselves. The submenus have right-pointing arrows next to them.

4. Point to a submenu to open it, or click a program to run it. In the example shown, I have selected the Accessories submenu and have also selected Calculator as the program I want to open.

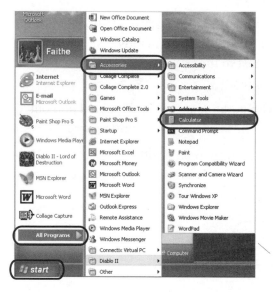

You'll learn more about starting programs in Chapter 5.

Shortcut Menus

Right-click

To click (press and release) using the right mouse button.

For most items in Windows, there are several possible actions. When you double-click (or single-click in some cases), the default action happens. But if you want one of the other actions instead, you must **right-click** the item to open a shortcut menu.

What commands you see on the shortcut menu depend on what the mouse pointer was pointing at when you right-clicked—that is, the commands depend on the context. Another name for shortcut menus is *context menus*.

Almost everything in Windows has a shortcut menu associated with it, and the commands on each shortcut menu are appropriate for the specific item. For example, when you right-click a document file, you see commands for renaming, deleting, copying, and so on. In contrast, when you right-click on the taskbar, you see commands for changing settings, arranging windows, and controlling the taskbar's toolbars.

To select a command from a shortcut menu:

1. Right-click the item or area that you want to act upon. The shortcut menu appears. When you right-click on the desktop itself, for example, this shortcut menu appears:

Arrange Icons By   ▸
Refresh

Paste
Paste Shortcut
Undo Delete   Ctrl+Z

New   ▸

Properties

2. Click (with the *left* mouse button) the command you want.

Working with Dialog Boxes

Some commands can be executed in a variety of ways, and Windows needs some guidance as to your wishes. Such commands have an ellipsis (...) after their name on the menu and open a dialog box when you select them.

Some dialog boxes are extremely simple, asking a single question and providing only a few **command buttons** for your answer.

Microsoft Word

⚠ Do you want to save the changes to "chapter 2"?

Yes   No   Cancel

Other dialog boxes have many more settings and many different types of controls with which you may specify your preferences. Here are some of the control types that you might encounter:

Tab Click to display a different page that's full of controls. Tabs are used to help organize large numbers of settings while keeping the size of the dialog box manageable.

Check box Click to toggle on or off.

Increment buttons Click the up or down arrows next to a text box to increase or decrease a numeric value incrementally, as an optional alternative to typing the number manually.

Some programs that you install place extra commands on the shortcut menus for certain types of items, so your shortcut menus may not be exactly like the ones shown in this book.

Command button
A button that makes a decision (such as accepting or rejecting your changes), answers a question posed by the dialog box, or opens a different dialog box.

Command button   Click to do something apart from this dialog box. Most dialog boxes have an OK command button that closes the dialog box and accepts the changes, as well as a Cancel button that closes the dialog box and abandons the changes. Other command buttons open additional dialog boxes.

Option button   Click a button to select a single item from a group of options. Like radio buttons on a car, when you make a new selection, the previous selection becomes deselected. (In fact, these buttons are sometimes called *radio buttons*.)

Text box   Type the desired value or setting.

Drop-down list   Click the down arrow next to the present selection, and then make a new selection from the list that appears.

Dimmed items in a dialog box are unavailable, as in menus.

Working with Toolbars

Toolbar
A collection of on-screen buttons, in which each button is a shortcut for running a certain program or issuing a certain command.

Toolbars are almost as central to the Windows operating system as menus are. You'll find toolbars in Windows XP windows, in application windows, and on the taskbar.

What's the difference between a button and an icon? Recall from Chapter 1 that an *icon* is a little picture that represents a file, folder, or application. You'll find icons on the desktop and in file management windows, and you double-click them to activate them. You'll see lots of icons in Chapter 3, when you begin working with files and folders. A *button*, in contrast, is a rectangular area on a toolbar that provides a shortcut to a particular command or program feature. Some buttons are graphical (that is, they display a picture); others are text-only. You single-click a button to activate it.

Toolbars in Windows

One of the most common toolbars in Windows XP is the Standard Buttons toolbar. It appears in file management windows, as shown below. You'll learn more about it in Chapter 3.

Many Windows-based programs also have toolbars; some programs have more than one. For example, Microsoft Word has two toolbars across the top of its window:

Toolbars in the Taskbar

You can also have toolbars in your taskbar. The most common one is the Quick Launch toolbar, which displays shortcuts to Internet Explorer, Outlook Express, and perhaps other programs too, depending on what you have installed. It appears directly to the right of the Start button.

If the Quick Launch toolbar doesn't appear, you can turn it on by doing the following:

1. Right-click the taskbar. A shortcut menu opens.

2. Point to Toolbars. A submenu opens.

3. Click Quick Launch.

One of the most useful buttons on the Quick Launch toolbar is the Show Desktop button . Clicking it minimizes all open windows, giving you instant access to the desktop. This is handy if you need access to a desktop icon, such as the Recycle Bin, but several open windows are obscuring your view of it.

There are other toolbars available in the taskbar, as you may have noticed from the submenu shown above. None are quite as useful as the Quick Launch toolbar, but you might want to experiment with them on your own:

Address   Provides an Address box into which you can enter the path to a file, folder, or Web page you want to view.

Links   Displays a toolbar based on the Links list from Internet Explorer, providing easy access to some popular Web sites.

Desktop   Displays a toolbar containing the icons on your desktop.

WARNING   If you turn on the display of multiple toolbars in the taskbar, there won't be much room left there for the names of open windows and running programs. I recommend that you use only the Quick Launch toolbar.

3 Managing Files, Folders, and Disks

F iles are the basis of almost all computing. Whatever you do—whether it's running a program, typing a memo, or optimizing system performance—you are working with a file. Folders and disks contain and organize those files. This chapter focuses on file, folder, and disk management in Windows XP, familiarizing you with concepts and skills you will use over and over in the rest of the book.

File

Computer data collected under a unique name (or at least unique to its storage location). A file can be a word processing document, an actual software program, an image, or many other types of data.

Disk

A circular platter coated with magnetic material that can store computer files. Hard-disk platters are metal; most removable disks are made of some type of plastic.

Drive

A mechanical device that reads a disk. With a hard disk, the disk and the drive are inseparable, so the terms *hard disk* and *hard drive* are synonymous. With a floppy, however, the drive is permanently mounted in the computer, and removable disks slide in and out of it. A drive has a letter assigned, such as A: for a floppy disk or C: for a hard disk.

Folder

A storage place for files. Each folder has a unique name (or at least unique to its location). A folder can also contain other folders, so you can have multiple levels of child folders within a folder.

Windows Explorer is an atypical program in that its name doesn't appear in the title bar. Instead, the name of the folder being browsed appears there.

File Management Overview

Files are necessary because computer memory is volatile—that is, whatever it contains is erased when you shut down the PC. In that way, memory is like a worktable that gets cleared off at the end of each workday, and its contents discarded. When you save something as a file, you store it on a **disk**, where it is safe until you need it again. You can think of a disk as a file cabinet in which you store files for safekeeping.

A computer has at least one hard disk, which is inside the case and cannot be removed easily. In addition, most computers have at least one type of removable **drive**, such as a floppy-disk drive, a Zip drive, or a CD-ROM drive.

Because a disk can potentially hold hundreds or even thousands of files, **folders** are used to help keep them organized. If a disk is like a file cabinet, then a folder is like a drawer in the cabinet, or like an expandable cardboard folder within a drawer. (The latter is actually a more apt analogy because computer folders are not fixed in size, but expand or contract to hold whatever you place in them.)

Folders can contain other folders—a folder can be the **parent folder** of one folder and the **child folder** of another. This allows you to create sophisticated file-organization systems. For example, you might have a Projects folder, and within that folder, you could have some word processing files that pertain to all projects in general, plus several child folders for your specific projects. Within each of those individual child folders, you could have more files that pertain generally to that project, plus more child folders for files dealing with certain aspects of the project.

In Windows, all these abstract concepts like file, folder, and disk take on a visual appearance. You can see and work with icons that represent specific files, folders, and drives on your system. You use a program called Windows Explorer to view and manipulate the files, folders, and drives on your system.

For example, on the right-hand side of the following figure, the contents of the D: drive appear. Folders are represented by an icon that looks like a paper folder, along with the folder's name. Files are listed with their name, but the icon can vary depending on the type of file. Notice in this figure that the D: drive contains a number of folders, and at the very bottom of the list, there's a single file called Log, with an icon that looks like a notepad.

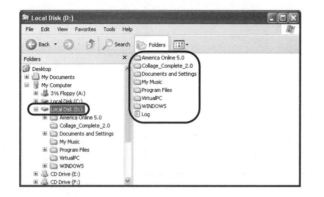

Most files on your hard disk were placed there when Windows or one of your applications was installed, and they don't require any special handling. The primary reason you will want to work with the file system is to manage the data files you create using various applications such as your word processor. You might need to move, copy, or delete those files, check on a file's name, protect a file from changes, or perform some other operation.

The following sections explain how to open a file management window and display the contents of a folder in which a particular file resides. Then the latter part of the chapter explains how to do things to the files themselves.

Opening a File Management Window

There are two main ways to open a file management window, and each results in a slightly different default display, or view:

> **My Computer** Displays an overview of all the disks on your PC, from which you can begin browsing for a specific disk or folder. It includes a System Tasks pane to the left of the listing instead of a folder list.

Parent folder
A folder that contains another folder (a child folder).

Child folder
A folder that's within another folder. The folder in which it resides is its parent folder.

In earlier versions of Windows, there was a sharp distinction between My Computer and Windows Explorer because only Windows Explorer could contain a folder list. In Windows XP, however, you can switch between the folder list and the System Tasks pane by simply clicking the Folders button on the toolbar.

Windows Explorer   Displays the contents of the My Documents folder (on the same disk that Windows is installed on) by default. This display includes the folder list, for easy navigation to some other folder or disk.

Both of these displays are "file management windows" in a generic sense because they help you manage your files. Throughout this book, if the instructions say to start in My Computer or Windows Explorer, you should open that particular window; if the instructions say simply to use a file management window, you may start in either one.

In both displays, when the folder list is turned off, the System Tasks pane appears; it goes away when you turn the folder list back on (by clicking the Folders button on the toolbar). This System Tasks pane contains shortcuts to popular activities such as moving, copying, and deleting, and you'll see it in use later in this chapter.

Opening the My Computer Window

When you want to start looking for a particular folder at a bird's-eye level of your system—with all the available drives to choose from—My Computer is the best place to start. To open My Computer, choose Start ➤ My Computer.

> **NOTE** In other words, click Start and then click My Computer. Throughout this book, I'll write multiclick commands with the ➤ symbol separating them.

In earlier versions of Windows, there was a My Computer icon on the desktop that opened My Computer; it didn't appear on the Start menu. If you miss the convenience of that icon, you can create a shortcut to My Computer on the desktop. See Chapter 7 to learn how to create your own desktop shortcuts.

Opening the Windows Explorer Window

When you start with Windows Explorer, the folder list appears automatically. The contents of the My Documents folder also appears by default. To open

Windows Explorer, choose Start ➢ All Programs ➢ Accessories ➢ Windows Explorer.

Windows Explorer is a little bit more trouble to open than My Computer, because you have to wade through several menu levels to get to it. However, if you find yourself using Windows Explorer frequently, you can create a shortcut to it on your desktop or in the Quick Launch toolbar, for quicker access. See Chapter 7 to learn how.

Opening Other File Management Windows

The Start menu also offers shortcuts to several special-purpose folders; you might want to use one of them to jump to a particular folder that you know you need to work with. Each of these shortcuts opens the folder *without* the folder list, although you can easily display it if you want it.

My Documents   Opens the My Documents folder, which most business applications use to store data files.

My Pictures   Opens the My Pictures folder, which is a child folder of My Documents and is used primarily to store pictures acquired from scanners and digital cameras (see Chapter 8).

My Music   Opens the My Music folder, also a child folder of My Documents. It's used to store music clips for Windows Media Player (Chapter 9), and some other music programs might utilize it as well.

My Network Places   Opens the My Network Places folder, which enables you to browse your local area network for access to other computers and shared resources. (More on this in Chapter 15.) If you don't have a network, you won't see this option on the menu.

Navigating between Folders

Once you've opened a file management window (either through My Computer or Windows Explorer), you can choose which drive's or folder's content you want to display. This process of navigating between folders is a very important skill that you'll use over and over as you work with Windows.

Selecting from the Folder List

One of the easiest ways to switch to a different folder is to select it from the folder list (sometimes called a folder tree, because its branches look something like a tree). When you select a folder on the list, its contents appear in the right-hand pane of the file management window.

NOTE Remember, if the folder list doesn't appear, click the Folders button on the toolbar.

Notice on the folder list that some drives and folders have plus signs next to them. They indicate that there are child folders beneath that don't currently display in the folder list. Click the plus sign to expand the list.

Some people don't like to leave the folder list displayed because it takes up so much room on-screen; they prefer to close it and leave that space for the display of the chosen folder's contents. In upcoming sections, you'll learn ways to navigate between folders that don't involve the folder list.

Conversely, a minus sign indicates that all the child folders for that folder currently appear. Click the minus sign to collapse the list and to change the sign back to a plus sign.

Moving Up and Down in the Folder System

Root folder

The top level of a disk's hierarchy, which contains all the first-level folders. This used to be called the root directory back in the days of MS-DOS, when folders were referred to as directories.

Think of the folder list as a branching root system, in which you start off with the disk at the top (the granddaddy parent folder) and then child folders within that disk, and then further child folders within some of the folders, and so on. Moving "up" in the system means moving closer to the top, or toward the **root folder**. Moving "down" means moving into a child folder within the current folder.

You have already seen in the preceding section that you can move freely between folders using the folder list. But if the folder list isn't displayed, you'll need a different method. (You might even prefer the alternative method to the folder-list method.)

Moving to a Child Folder of the Current Folder

To move down into a child folder, display the folder or disk containing the folder you want, and then double-click the icon for that folder. In this example, I'll double-click the Helpnote folder to view its contents.

The folder's contents now appear in the right-hand pane. Notice that the title bar of the screen now displays the name of the folder.

Moving Up One Level to the Parent Folder

To move back up to the parent folder of the currently displayed one, click the Up One Level button 🗗 in the toolbar. The contents of the parent folder now appear in the right-hand pane.

Using Back and Forward Buttons

When you display a different disk's or folder's contents, whatever contents were previously displayed in the right-hand pane are replaced by the new display.

If you want to return to the previously displayed contents, click the Back button 🔙 .

If you want to move ahead again to the display as it was before you clicked Back, click the Forward button ➡ .

Notice that each of these buttons has a down-pointing arrow to its right.

Clicking that down arrow opens a list of all the locations that have displayed since you opened the window, and you can choose the one you want rather than having to click Back or Forward repeatedly until your desired location appears.

In some earlier versions of Windows, such as Windows 95, whenever you double-clicked a folder to display its contents, by default it opened in a new window instead of replacing the contents in the existing one. If you want to duplicate this behavior in Windows XP, choose Tools ➤ Folder Options ➤ Open Each Folder in Its Own Window, and click OK. However, if you do this, the steps in the rest of this book may not match what happens on your screen.

The file management window in Windows is related to Internet Explorer, the Web browser program built into Windows XP, to the point where they share many of the same buttons and commands, such as the Back and Forward buttons. The History command on the Back button's menu opens the Explorer bar with history information displayed in it. This history, however, pertains only to Web pages, not to folders on your local PC—so it won't be important until you get to Chapter 17.

Manipulating Files and Folders

Now that you know how to display the desired folder, it's time to learn what you can actually *do* with the contents of that folder, and why you might want to do it.

> **NOTE** When you perform an action on a folder, everything within it (files and child folders) is also affected. For example, if you copy a folder to another disk, everything in that folder gets copied, too.

Selecting Files and Folders

As I mentioned earlier, the primary reason that most people open a file management window is to do something to a data file they've created in some program. For example, you might want to delete a letter you created using your word processor, or to copy it onto a floppy disk.

Select

To choose the object(s) that the next command you issue will affect. You can select icons representing files, folders, and disks in a file management window; you can also select text, graphics, and other data in certain applications.

Before you can act on a file or folder, however, you must **select** it. No matter what the activity, it's always a two-part equation, like a subject-verb sentence: First you select what you want to act on (the subject); then you select the activity (the verb).

To select a single file or folder, simply click it. To deselect it, click somewhere else (away from it). A selected file appears in white letters with a dark background, the opposite of unselected ones. In the following figure, I've selected the "chapter 3" file.

> **NOTE** In the default Windows XP color scheme, that dark background is blue, but yours might be different depending on the appearance options you've chosen. (See Chapter 11.)

You can select multiple files and/or folders and act on them as a group. For example, if you needed to delete 10 different files in the same folder, you could select them all and then issue the Delete command once. (You can't select multiple files or folders in different locations at once.)

If all the files/folders you want to select are contiguous (that is, listed one right after another), you can select them like this:

1. Click the first file or folder you want to select (for example, the AR folder in the next figure).

2. Hold down the Shift key, and click the last file or folder in the group (G0303 in the figure). That file and all the files in between become selected.

3. Release the Shift key. You can now perform the task, and all the selected files or folders will be affected.

If the files are noncontiguous, use this method instead:

1. Click the first file or folder you want.

2. While holding down the Ctrl key, click each additional file you want to select.

3. Release the Ctrl key. Any action you perform now will affect all the selected files or folders.

You can also select files and folders located in a cluster in the window (but not necessarily contiguous in the strict sense) by enclosing them in a "box." To do so, follow these steps:

1. Point to an area above and to the left of the first file you want to include (M0301 in the following figure).

Is "contiguous" determined by rows, or by columns? It depends on the view. You'll learn about displaying the folder content in various views in Chapter 4. In Icons and Thumbnails views, contiguous runs by rows, from left to right and then down to the next row. In List view, contiguous runs by columns, from top to bottom and then to the next column. In single-column views such as Details and Tiles, it's a non-issue. The figure shown here is in Icons view.

2. Hold down the left mouse button and drag down and to the right, creating a box around your targeted files.

3. Release the mouse button. Any files that fell within the box you drew are selected.

Moving and Copying Files and Folders

Now that you know the various ways to select files and folders, it's time to learn what actions you can take with them. Two very common actions are moving and copying. You might want to copy a file to a floppy disk to share with a friend, for example, or move some infrequently used data files to a secondary hard disk to free up space on your primary disk.

You have a couple of options for moving and copying: You can use the drag-and-drop method with the mouse, or use menu commands. I'll show you both methods in the following sections.

Moving Files and Folders

To move a file using the drag-and-drop technique, do the following:

1. If the folder list doesn't appear, click the Folders button to display it.

2. Display the folder containing the file(s) or folder(s) to be moved.

3. In the folder list, make sure the destination folder's or drive's name is visible (but don't click it to select it). If necessary, click a plus sign to expand the folder list and make the destination visible.

4. Select the file(s) or folder(s) to be moved.

WARNING Don't move program files or folders—that is, files or folders needed to run particular programs. Most programs will not work anymore if you move their files. Your safest bet is to move only the data files you have created yourself. You can *copy* any files without fear, however.

5. If you are moving from one disk to another, hold down the Shift key. (Otherwise, Windows will copy rather than move.)

6. Drag the selection to the destination folder or drive on the folder list. For example, in the following figure, I'm dragging the folder named LOD_108 to the A: drive. Then release the Shift key.

NOTE If there is a plus sign on the mouse pointer as you drag, you are copying rather than moving; press Esc and try again. If there is no plus sign, you are moving.

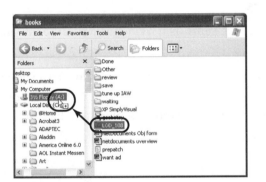

Windows attempts to guess what you want to do based on the source and destination locations. If you drag from one drive to another, it assumes you want to copy unless you hold down Shift while dragging. If you drag from one folder to another on the same drive, it assumes you want to move unless you hold down Ctrl. If you don't want to remember all that, just get in the habit of always holding down Shift when moving and always holding down Ctrl when copying.

Another way to move a file is to use the Move to Folder command on the Edit menu. This method has the advantage of not requiring the folder list to be visible.

1. Select the file(s) or folder(s) you want to move and then choose Edit ➢ Move to Folder.

The Make New Folder button lets you create a new folder on the fly. To use it, be sure to first select the drive or folder that you want as the parent for the new folder. Then click Make New Folder, type a name for the new folder, and click OK. Then click Move to complete the move. You'll learn other ways to create new folders later in this chapter.

2. In the Move Items dialog box, click the plus signs next to drives and folders until the destination location appears, and then select it. (In this example, I want to move the file to the ADAPTEC folder.)

3. Click Move.

Copying Files and Folders

Copying works almost exactly the same as moving, except for a few minor details.

When you copy with drag-and-drop, you must hold down Ctrl as you drag if you are copying within the same drive; otherwise a plain drag-and-drop will move. While copying, the mouse pointer shows a plus sign, like so:

You can also copy using the Copy to Folder command on the Edit menu, which works just like the Move to Folder command you just learned about.

Deleting Files and Folders

You will probably want to delete old data files that you no longer have any use for, to save space on your hard disk and to make it easier to locate the data files you currently need.

To delete one or more files or folders:

1. Select the file(s) and/or folder(s) you want to delete.

2. Press the Delete key.

> **TIP** To delete the selection permanently without sending it to the Recycle Bin, hold down the Shift key as you press the Delete key in step 2.

3. In the confirmation box that appears, click Yes.

There are many alternatives to step 2. Here are some of them:

◆ You can right-click your selection and choose Delete from the shortcut menu that appears.

◆ You can click Throw Away This File from the System Tasks pane.

◆ You can choose File ➣ Delete.

Renaming Files and Folders

Many people, when they start out in computing, give their data files rather generic names, such as Letter1, Memo99, and so on. They don't realize that over time, they will probably write dozens of letters, and it will be difficult to remember which letter is which.

You can rename a file easily in Windows, to give it a better or more descriptive name than the one you originally assigned.

> **WARNING** Don't rename files or folders needed to run a program, or the program might not work anymore. Rename only data files and folders that you have created yourself.

When you delete a file or folder, it isn't destroyed immediately; instead, it is moved to the Recycle Bin. You can get it back later by fishing it out of the Recycle Bin, as you'll learn later in this chapter.

As an alternative to deleting old files, you might consider moving them to a floppy disk for archival purposes, or creating a writeable CD containing those files. You'll learn about writeable CDs near the end of this chapter.

To rename a file or folder:

1. Select the file or folder.

2. Press the F2 key. The name becomes selected.

> **TIP**   Instead of pressing F2 in step 2, you can select File ➤ Rename, or you can right-click the file and then click Rename from the shortcut menu.

3. Type a new name.

4. Press Enter.

Do you need to type the **file extension** when renaming? Well, it depends. By default, file extensions are hidden for known file types; so if the file's original name doesn't show a file extension, you don't have to type one when you rename the file. In fact, if you do type one, the file's actual name ends up with two extensions, like `MyFile.doc.doc`.

However, in Chapter 4, you'll learn how to set file extensions to display in file management windows. If you rename a file with a displayed extension, you must retype the period and the extension when you type the new name; otherwise, the file will lack an extension, and Windows won't be able to determine its file type.

Creating New Folders

As you saw earlier, you can create new folders on the fly while moving or copying files with the Move to Folder or Copy to Folder command. You can also create new folders at any other time, for any purpose.

For example, suppose you want to organize your documents in the My Documents folder into separate child folders for each member of your family. You could create a folder for each person, and then move that person's document files into that folder.

You can rename only individual files and folders; you cannot rename them as a group. The Rename command isn't available when multiple files or folders are selected.

File extension

A code (usually three characters) following the filename and separated from it by a period. The extension indicates the file type, such as `.jpg` for a JPEG graphic or `.doc` for a Microsoft Word document.

To create a new folder:

1. Display the folder that should be the parent folder for the new one.

2. Choose File ➢ New ➢ Folder. A new folder appears with the name New Folder. The name is highlighted, and ready to be typed over with a new name.

Instead of choosing File ➢ New ➢ Folder in step 2, you can right-click the background of the current folder display and then choose New ➢ Folder from the shortcut menu.

---

3. Type the name for the new folder and then press Enter.

Searching for Files and Folders

It's easy to forget in which folder you have stored a particular file, but Windows makes the process of finding lost files painless. Here's what you do:

1. Choose Start ➢ Search.

A Search Results window appears, with a Search Companion pane at the left.

2. Click the category that best represents what you want to search for. These search categories restrict your search to files with certain extensions. If you don't want that restriction, choose All Files and Folders as the category.

What do you want to search for?

→ Pictures, music, or video

→ Documents (word processing, spreadsheet, etc.)

→ All files and folders

→ Computers or people

→ Information in Help and Support Center

The Search Companion pane then changes to show additional controls.

NOTE   Each of the specifications in steps 3 through 6 is optional; you can use any combination of them to build your search criteria. The more specific your criteria are, the fewer files will be returned. At any point, you can skip to step 7 to run the search.

3. (Optional) In the Part or All of the File Name text box, type the filename if you know it, or any portion of it that you do know.

To represent unknown parts of the name, you can use **wildcard** characters. For example, if you know only that it begins with W, you would use W*. Or, if you know it begins with W and contains exactly six letters, you could use W?????.

4. (Optional) If you remember that the filename contains a certain word or phrase, type it in the A Word or Phrase in the File text box.

Search by any or all of the criteria below.

All or part of the file name:

W*.*

A word or phrase in the file:

5. (Optional) If you don't want to search all hard drives on your system, open the Look In drop-down list and select a single drive that you want to search, such as the C: drive in this example.

Wildcard

A symbol that can stand for any character. There are two wildcards in Windows-based computing: * for any number of characters and ? for a single character. These same wildcards were used in MS-DOS as well.

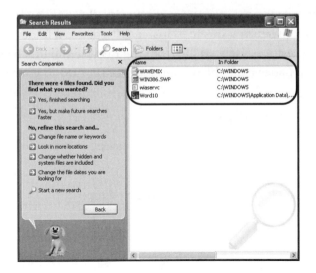

You can also click Browse from the Look In drop-down list and pinpoint a specific folder from which to start the search. That way, your search results will reflect only that folder and its subfolders.

6. (Optional) To set any other criteria for the search, click one of the other buttons to display additional controls, and make your selections. Here, for example, I have chosen When Was It Modified? and filled in some date criteria.

7. Click Search to begin the search.

Any files that match all the specifications appear on a list in the right-hand pane.

Working with Search Results

As you can see in the preceding figure, the Search Companion makes it very easy to refine your initial search after you see the results. Just follow the prompts in the Search Companion pane if you need to make changes.

Let's assume for the moment, though, that the file you were searching for *did* appear in the search results. What can you do with it now?

Locate it.   Make a note of the location listed in the In Folder column. Now you know where the file is stored, and you can find it later in Windows Explorer or through whatever program you used to create it.

Open it.   You can double-click the file to open it in the program you used to create it. (You can open a file this way from any file management window, not just from a search.)

Move, copy, rename, or delete it.   The same file management operations that you learned earlier in this chapter can be employed in the Search Results window.

Working with the Recycle Bin

As I mentioned earlier in the chapter, when discussing deleting, a file is not immediately destroyed when you delete it. Instead, it goes to a folder called Recycle Bin. You can restore a deleted file from the Recycle Bin much as you can fish out a piece of paper from the wastepaper basket next to your desk.

Restoring a Deleted File

The Recycle Bin's icon sits on the desktop, so you can open it and retrieve a deleted file at any time:

1. Double-click the Recycle Bin icon on the desktop.

The Recycle Bin window opens.

2. Select the file you want to restore. (In the following figure, I've selected Introduction.)

3. In the Recycle Bin Tasks pane, click Restore This Item. (Notice the name change here; this pane is usually called System Tasks.)

NOTE There are many alternatives to step 3. You can choose File ➤ Restore, right-click the file and choose Restore from the shortcut menu, or drag the file out of the Recycle Bin window and into some other file management window or onto the desktop.

Emptying the Recycle Bin

If you are certain you don't want any of the files in the Recycle Bin, you can empty it to free up the hard-disk space that those files are occupying. If there are only a few small files, the difference might be negligible; but when the Recycle Bin contains many large files and your hard-disk space is running short, emptying the bin is a worthwhile proposition.

You need not open the Recycle Bin window in order to empty the bin; simply do the following:

1. Right-click the Recycle Bin icon on the desktop and then choose Empty Recycle Bin.

If you are trying to delete some files to free up hard-disk space for some other purpose, keep in mind that the space is not actually freed until the Recycle Bin is emptied.

2. A confirmation message appears. Click Yes.

You can also empty the Recycle Bin while its window is open.

1. With no files selected in the Recycle Bin window, click Empty the Recycle Bin in the Recycle Bin Tasks pane.

> **NOTE** Instead of the clicking in step 1, you can choose File ➤ Empty Recycle Bin. If you do that, you don't need to worry about making sure no files are selected beforehand.

2. Click Yes to confirm.

Formatting Disks

Formatting

Preparing a disk by wiping out any existing content and creating an organizational structure in which files and folders can be stored.

IBM was the maker of the original personal computer many years ago, and its standard of disk formatting is still the standard today.

Formatting a disk creates an organizational structure called a file allocation table, or FAT, that makes it possible for files and folders to be stored on the disk. You can format both hard and floppy disks, but because formatting a disk wipes out any existing content, you will probably never have occasion to format a hard disk.

Many floppy disks sold these days are preformatted, so you may not need to format new floppy disks either. When shopping for floppies, look for disks marked "IBM Formatted." IBM-compatible formatting will work on both MS-DOS and Windows PCs.

Formatting a floppy disk can be a useful skill to know, however, in case you buy unformatted floppies (which are a little cheaper than formatted ones) or you want to reformat a floppy. Since reformatting wipes out all the content on a disk, you can reformat the disk as an alternative to deleting all the disk content using the method you learned earlier in the chapter.

To format a floppy disk, do the following:

1. Place the disk to be formatted in your floppy drive.

2. Open the My Computer window.

3. Right-click the floppy drive icon and then choose Format from the shortcut menu.

4. You should now see the Format dialog box. Leave the Capacity, File System, and Allocation Unit Size settings at their defaults.

5. If you would like a **volume label** for the disk, enter it in the Volume Label text box, replacing the label that's already there.

6. (Optional) If you are reformatting an already-formatted disk, you can mark the Quick Format check box to make the formatting happen faster.

Reformatting a disk is not necessarily better than deleting its content manually; it's just an alternative.

If the items in your My Computer window look different from the ones shown here, don't worry. You'll learn how to switch between different views in Chapter 4.

Volume label
An internal label for a disk, which shows up in My Computer next to the drive letter whenever that disk is inserted. You can use a volume label to help you remember what's on a particular disk. The label can contain up to 11 characters with the FAT file system, or 32 characters with NTFS.

When you use Quick Format, the disk's FAT is simply rewritten; the disk itself is not checked or prepared in any way. That's why you can use Quick Format only with already-formatted disks.

The Create an MS-DOS Startup Disk option enables you to create a bootable floppy that you can use to start your computer if it won't start normally. If you just want a blank, formatted floppy disk, however, you don't want a startup disk.

7. Click Start.

8. A warning message appears. Click OK to begin the formatting.

Format 3½ Floppy (A:)

⚠ WARNING: Formatting will erase ALL data on this disk.
To format the disk, click OK. To quit, click CANCEL.

[OK]   [Cancel]

9. Wait for the formatting to finish, and then click OK to accept the confirmation message.

Formatting 3½ Floppy (A:)

ⓘ Format Complete.

[OK]

10. Click Close to close the Format dialog box.

Copying a Floppy Disk

If you have a floppy disk that contains important data, you might want to make a copy of it. You can copy its contents to your hard disk and then to another floppy, but going floppy-to-floppy is faster. You can make the copy using a single floppy drive, by swapping the disks out as prompted.

To copy a floppy disk:

1. In My Computer, right-click the floppy drive and then choose Copy Disk.

3½ Floppy (A:)
Open
Browse with Paint Shop Pro
Explore
Search...

Sharing and Security...

Copy Disk...

Format...

Cut
Copy
Paste

Create Shortcut
Rename

Properties

2. In the Copy Disk dialog box, click Start.

3. Insert the disk to be copied and then click OK. Then wait for the disk to be copied into your computer's memory.

4. When prompted, insert the disk to contain the copy and then click OK.

5. When a Copy Completed Successfully message appears, click Close.

Copying Files to a Writeable CD

A new feature in Windows XP is the ability to write directly to a writeable or rewriteable CD-ROM disk. With earlier versions of Windows, you needed to use a special utility program that came with your drive.

Not all CD-ROM drives are writeable; most of them are read-only. If you have a writeable CD-ROM drive, you can use the following procedure to copy files to a blank writeable CD:

1. Open a file management window, and display the folder containing the files/folders you want to copy to the CD.

2. Place a blank writeable CD (or one with some remaining space on it) in your writeable CD drive.

There are two types of writeable CD-ROMs: CD-R and CD-RW. Generally, CD-R can be written to only once, while CD-RW can be written to multiple times. You might use a CD-R to make a backup copy of a CD-ROM, while a CD-RW might be more useful for storing daily backups. Windows XP's technique for writing to a CD-R is to assemble all the files to be written in a "staging area," and then, when you are ready, to write them as a group. As you are dragging files into the CD-R's window, it appears that you are copying them one-by-one, but the actual write operation is delayed.

Depending on your system configuration, a box may appear, asking what you want to do with the CD. If it does, as shown here, click Open Writable CD Folder Using Windows Explorer. To skip this step in the future, mark the Always Do the Selected Action check box. Then click OK.

A file management window for that disc appears.

3. Drag and drop files/folders into the window for the CD. The file and folder names appear there; a down arrow on the icon of each file/folder indicates that it hasn't actually been written to the CD yet.

4. Drag other files/folders from other locations to the CD's window if needed. Repeat until you have assembled all the content for the CD in the CD's file management window.

5. In the CD Writing Tasks pane, click Write These Files to CD.

One advantage of writing to a CD using Windows XP is that a technique called "packet writing" enables you to add more data to a CD even after you have written to it initially. The mechanics behind this aren't important for the average user to understand, but basically, it creates a new FAT for the disc each time it writes to it, including all the old content plus the content being added.

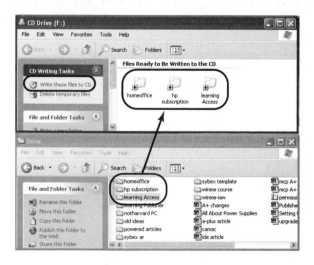

6. You should now see the CD Writing Wizard window. Type a label for the CD in the CD Name box if desired, or leave the default name (today's date); then click Next.

7. Wait for the files to be written to the CD. A progress indicator shows you how much time is left.

8. When the writing is completed, click Finish.

9. Check your newly created CD-ROM in a file management window to make sure it contains all the files and that the files can be accessed.

4

Setting File Management Options

●●●●●●●●●●●●●●●●●●●●●●●●●●●●●●●●●●●●●●

Windows XP is extremely flexible—it lets you customize almost every aspect of its operation, from how it looks to how it behaves. One of the areas you can customize is the file management window, which you worked with in Chapter 3. As you'll see in this chapter, you can make a wide array of choices about how files and folders appear and how you manipulate them.

This chapter picks up where Chapter 3 left off in describing file management, but if you're a beginner just starting out with Windows, you might want to learn more about running programs first, in Chapter 5. If that's the case, skip this chapter for now, and come back to it later.

Choosing How Files Are Displayed

Back in Chapter 3, you may have seen some file listings that didn't look exactly the way they did on your own screen. That's because you have a choice of how you want the file listings to appear. In the following sections, you'll learn how to change their appearance.

Some file settings affect only the window you are working with at the moment, or only the folder currently displayed; other settings affect all file management windows globally. In this chapter, we'll start out with the more temporary settings, and work our way to the global settings at the end.

Selecting a View

There are five views to choose from in most file management windows, ranging from very large icons to very small ones, and from very little detail to lots of detail. Each view has its own usefulness. Before I describe each of the views, however, I'll tell you how to change your view from within any folder.

To change the view, open the View menu and then click the view you want: Thumbnails, Tiles, Icons, List, or Details.

Windows saves your view preference for that folder, and the next time you display its contents, the files will appear in your chosen view. However, the setting doesn't affect any other folders, so if you change to a different folder, you must set the view again.

Here are brief descriptions and illustrations of the five views:

> **Thumbnails view**   If the file is a graphic in a supported format, a miniature (that is, "thumbnail") version of the picture appears in place of the icon. Or, if the item is a folder that contains files in supported formats, tiny versions of the first few files appear on the folder icon's face.

Tiles view   The filename appears to the right of the icon, along with the file type (if known) and the file size.

Icons view   This view is the same as the Large Icons view from previous versions of Windows. It shows the icons at a medium size with the name (and no details) beneath, and it fits even more files in the window at once without scrolling.

Recall from Chapter 3 that a file's extension is a three-character code after the filename that tells Windows the file's type. For example, you might have `Config.bak` and `Config.sys` in the same folder; the `.bak` extension indicates that `Config.bak` is a backup copy.

List view   The most compact view, List view displays the names of the files in columns; it can fit many more files in a window than other views.

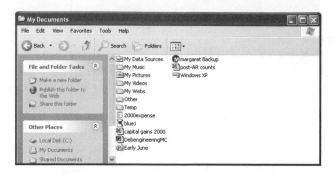

Details view   This view is like List view except that the filenames appear in a single column and there are additional columns containing other information such as file size and date last modified. You can sort by any of the columns by clicking its heading.

Changing the Displayed Details

In Details view, certain details about the files appear in columns. You can change what details appear there:

1. Choose View ➢ Choose Details.

2. You should now see the Choose Details dialog box. Select or deselect the details you want to appear. To do so, you can either click the check box next to a detail or click its name and then click the Show or Hide button.

3. To change the default width of a particular column, select its title in the list and then change the number in the Width of Selected Column (in **Pixels**) text box. Decrease the number to make a column thinner; increase it to make the column wider.

4. To rearrange the column order, click a detail and then click Move Up or Move Down.

5. Click OK to close the dialog box.

Changing File Sort Order

When you are trying to locate a certain file or folder in a long list, you might want to sort the listing by a particular criterion. Some examples: If you are looking for all your Excel files, you can sort by file type; or if you are looking for a file that begins with a certain letter, you can sort by filename. And if you are looking for a file you worked on earlier today, you can sort by date.

To change the sort order:

1. Choose View ➤ Arrange Icons By.

If you select a lot of details, you will probably need to scroll to the right to see all the details unless your file management window is very large or even maximized.

Pixel

A colored dot that makes up the display. The number of total pixels on the display depends on the screen resolution you are using, as you'll learn in Chapter 11. An average resolution is 800 pixels across by 600 pixels down.

2. In the submenu that appears, click the way you want the icons arranged (such as Size in this example).

The files re-sort themselves to match the order you specified. Folders appear first, followed by files.

The Show in Groups option on the submenu creates a heading for each sort category. (Shown in the following figure are the headings for Type.) If you sort by Name, the first letter of each name is a category. If you sort by Modified date, the divisions are based on the last access to the file, such as This Year and Last Year. Each sort option has its own grouping method.

The Auto Arrange option sets the display to automatically re-sort the list whenever it becomes out of order. For example, when you create a new folder within the current folder, that new folder is placed, by default, at the bottom of the window. When you close and reopen the window, the new folder gets sorted in with the others; but until you do so, or until you refresh the display or change the sort method, the folder remains at the bottom. If you turn on Auto Arrange, however, it snaps into its appropriate spot immediately.

Displaying or Hiding Window Controls

There are a number of optional features in a file management window, and you can turn them on and off using the View menu. These settings apply to the window for as long as it is open, no matter which folder's contents you are viewing; but when you close the window, the settings are not retained.

Displaying or Hiding the Status Bar

The status bar, when displayed, appears at the bottom of the window and provides information about whatever is selected. For example, when you select a group of files, the status bar reports the total number of files selected and the disk space they collectively occupy.

The status bar is hidden by default. To turn it on (or off again), choose View ➤ Status Bar.

Controlling the Explorer Bar

The Explorer bar is an extra pane that sometimes appears in a file management window to help with certain tasks. For example, the Folders list that you worked with in Chapter 3 when managing files appeared in the Explorer bar. The Folders list is only one of several different displays that can appear in that space.

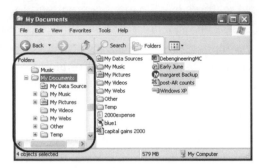

Other displays that can appear in the Explorer bar include the Search pane, which you can use to search your hard disk for misplaced files (covered in Chapter 3), and a History list that displays the names of Web pages you have visited recently using Internet Explorer.

Since, in most cases, content appears in the Explorer bar as part of some other activity, such as searching or Web browsing, you will seldom need to turn on the Explorer bar manually and select content to appear in it.

But if you do want to change the content of the Explorer bar, simply choose View ➤ Explorer Bar and then click the content that you want to appear in it (such as Folders in this example). The Explorer bar opens at the left side of the file management window, with the chosen content displayed.

Unlike other optional window features, you don't turn the Explorer bar off by reselecting it from the menu. Instead, you click the Close (X) button in the bar's top-right corner to close it, as you would close a separate window.

In case you are curious about the various content choices you can make on the Explorer Bar submenu, here's a quick summary of them:

Search   Displays the Search pane, the same as if you had opened the Start menu and clicked Search.

Favorites   Displays the Favorites list from Internet Explorer. The Favorites list is a collection of Web addresses you create yourself, as you'll learn in Chapter 17.

Media   Displays a media player, which you can use to control media clips. For example, if you display the contents of a folder that contains audio clips, you can select one of them and then use the controls in the Media pane to play it. This is different from the stand-alone Windows Media Player, which you'll learn about in Chapter 9.

History   Displays the History list from Internet Explorer. The History list is a log of the Web sites you have visited recently.

Folders   Displays the Folders list that you are already familiar with from Chapter 3.

The remaining two options on the Explorer Bar submenu don't control the Explorer bar content per se, but rather an additional pane at the bottom of the window:

Tip of the Day   Displays helpful hints for using Windows XP.

Discuss   Displays a toolbar of buttons that are useful when working with newsgroups or other online discussions.

Setting Folder Options

Folder options apply to all folders, not just the selected one, and they apply permanently, not just as long as the current file management window is open. These are global settings that you adjust once and then don't have to change again (unless you change your mind about your preferences, of course).

To change folder options, open the Folder Options dialog box from any file management window:

1. Choose Tools ➢ Folder Options.

2. In the Folder Options dialog box, change the folder settings as desired:

Tasks   You can choose whether to show the File and Folder Tasks pane (the blue-framed pane that contains shortcuts to common tasks and that appears when the Explorer bar is not present) or whether to use Windows classic folders instead, which does not include the pane.

Browse Folders   The default is Open Each Folder in the Same Window. When you double-click a folder to open it, its contents replace the previous contents in the same window. This prevents a lot of windows from opening that you will need to close later, thereby saving you time. Alternatively, you can select Open Each Folder in Its Own Window.

Click Items as Follows   The default here is Double-Click to Open an Item (Single-Click to Select). That's the way you've been taught to do things throughout this book. The alternative, Single-Click to Open an Item (Point to Select), makes Windows work more like a Web page.

3. Click OK to accept your changes.

Opening each folder in its own window was the default in Windows 95, so you might want that setting if you've upgraded from Windows 95 recently and want to feel more at home in Windows XP.

Setting Folder Viewing Options

The final options you'll learn about in this chapter deal with file management in a very global way. They are options that affect all displays in which filenames appear. This can include the Save and Open dialog boxes in applications, for example, and your e-mail program when you are selecting file attachments for e-mail.

To control the way files and folders are displayed in a global way:

1. Choose Tools ➤ Folder Options.

2. Click the View tab.

3. In the Advanced Settings pane, under Files and Folders, select or deselect any of the check boxes as desired.

There are many more settings than can be covered in a book of this size, but here are a few of the most common ones:

Hidden Files and Folders   The default is Do Not Show Hidden Files and Folders. If you choose Show Hidden Files and Folders instead, any files or folders that have the Hidden attribute will appear in file listings, but they will appear slightly dim or faded to indicate that they are hidden.

Hide Extensions for Known File Types   This option is turned on by default. More experienced Windows users might want to turn it off so that they can see the file extensions; this can help distinguish between listed files that have the same name but different extensions.

> To set a file or folder to have the Hidden attribute, right-click it, choose Properties, and then mark the Hidden check box in its Properties box.

NOTE   You'll need to scroll down in the Folder Options dialog box to access some of the options listed here.

73

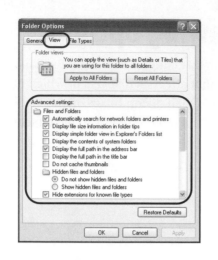

Remember Each Folder's View Settings   Also on by default, this setting is what makes it possible for Windows to reopen a folder using the same view settings as you were using the last time you closed it.

Restore Previous Folder Windows at Logon   This option is off by default, but you might want to turn it on. If you shut down Windows with file management windows open, those same windows will reopen at startup if you mark this check box.

Show Control Panel in My Computer   This setting is also off by default. Earlier versions of Windows included a Control Panel icon in the My Computer window. Mark this option to have that happen in Windows XP as well.

4. Click OK to close the dialog box.

Part 2

Running Programs with Windows XP

In this part of the book, you'll learn about programs—how to run them, how to install and remove them, and how to organize them on your desktop for quick, easy access. You'll start learning about programs by using the Windows accessories as examples. Then you'll learn how to install new programs that you buy on your own, and how to manage the list of installed programs. Finally, you'll learn how to customize the Start menu and the desktop with shortcuts to your favorite programs.

Running Programs with Windows XP

5 Program Basics and Exploring Accessories

N ow that you've got a handle on windows and files, it's time to learn about the activity that you probably bought a computer for in the first place—running programs.

This chapter has two purposes: to teach you about Windows programs in general and to introduce several of the most popular and versatile Windows accessories. As you learn about each of the accessories discussed here, you'll pick up progressively more program skills—skills you'll use over and over again. We'll begin with something very simple—the Calculator—and learn about program menus. The Notepad text editor will introduce you to file saving, opening, and printing; WordPad will help you understand text formatting; and Paint will demonstrate graphics editing.

Starting a Program

The Start menu is your one-stop shop for starting any program. There might be alternative ways to start certain programs, such as shortcuts on the desktop, but the Start menu method always works, too.

1. Click the Start button. The Start menu opens.

2. If the program's name appears, click it, and you're done. The program starts. If not, continue to step 3.

If the program you want to start isn't on the Start menu, perhaps it hasn't been installed yet; see Chapter 6 to learn about installing programs.

NOTE The first level of the Start menu shows shortcuts to programs you have run most frequently or most recently. You'll learn how to change which programs appear here in Chapter 7.

3. Point to All Programs. A submenu appears.

4. If the program you want appears on the menu, click it and you're done. If not, continue to step 5.

5. Point to the folder containing the program. Another submenu opens.

You can either point to or click All Programs and other submenu names; they open either way.

6. Keep moving through levels of submenus until you find the program you want to run (such as Notepad in this example), and then click it.

The program starts.

Exiting a program is the same as closing any other window: Click the Close (X) button in the top-right corner of the window.

As practice, try starting the Calculator **accessory**. To do so, choose Start ➢ All Programs ➢ Accessories ➢ Calculator.

Accessories

Small, useful programs that come with Windows. Each of these accessories serves a unique function, such as word processing, drawing, or performing math calculations.

79

A program window is much like a file management window, so you'll feel right at home after your experiences in Chapters 3 and 4. Each program window, for example, has a title bar, a menu bar, and window controls, and they work the same as in a file management window.

The menu content is different, of course, because the menus are designed for the specific activities of that program. For example, Calculator has three menus: Edit, View, and Help.

The main difference between programs is the content of the center area, also called the *work area*. In some programs, such as a word processor, the work area is a big blank space. In other programs, such as a spreadsheet, it's a grid. Still other programs, such as Calculator, provide buttons there that you can click. Every program is different, so let's look at a few examples.

Playing with Calculator

The main part of the Calculator window resembles a real hand calculator, with number and math-operator buttons. You can click the buttons the same as you would press the buttons on a hand-held model, and a text box displays the result just as an LED on a calculator would.

For example, let's say you want to multiply 128 times 35.4. Here's how you would do it:

1. Enter the number 128 by clicking the calculator buttons, or by typing it using the number keys on your keyboard.

2. Click the * button (which stands for Multiply), or press the * key on the numeric keypad on your keyboard.

Many people find it easier to use the keyboard's numeric keypad (at the right end of the keyboard) than to click the number buttons. Make sure NumLock is set to On, however, or the numeric keypad will function as arrow keys rather than numbers.

3. Enter the number 35.4.

4. Click the = button, or press Enter.

The result, 4531.2, appears in the Calculator window.

5. Click the C button (which stands for Clear) to clear the calculation and make way for another.

Most programs—Calculator included—have additional features besides the obvious, and you can look for them by opening the menus and seeing what commands you have to choose from. For example, Calculator's Edit menu shows two commands: Copy and Paste. The Copy command gives a clue that you can copy the results of your calculation onto the **Clipboard** and then paste them into some other program. The Paste command's presence indicates that you can also paste numbers copied from some other program into Calculator.

Calculator's View menu offers a choice between Standard and Scientific. If you choose Scientific, a wider array of buttons appears, allowing you to use extra functions useful for scientific calculations. To change to Scientific view, choose View ➤ Scientific.

The CE button stands for Clear Error, and it clears only the last entry, not the entire formula.

Clipboard
A holding area in memory, into which you can place snippets of data from various programs, and then paste them into other programs (or into a different location in the same program). This makes it easy to transfer data of different types between programs.

The controls of Calculator change to the Scientific ones, as shown here.

Notice the keyboard short-cuts listed next to some of the items on the View menu. You have the option of pressing the listed key instead of opening the menu and selecting the command.

Exploring a Program's Help Feature

Almost all programs have a Help menu, through which you can access a help file designed specifically for that program.

Let's look at the help system in Calculator, since it's fairly typical of the help systems in all Windows accessory programs.

1. Choose Help ➢ Help Topics.

A Calculator help window opens.

2. To browse the help system, click the book icon at the top of the left pane. A series of sub-books opens. Continue clicking through book levels to find the topic you want to read about.

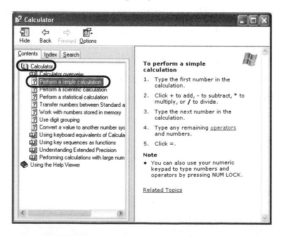

3. To look up a topic in an alphabetical index, click the Index tab. Then enter the word to look up, just as with the Windows help system (Chapter 1). In this example, I wanted directions for calculating the standard deviation.

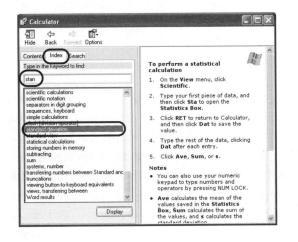

4. To search for a topic, click the Search tab. Then enter the word for which you want to search, and click List Topics.

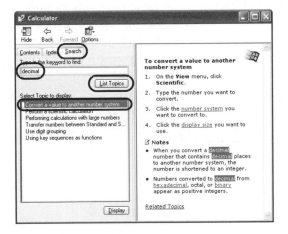

5. To close the help window, click its Close button.

Working with Notepad

Notepad is a text editor. You can use it to read, compose, and edit **plain-text** files. This is not the same as word processing; word processing involves both

Plain text

Text without any formatting—that is, the characters (letters, numbers, and symbols) only. Other names for this format include *text-only* and *ASCII*.

text and formatting, and you'll see it in action in the upcoming section on WordPad.

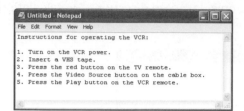

A text editor can be useful when you are creating a document to be delivered electronically—perhaps sent as an e-mail attachment or placed on a floppy disk—and you aren't sure what word processing software the recipient will have access to. This is more of an issue with recipients who don't use Windows, because anyone who uses Windows can work with the WordPad word processing format. But for people on Macintosh, **Unix**, or **mainframe** computer systems, you can't assume that any word processor you use will produce a document that they can read. So, to ensure compatibility, you must fall back to the text-only format that Notepad generates.

> **NOTE** Most word processing programs, including WordPad, have the option to save the file in a text-only format, so you don't necessarily have to use Notepad whenever you want to create a text-only file. It's being covered in this chapter primarily because it's a simple example of a text program.

To start Notepad, choose Start ➢ All Programs ➢ Accessories ➢ Notepad.

Unix

An alternative operating system to Windows, mainly employed these days by Internet hosting services and large corporate network servers. The very popular Linux operating system is a close, younger relative of Unix.

Mainframe

A large computer, typically in a big-business setting, that concentrates all the processing power in a single machine. It then doles out its abilities as needed to "dumb terminals"— workstations with keyboards and monitors but no processors or memory of their own. Such systems are typically incompatible with programs that run on Windows-based PCs.

The Notepad program opens, displaying a blank area into which you can type.

Typing in Notepad

To start using Notepad, simply start typing. The text appears in the work area. Press Enter to start a new paragraph. You don't need to press Enter to start a new line. (If you can't see the whole paragraph at once, turn on word wrap, as described in the next section.)

To edit the text, use the following procedures:

To	Do This
Move the **insertion point**	Click where you want it, or use the arrow keys
Delete the character to the left of the insertion point	Press Backspace
Delete the character to the right of the insertion point	Press Delete
Delete a block of text	Drag across the text to select it and then press Delete

Turning on Word Wrap in Notepad

By default, Notepad doesn't use **word wrap**. If you keep typing after you reach the right edge of the screen, the display will scroll—the cursor will not move to the next line. This is by design, because some people use Notepad to write programming code, in which line breaks are significant.

Insertion point
The flashing vertical line that indicates where text you type will be inserted. Also called the *cursor*.

Word wrap
A standard feature in most word processing programs (and optional in most text editors) that automatically breaks a paragraph to the next line when it becomes too wide to fit on-screen in the program window's current size. It doesn't affect the document, only the display. If you resize the window, the lines break differently.

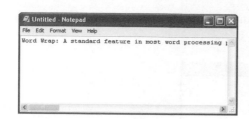

However, if you would like to be able to see all the text without having to scroll, you can turn on word wrap, so that the entire paragraph flows from line to line, changing as needed as the size of the window changes.

To turn on word wrap, choose Format ➢ Word Wrap.

You must turn on word wrap every time you use Notepad; it doesn't remember your preference.

Working with Data Files

Once you create something in a program like Notepad, you will probably want to save it and/or print it. The skills for saving and printing are basically the same in almost all programs, but since you're already working with Notepad, we'll use it as our example here. Then, when you learn about other programs like WordPad and Paint later in the chapter, you'll already be familiar with the operations.

Saving a File

When you save a file, you copy what is on screen to your hard disk, and give it a name, so that you can reopen it later. If you don't save your work, it's lost when you exit the program in which you created it.

To save in Notepad—or almost any other program—follow these steps:

1. Choose File ➢ Save.

TIP Instead of step 1, you can press Ctrl+S.

If you saved this file previously, you are done at step 1. Notepad resaves the file with the same name and in the same location as before. See the next section, "Resaving with a Different Name," if needed.

2. In the Save As dialog box, type a name for the file. The insertion point should already be in the File Name text box, but if it's not, click there to select the default name already there and then type to replace it.

3. Click Save. The file is saved under the name you specified.

If you are going to share the file with someone who doesn't use Windows, limit the filename to eight characters and no spaces. This will ensure compatibility, because some operating systems, such as MS-DOS, require filenames of eight characters or less.

Resaving with a Different Name

If you want to rename the file, use a file management window, as you learned in Chapter 4. You can also use a file management window to copy the file and then rename the copy if you want an additional copy under a different name.

However, you might find it easier to simply resave the file under a different name. You can do this from the program in which you created the file, so you don't have to go to the trouble of opening a file management window.

1. Choose File ➢ Save As.

2. In the Save As dialog box, type a different name in the File Name text box.

3. Click Save. The copy is saved.

Saving in a Different Location

The default save location for most programs is the My Documents folder. In most cases, it's a good idea to accept this default, because then you don't have to remember where you have saved this or that file—they are all in a central location. You can create child folders within My Documents to organize files if needed (see Chapter 3).

However, if you do want to save directly to a different location, you can specify that location in the Save As dialog box by navigating to a different folder. This is somewhat like navigating between folders in a file management window, but the interface is different.

To change the save location in the Save As dialog box:

1. Click the down arrow next to the Save In box. A list of the drives on your system appears. This list also includes some special locations not associated with a particular drive, such as Shared Documents and My Network Places.

2. Click the drive or other location to which you want to save. In this example, I chose Local Disk (C:).

NOTE   In some programs' Save As dialog box, a Places bar appears to the left of the folders, providing icons for My Documents, Desktop, and a few other special locations. If you are working in such a program, you can click one of those icons to jump to one of those folders.

---

3. You should now see a list of all the folders in that location. Double-click the folder you want ("books" in this example). You might have to double-click through several layers of child folders to get to it.

4. Continue saving normally.

To move up a level in the folder hierarchy (for example, if you made a mistake in double-clicking a particular folder), click the Up One Level button 🗁. It's the button that looks like a folder with an up arrow on it. The exact appearance of the button varies depending on the program.

To create a new folder on the fly, display the folder in which you would like to place the new folder, and then click the New Folder button 🗁. You'll be prompted for a name; enter it and click OK.

Opening a File

After you have saved a file, you can reopen it at any time. You might want to make changes to it, for example, or print additional copies. (Printing is covered in the next section.)

To open a file:

1. Choose File ➢ Open.

If the file you want to open doesn't appear on the list, but you are sure it's in the current folder, check the Files of Type setting. You might need to open that drop-down list and choose another file type. Reason: Some programs can open files with more than one extension, but only the files of one particular extension are shown by default in the Open dialog box. For example, sometimes a text file will have the name **Read.me**. Since **.me** is not a recognized file extension for a text file, it won't appear in Notepad's Open dialog box by default; you must change the Files of Type setting to All Files in order to see and select it.

2. The Open dialog box that appears looks a lot like the Save As dialog box. Click the file you want to open. If needed, change to a different location, as you learned in the preceding section.

3. Click Open.

The file opens.

Printing a File

In most cases, you will distribute your work to other people on paper rather than via computer, so printing is an important skill to master. Windows interacts directly with your printer, sending it the appropriate codes automatically; all you need to do is issue the Print command and specify a few details like the number of pages, and Windows will do the rest.

To print a file, you first need to make sure your printer is set up correctly in Windows. Chapter 13 covers this, so turn there if printing doesn't work as expected.

1. Choose File ➤ Print.

File	Edit	Format	View	H
New		Ctrl+N		
Open...		Ctrl+O		
Save		Ctrl+S		
Save As...				
Page Setup...				
Print...		Ctrl+P		
Exit				

2. Adjust any print settings in the Print dialog box as needed.

The Print box's controls vary somewhat depending on the program, but almost all programs let you specify a number of copies. Some of them also let you enter a page range (if you don't want to print every page of a multipage document) and choose which printer to use (if you have more than one available).

3. Click Print. (In some programs, the button is named OK instead.)

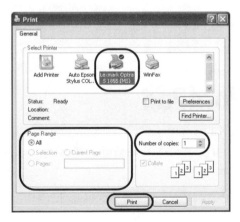

Your document prints.

Exiting a Program

As mentioned earlier, you can exit from a program the same way that you close any window: by clicking its Close (X) button in its top-right corner. If you have any open data files with unsaved changes, you are prompted to save your work as shown in the next figure; then the program closes.

There are sometimes alternative ways to exit a program, depending on the program. For example, some programs have an Exit command; choose File ➤ Exit.

You are prompted to save any open data files, and then the program closes.

Working with WordPad

WordPad is a word processing program. It's a lot like Notepad, except that it allows you to format the text. You'll probably find yourself using it a lot more than Notepad because of its greater flexibility.

To start WordPad, choose Start ➤ All Programs ➤ Accessories ➤ WordPad.

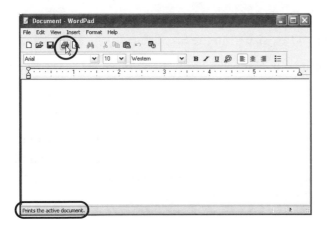

The WordPad program opens, with a blank document ready for your typing.

The first thing you will probably notice in WordPad is that, in addition to the regular menu bar, there are two toolbars across the top, plus a ruler. These are just like the file management window toolbars you learned about in Chapter 3. Each button is a shortcut to an equivalent menu command. To find out what a button does, point the mouse at it, and a description will appear in the status bar. In the following figure, I'm pointing to the Print button.

If you also have Microsoft Word or some other word processor on your PC, such as Corel WordPerfect or Lotus Word Pro, you might prefer to use it instead of WordPad. Even so, it's still worthwhile to take a few minutes to learn about WordPad here, since all word processors are similar.

The main way in which WordPad differs from Notepad is in its ability to format text, so let's look briefly at the various kinds of formatting it can do.

Font

A style of lettering, or type-face. Windows XP comes with several fonts, and you might have others, too, depending on your printer and on what other programs are installed on your computer. For example, Microsoft Office installs dozens of fonts when you run its Setup program.

Formatting Text

The most basic kind of formatting involves individual characters. For example, you could make a certain word in a sentence boldface to make it stand out, or you could change the **font** or size of certain text.

There are two ways to format text: using the Format menu or using the toolbar buttons. Let's look at the menu method first:

1. Select the text you want to format.

| NOTE | To select text, drag the mouse across the text to be selected. You learned about dragging in Chapter 1: Hold down the left mouse button while you move the mouse. |

2. Choose Format ➤ Font.

3. In the Font dialog box that appears, make selections to define the for-matting you want. You can:

◆ Choose a font from the Font list.

◆ Choose a font style from the Font Style list (Bold, Italic, neither, or both).

◆ Choose a text size from the Size list.

◆ Use Strikeout, Underline, or both by marking the respective check boxes.

◆ Choose a text color from the Color drop-down list.

◆ Choose a script (for certain fonts only) from the Script drop-down list. These are useful primarily for languages other than English. For example, if you were writing in French or Spanish, you might choose Central European.

Fonts with an *O* icon next to them are OpenType fonts. OpenType is a new kind of font introduced in Windows XP. It's an improved version of the TrueType font standard. TrueType fonts are repre-sented by a *TT* icon on the list. Both OpenType and TrueType fonts are fully sizeable and look good at any size, both on the screen and on paper; and either will work equally well in your document.

The Script setting might appear to have no effect, because you are using a U.S. keyboard and have no international keyboard layouts installed. If you work regularly with some other language, you might want to install additional keyboard layouts from the Keyboard settings in Control Panel. See Chapter 12.

4. Click OK to apply the settings.

The advantage of the dialog box method, as you just saw, is that you can set many different text formatting attributes in a single dialog box. You can also control individual formatting attributes from the toolbar, as follows:

Font   Open the Font drop-down list on the toolbar and select a font.

Font Size   Open the Font Size drop-down list on the toolbar and select a size.

Script   Open the Script drop-down list and select a region (if applicable).

Bold, Italic, and Underline   Click the Bold, Italic, or Underline button on the toolbar.

Color   Click the Color button (which looks like a palette) and click a color on the list that appears.

Indentation

The horizontal position of the paragraph in relation to the overall page margins. For example, if the document has a 1" left margin and the first paragraph has a 0.5" left indent, that paragraph will start 1.5" from the left edge of the paper when printed.

Alignment

The horizontal alignment of each line of the paragraph. The default is Left—each line begins flush against the left margin (or indent), and the lines don't necessarily have to end at exactly the same place at the right margin. Right-alignment forces each line to align neatly at the right margin, allowing the left edge to be ragged. Center alignment centers each line of the paragraph between the right and left margins (or indents).

First-line indent

A first-line indent applies a different indentation setting to the first line of the paragraph than to subsequent lines. In many letter and magazine styles, it's customary to indent the first line of each paragraph by a half-inch.

Formatting Paragraphs and Pages

WordPad also enables you to format entire paragraphs and entire documents. Although this chapter doesn't cover all those features in detail, here's a quick review.

Paragraphs

Paragraph formatting includes **indentation**, **alignment**, tabs, and bullets. This type of formatting can be applied only to whole paragraphs, not to individual characters.

You can control indentation and alignment in the Paragraph dialog box, shown here. Choose Format ➤ Paragraph to display it.

You can also drag the markers on the ruler to adjust indentation. There are two triangles at the left; the top triangle controls the **first-line indent**, and the bottom triangle is for subsequent lines. The square beneath the triangles represents the entire paragraph (all lines together). At the right, there is a single triangle, representing the right indent. Make sure the insertion point is in the paragraph you want to format, and then drag the desired markers to the left or right to change the paragraph's indentation settings.

The toolbar contains buttons for alignment settings. To change to a different alignment, click the toolbar button for the alignment you want: Left, Center, or Right ▤ ▥ ▦ .

To change a paragraph to a bulleted one, simply select it and then click the Bullet button ▤ on the toolbar.

Pages

Page formatting affects the entire document, not just individual paragraphs. There are two primary page formatting settings that you can adjust: the margins and the **page orientation**. You can also set a paper size, in case you want to print on nonstandard paper such as legal.

Set page formatting by choosing File ➢ Page Setup to open the Page Setup dialog box, shown here:

Page orientation
The direction that text runs on the page—across the wide edge (landscape orientation) or across the narrow edge (portrait orientation).

Working with Paint

Paint is a very simple drawing program included with Windows. Kids love it, and grown-ups can also use it to create simple artwork for business and hobby use. Let's take a look at it as a final example of a Windows accessory program.

To start Paint, choose Start ➢ All Programs ➢ Accessories ➢ Paint.

The Paint program starts, with a blank area for your drawing.

Choosing a Color

First, you will want to select the color with which you will draw. You can choose two colors at once: foreground and background.

To select a color, click the color you want from the color grid. Click with the left mouse button to select the foreground color, or with the right mouse button to select the background color. The selected colors appear to the left of the color grid, in case you forget what you've chosen.

To draw with the foreground color, you will drag with the left mouse button. To draw with the background color, you will drag with the right mouse button.

Drawing a Line or Shape

Next, choose the tool with which you want to draw. There are many choices, including lines, shapes, a free-form paintbrush, an airbrush, and so on. You will want to experiment with the tools on your own.

As an example, let's draw an oval:

1. Click the Oval tool 🔘 on the side toolbar. The drawing style choices for ovals appear below that toolbar.

2. Click your desired drawing style. Your options, from top to bottom, are:

   Outline   Draws a shape with a transparent center.

   Filled Outline   Draws a shape filled with background color.

   Filled   Draws a filled shape with no border.

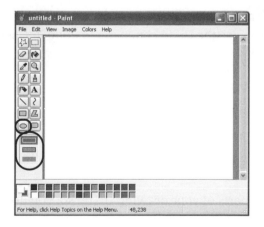

The choices are different for different tools, but the ones shown in the preceding figure apply to all filled shapes, such as rectangles, ovals, and rounded rectangles.

3. Position the mouse pointer on the work area where you want the oval to start.

4. Hold down the left mouse button and drag, creating the shape. Release the mouse button when finished.

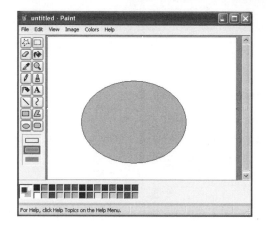

TIP   If you use the right mouse button instead of the left one to draw, the color usage is reversed. For example, if you are drawing a filled outline, the outer border is the background color and the inner fill is the foreground.

Undoing and Erasing

If you make a mistake, you can use the Undo command to undo it. Choose Edit ➤ Undo.

You can also erase unwanted parts of your drawing. To do so, you use the Eraser tool.

WARNING Erasing doesn't remove the color in that area—it simply changes that area's color to the background color. Therefore, you must make sure that you have selected the desired background color (by right-clicking on the color) before you use Eraser. For example, if you are working with a white background for your drawing, select white as the background color first.

1. Right-click the color in the color grid that matches your drawing background (probably white).

2. Click the Eraser tool ✐.

3. Click the thickness you want for the Eraser tool.

TIP A very thick eraser is good for covering large areas; a thin one allows you to be more precise.

4. Drag the mouse across the area you want to erase.

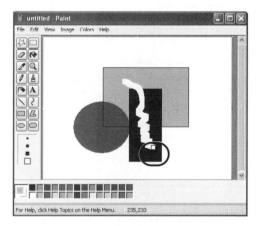

Sharing Data between Programs

Windows programs all share a common area called the Clipboard. Like a real-life clipboard, it holds data until you are ready to use it. You can copy or cut some data from a program to the Clipboard in Windows, and then paste it into any other program (or back into the same program in a different document or a different spot in the same document).

You place things on the Clipboard with either the Copy or the Cut command, from the program's Edit menu. Copy leaves the original intact, while Cut deletes the original. Then you use the Edit ➤ Paste command in the program in which you want to paste the data. The pasted data is placed in the active document, at the insertion point position.

To try out the Clipboard, let's create a picture in Paint and then paste it into WordPad:

You can use Ctrl+C as a shortcut for Copy and Ctrl+X for Cut. To paste, use Ctrl+V. Some programs also have Cut, Copy, and Paste buttons in a toolbar. Yet another method is to right-click a selection and choose Cut or Copy from its shortcut menu.

1. Open Paint and draw a picture, as you learned in the preceding section.

2. Use the Select tool ⬚ to draw a dotted box around your drawing.

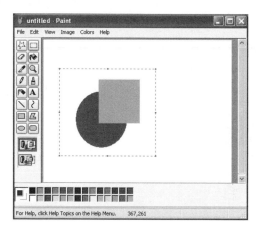

3. Choose Edit ➤ Copy. The picture is copied to the Clipboard.

NOTE Notice that Ctrl+C appears next to Copy on the Edit menu. That means that Ctrl+C is the shortcut key combination for that command.

4. Close Paint without saving your changes.

5. Open WordPad, as you learned to do earlier in the chapter.

6. Choose Edit ➤ Paste.

The picture is pasted into your WordPad document.

7. Close WordPad without saving your changes, since this was just for practice.

Some programs, such as Microsoft Office, come with an enhanced Clipboard that can hold multiple clips at once. In these programs, when you place something on the Clipboard, the existing Clipboard content is not erased. A special toolbar or pane enables you to choose which of the Clipboard's clips to paste.

When you copy or cut something to the Clipboard, whatever was previously on the Clipboard is erased. Therefore, you cannot rely on the Clipboard for storage. It's only for temporary use. The Clipboard is also cleared when you shut down Windows.

6 Installing New Programs

The Windows accessories are great, but sometimes you need a more powerful program to get the job done. That's when you buy and install an extra program. For example, if you max out the capabilities of WordPad, you might be ready to move up to Microsoft Word. This chapter covers installing new third-party programs, as well as installing and removing the Windows accessories themselves and getting updates to Windows itself from Microsoft.

Adding and Removing Windows Components

Not all of the Windows accessories can be removed; WordPad, Notepad, and Calculator are all permanent fixtures, for example.

When you install Windows XP (or when it comes preinstalled on a PC you buy), many accessory programs are installed, too. You saw some of them in Chapter 5. But some accessories are not installed by default; you must add them manually later. Besides the accessories, there are also other components you can add to Windows XP for special situations such as fax services and remote desktop connection support.

Most of the non-accessory components are special purpose items that the average home user will not find useful. For example, you will probably never need print services for Unix on your home PC.

Conversely, if disk space is in short supply on your hard disk, you might want to remove some of the Windows accessories or other components that you don't use.

To add or remove Windows components, follow these steps:

1. Choose Start ➤ Control Panel.

2. In Control Panel, click Add or Remove Programs.

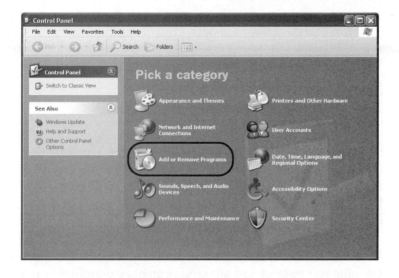

3. In the Add or Remove Programs dialog box, click Add/Remove Windows Components.

4. In the Windows Components Wizard, click a component category on the Components list (for example, Accessories and Utilities in the following graphic) and then click the Details button.

A list of components or subcategories within the clicked category appears.

Some categories are several levels "deep," such that choosing a category brings up another list of categories. Other categories present the individual components. You can make or clear the check box for entire categories at once, but unless you are an expert Windows user, you won't know exactly what's in each category without browsing.

5. Keep moving through categories until the component you want to add or remove appears. Then click to mark or remove its check box.

6. Click OK to close the category or subcategory window. Keep clicking OK until you have closed all the subcategory windows you moved through in step 5 and the Windows Components Wizard reappears.

7. Repeat steps 4–6 as needed to add or remove additional components.

8. In the wizard dialog box, click Next. If prompted, insert the Windows XP CD-ROM and then click OK to continue.

9. Click Finish.

10. Click Close to close the Add or Remove Programs dialog box. Depending on what you added or removed, you might be prompted to restart Windows after this procedure. If that happens, click Yes to restart.

11. Close Control Panel.

Installing a New Program

In many cases, you can simply insert the CD-ROM for a new program in your CD-ROM drive and the Setup program will start automatically. This happens because the CD has a file called `Autorun.inf` on it that specifies a program (such as Setup) that should run automatically whenever that CD is inserted.

If nothing happens when you insert the CD-ROM, or if you are installing from another source such as a floppy disk or a download from the Internet, you must start the Setup program in another way. One way is to use a file management window to locate the Setup file and double-click it to start the setup routine for the program. Another way—simpler for beginners who might not be sure which is the Setup file—is to do the following:

1. Choose Start ➣ Control Panel.

2. In Control Panel, click Add or Remove Programs.

Some `Autorun.inf` files are able to determine whether the program is already installed on your PC, and if so, to run the program upon insertion rather than reinstall it every time you insert the disc.

3. In the Add or Remove Programs dialog box, click Add New Programs.

4. Make sure the new program's disc is in your CD-ROM or floppy drive. Then click the CD or Floppy button.

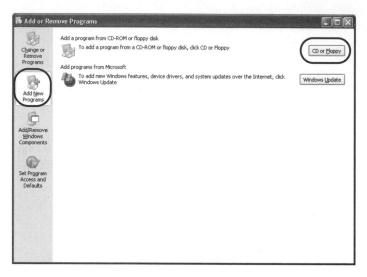

5. The Install Program from Floppy Disk or CD-ROM dialog box opens. Click Next.

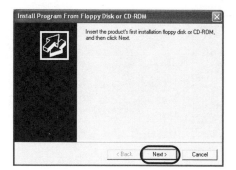

6. Windows now searches for Setup programs on your floppy and CD-ROM drives, and if one is found, a Run Installation Program dialog box appears. Click Finish.

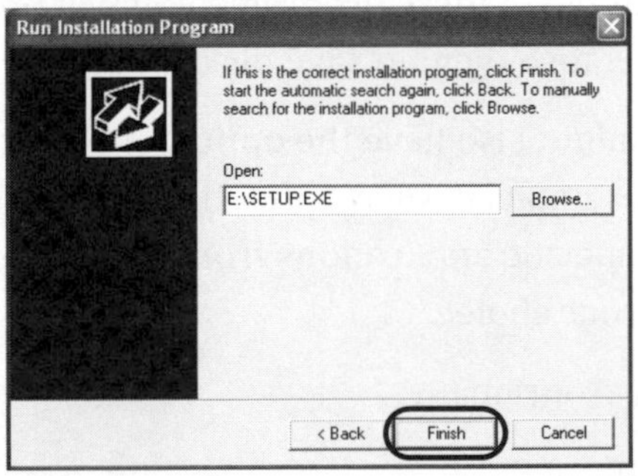

7. The Setup program starts. Follow the prompts. (Every program's routine is a little different, but most are self-explanatory.)
8. When the Setup program ends, you are returned to the Add or Remove Programs window. Click Close.
9. Close Control Panel.

The next time you open the Start menu after installing a new program, a bubble appears over the All Programs menu name, indicating that there are new programs.

Then, when you open the All Programs menu, the new programs appear shaded, so that you can quickly identify them. For example, in the next figure, two new programs have been added: WinZip and Microprose. (Actually Microprose is a folder, in which there is a new program installed. You can tell because of the right-pointing arrow to its right.)

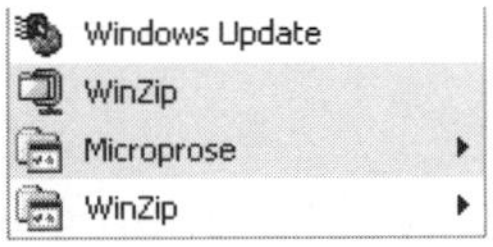

Microprose is actually the name of a game manufacturer; some programs place themselves in a folder having the manufacturer's name rather than the game's name.

Removing an Installed Program

Most computers that come with Windows preinstalled also come with a lot of other software preinstalled, too. Some of these programs you will probably never need or want, so why not remove them to save disk space?

Depending on the program, you might also have the option of changing the program's installed options. For example, if Microsoft Office has been installed, you can add or remove specific applications from that suite, or you can remove the entire package—your choice.

To remove or change an installed program:

1. Choose Start ➢ Control Panel.

2. In Control Panel, click Add or Remove Programs.

3. In the Add or Remove Programs dialog box, click the program you want to change or remove (LiveUpdate in this example). Buttons appear for changing or removing it.

NOTE　Depending on the program, there might be a single button named Change/Remove, or two separate buttons: Change and Remove.

4. Click the Change/Remove button (or Remove if they are separate buttons).

5. A confirmation box appears. (It's slightly different for every program.) Click Yes or OK, depending on the box.

6. Wait for the program to be removed. Depending on the program, another program might launch to handle the removal, or Windows might handle it transparently with no interaction.

7. If a confirmation box appears to tell you that the program has been removed, click OK. (You might not see this, depending on the program.)

8. Remove other programs if desired; then click Close to close the Add or Remove Programs dialog box.

9. Close Control Panel.

Bug

An error in a program that causes it to malfunction. The term bug supposedly comes from the days when computers were room-sized monstrosities that used vacuum tubes instead of electronic circuits. Bugs would be attracted to the tubes and would get caught and die there, causing problems with the tubes' operation. These *bugs* made the computer malfunction, and the term bug has gradually come to mean any problem with a computer.

Updating Windows XP

Microsoft periodically improves and updates Windows XP itself, by providing additional features and patches that fix **bugs** that users have identified. Windows comes with an AutoUpdate feature that automatically checks the Microsoft Web site and downloads the latest fixes and features. You can also access Microsoft Update manually at other times to check for new updates.

Getting Automatic Updates

Most security problems in Windows XP can be avoided simply by keeping Windows XP updated with the latest security patches from Microsoft. The best way to receive these updates is via Automatic Update. Some people might worry about their privacy when Microsoft is allowed to automatically download to their PCs, but rest assured that there's no gimmick here. Microsoft simply wants your system to be up-to-date.

To check whether your system is set up to receive automatic updates, follow these steps:

1. Click the Start button, and then right-click My Computer and choose Properties. The System Properties dialog box opens.

2. Click the Automatic Updates tab. Check the current setting for automatic updates. The exact options and wording will depend on whether you have Service Pack 2 (SP2) installed or not in Windows XP.

   Here's what you'll see if you do have SP2 installed:

And here's what you'll see if you don't:

WARNING I strongly recommend that you download Service Pack 2 right away if you don't have it yet. It provides much better security protection for your PC. After you configure Automatic Update, Windows might download and install the service pack automatically; if it doesn't, use Windows Update (as described later in this chapter) to download and install it.

In either case, choose the most automatic setting possible. If you have Service Pack 2, choose Automatic (Recommended). If you don't have Service Pack 2 yet, choose Download the Updates Automatically and Notify Me When They Are Ready to Be Installed.

If you don't have SP2 yet, notice that you don't have the option of allowing Windows to automatically install the updates—only to download them. That means that after a download has been completed, you will need to go through the process described in the following section. SP2 users will not have to install updates, because they will be installed automatically.

Installing an Automatic Update

If you do not yet have SP2 installed, or you have not configured Automatic Update to allow it to install updates automatically, the AutoUpdate icon will reappear in your system tray whenever an update is available. At that point, you can ignore the icon until you're ready, or click it to begin the installation.

1. When you see the AutoUpdate icon in the system tray, click it.

The Automatic Updates dialog box opens.

If you are curious about what the update is, click the Details button before moving on to step 2, to see a description of it.

If you don't want to install the update right now, click the Remind Me Later button, and then specify a time interval for receiving another reminder.

2. Click Install.

3. The installation begins. If a box appears, telling you to restart, click Restart. Otherwise, click OK to close the Automatic Updates dialog box.

Getting Updates Manually

If you chose not to use Automatic Updates, or if you want to check for updates when the AutoUpdate icon doesn't appear in the notification area, you can use Windows Update in manual mode. This type of update also has the advantage of enabling you to retrieve noncritical updates such as newer drivers for your hardware or newer versions of support programs like Windows Media Player.

Follow these steps to use Windows Update to retrieve both critical and optional updates:

1. Choose Start ➢ Control Panel.

2. In Control Panel, click Add or Remove Programs.

3. In the Add or Remove Programs dialog box, click Add New Programs.

4. Click Windows Update.

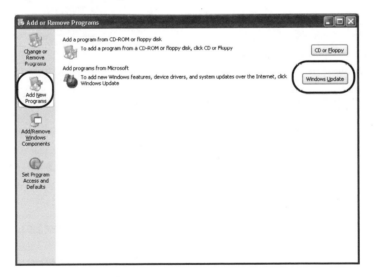

Critical updates

Updates that are important for the functionality of Windows. These can include security patches or bug fixes. In contrast, updates such as new versions of Windows Media Player or a keyboard layout for a newly supported foreign language would not be critical.

Internet Explorer opens and connects to the Internet, and a Windows Update page displays.

> **NOTE** The first time you use Windows Update, a Security Warning box appears, asking whether you want to install and run the Windows Update Control. Click Yes.

5. On the Windows Update Web page, click Custom Install.

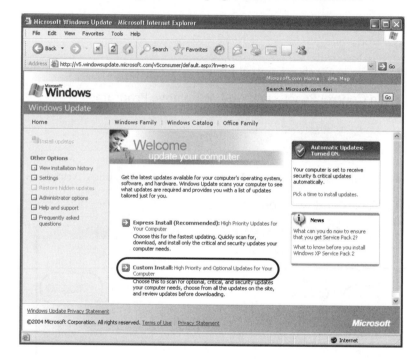

6. Review the high priority (critical) updates found, if any. If a check mark does not appear next to each of these updates, click to place one there.

> **WARNING** You should not decline critical updates unless you are a Windows expert and have a good reason to do so.

7. Click Select Optional Software and Updates.

8. Review the optional updates available. Mark or clear the check box for each item as desired.

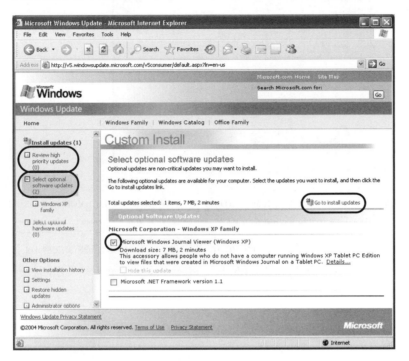

9. Click Go to Install Updates.

 Go to install updates

10. Review the selected updates and then click Install.

Install...

11. Depending on the update, a license agreement may appear. If it does, click Accept to accept the terms.

12. Wait for the update. A progress bar shows you the status of the download as it proceeds.

13. When the Web page displays "Installation Complete," close the Internet Explorer window.

14. If prompted to restart your PC, do so. Sometimes a restart is needed for an update to be applied.

7

Organizing Your Programs

● ●

As you install more programs in Windows XP, your Start menu may become cluttered with programs that you seldom use. One way to improve the menu's efficiency is to rearrange its structure so that the programs you use most often are more quickly accessible. In this chapter, you will learn how to change the Start menu, and also how to create shortcuts for starting programs on the desktop and on taskbar toolbars. You will also learn how to set a program to start automatically each time you turn on your PC, and how to disable one from starting automatically.

Classic

Windows XP's name for alternative settings that enable you to make Windows XP look or feel more like earlier versions of Windows.

Properties

Settings for a Windows feature, folder, or file. Each object in Windows has properties that you can set from its Properties dialog box by right-clicking it and choosing Properties from the shortcut menu.

Top-level menu

The portion of a menu that appears immediately when you open it, not including any submenus that you open later.

Changing the Start Menu's Appearance

If you have used earlier versions of Windows, you have probably already noticed that the Start menu in Windows XP looks different—and acts different, too. If you prefer the old look-and-feel, you can switch to a **classic**-style menu. You can also set appearance **properties** for the Start menu, regardless of the menu style you decide on.

Changing to the Classic Start Menu

In previous Windows versions, the Start menu consisted of one column, not two, and there were very few icons that appeared on the **top-level menu**. Almost every item required you to move through at least one level of submenu. If you would like Windows XP to emulate the old style, do the following:

1. Right-click the taskbar (any empty spot) and choose Properties from the shortcut menu.

2. In the Taskbar and Start Menu Properties dialog box, click the Start Menu tab and then click the Classic Start Menu button. The sample in the preview area above the buttons changes to show the classic Start menu.

3. Click OK. The change is applied.

4. If desired, click the Start button to confirm that the classic menu style is now in effect.

To switch back to the normal Start menu, repeat these steps but choose Start Menu instead of Classic Start Menu in step 2.

Changing Start Menu Properties

You can set properties for either the normal Start menu or the classic Start menu, and those properties will be separately retained.

To open the properties for either of the two Start menu views:

1. Right-click the taskbar (any empty spot) and choose Properties from the shortcut menu.

2. In the Taskbar and Start Menu Properties dialog box, click the Start Menu tab and then click the Customize button next to the style you have chosen.

When you switch to the classic Start menu, icons for My Computer, My Documents, My Network Places, and others appear on your desktop. On the normal Start menu, they appear in the right column of the menu, but in classic mode there is only a single column. So that you will continue to have access to these icons, they appear on the desktop as they did in earlier Windows versions.

The Customize Start Menu (or Customize Classic Start Menu) dialog box appears. From here, the procedures diverge, because the options for the two Start menus are dissimilar.

3. Make any changes to the settings, as described in the following sections.

4. Click OK to return to the Taskbar and Start Menu Properties dialog box.

5. Click OK to close the dialog box.

Properties for the Windows XP Start Menu

The Customize Start Menu dialog box has two tabs: General and Advanced.

On the General tab, you'll find the following settings:

Select an Icon Size for Programs Choose between Large Icons and Small Icons. Large is the default. This refers to the icons that appear next to the program names on the top-level Start menu. If you choose Small Icons, more of your recently used programs will fit on the top-level menu, like this:

Notice that the icon size affects only items in the left-hand column on the top-level Start menu. The icons in the right column remain large regardless of the chosen setting.

Number of Programs on Start Menu   This controls how many recently used programs will appear on the Start menu. Setting this to a number larger than 5 (the default) changes the height of the top-level Start menu, because the more programs to be shown on the menu, the larger it must be to accommodate them.

Clear List   This button clears the recently used program data. You might use Clear List, for example, to ensure your privacy if you don't want others to know what programs you have been running.

Show on Start Menu   There are two settings here: Internet and E-Mail. Select your favorite Web browser and e-mail program. They will appear at the top of the Start menu, like this:

These settings enable you to use some other brand of Web browser or e-mail program if desired. To prevent *any* programs from appearing at the top of the Start menu, clear the check boxes next to them.

On the Advanced tab are a variety of less-common settings:

Open Submenus When I Pause on Them with My Mouse   On the All Programs menu system, when this setting is turned on (the default), you can point at a submenu to make it open. When this setting is off, you must click the submenu name to open it.

Your new setting for Number of Programs doesn't take effect until you clear the current list with the Clear List button.

Highlight Newly Installed Programs   When this is on (the default), after you install a new program, it appears highlighted on the Start menu, and a little bubble appears saying, "New Programs Installed." This feature can help beginners locate new programs they have installed.

Start Menu Items   Here you can select or deselect check boxes to control what items appear on the right-hand side of the Start menu. For some items, you can also choose *how* they appear on the Start menu. The default for many of them is Display as a Link, which means that the name appears and you click it to display its content in a window. The alternative is Display as a Menu, which makes a submenu instead of a separate window. Here's what Control Panel would look like that way, for example:

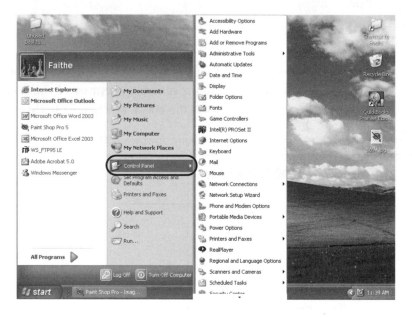

List My Most Recently Opened Documents   When checked, this adds an extra item to the right-hand column for My Recent Documents. It opens a submenu containing shortcuts to the data files you have most recently opened, so that you can easily reopen them. You can clear the list by clicking the Clear List button.

Properties for the Classic Start Menu

The classic Start menu's properties are much like those of previous Windows versions. This book won't spend a lot of time on the classic Start menu, but here's a brief summary:

Start Menu The controls at the top of the Customize Classic Start Menu box are for adding, removing, and organizing the programs on the Start menu. See the next section, "Changing the Start Menu's Content."

Clear A single Clear button clears the list of recent documents, the Web history in Internet Explorer, and several other history lists.

Advanced Start Menu Options Check marks appear for a variety of items and settings. Select or deselect check boxes as desired.

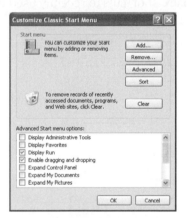

Marking one of the Expand... check boxes in the Advanced Start Menu Options section is the same as choosing As Menu for the corresponding feature in the normal Start menu properties.

Changing the Start Menu's Content

You just saw how to modify the Start menu's look and behavior; now let's turn to modifying its content. As you install more software, you might find that the All Programs submenu grows to an unmanageable size, making it difficult for you to easily locate the programs you use the most. In the following sections, you will learn ways to place shortcuts to commonly used programs closer at hand.

Changing the Top-Level Start Menu

Let's briefly review the main features of the top-level Start menu.

> **WARNING** This section assumes that you are using the normal Start menu. If you have switched to the classic Start menu, switch back now to the default, or you won't be able to follow along with these steps.

The right-hand column is occupied by shortcuts to Windows utilities and special folders, and you can change its content in the Customize Start Menu dialog box, as you learned in "Properties for the Windows XP Start Menu" earlier in this chapter.

The left-hand column has an upper and lower section. In the upper section are shortcuts to your Internet and e-mail programs. You learned how to select which e-mail and Internet programs will appear there, and how to turn off their display altogether if desired. In the lower section are shortcuts to recently used programs.

You can't control what programs appear in the lower-left section, but you can clear the list, as you learned earlier. However, in the upper-left section, you can add shortcuts to additional programs, placing shortcuts for a few favorite programs in a very convenient location.

Adding a Program to the Top-Level Start Menu

To add a shortcut to the top-left portion of the Start menu:

1. Choose Start ➤ All Programs.

There are other ways to keep shortcuts for favorite programs close at hand. You can place shortcuts directly on the desktop, or on a toolbar on the taskbar. Both are covered later in this chapter.

2. Locate and point to the program that you want to add to the top-level Start menu.

3. Drag the program's name to the upper-left area of the top-level Start menu. A black, horizontal line indicates where the shortcut is going.

4. Move the mouse up or down to reposition the black line; when you are satisfied with the position, release the mouse button to drop the short-cut into place.

Removing a Program from the Top-Level Start Menu

After adding a program shortcut to the Start menu, you can remove it at any time by following these steps:

1. Click the Start button.

2. Right-click the shortcut you want to remove and then choose Remove from This List. (In the following figure, I'm removing Microsoft Word.)

The shortcut disappears.

Changing the All Programs Menu

A few shortcuts appear on the top-level Start menu, but most computers have far too many programs installed for them all to be on the top-level menu. The All Programs menu organizes the complete list of installed programs in a hier-archical menu structure from which you can select, as you saw in Chapter 6.

Repositioning Items on the All Programs Menu

You can move items up or down on the All Programs menu simply by dragging them:

1. Choose Start ➢ All Programs.

2. Point to the item you want to move.

> Remote Assistance
> Windows Media Player
> Windows Messenger

3. While holding down the mouse button, drag the item up or down on the All Programs menu. A black, horizontal line shows where the item is going.

4. When the black line is in the desired spot, release the mouse button.

> Microsoft Money
> Microsoft Outlook
> Microsoft Word
> MSN Explorer

The item drops into its new position.

Creating New Folders on the All Programs Menu

One way to organize a full All Programs menu is to create new folders (that is, submenus) to categorize your programs—for example, Games, Internet, and Business might be good names for them. Then you can drag each program or existing subfolder into one of those categories.

To create a new folder on the All Programs menu:

1. Click the Start button.

2. Right-click All Programs and then choose Open.

> You can drag within the same menu, or you can drag over a submenu name to open it and then drag onto the submenu. To move something onto a submenu, pause for a moment with the mouse pointer over the submenu name; it will open shortly. Then drag straight across, onto the submenu, and then up or down on it.

3. A Start Menu file management window opens with a Programs folder in it. Double-click the Programs folder to display its content.

4. Create the new folder in the Programs folder, as you would in any file management window. (Refer to Chapter 3 if needed.)

5. See the preceding section, "Repositioning Items on the All Programs Menu," to move items from existing locations on the All Programs menu into the new folder.

Deleting an Item from the All Programs Menu

Ordinarily, you should not delete items from All Programs. Each item represents an installed program, and if you delete it from the Start menu, you lose out on one of the easiest ways to start that program. To remove a program from your computer, uninstall it, as you learned in Chapter 6.

However, if you have already uninstalled the program but it persists on the All Programs menu, you can safely delete the reference to it by doing the following:

1. Choose Start ➤ All Programs.

2. Locate and point to the program you want to remove from the menu (MSN Explorer in this example).

3. Right-click that program and choose Delete from its shortcut menu.

The All Programs menu actually takes its content from a combination of the content of two separate folders on your hard disk: the one for your user logon (Owner, for example) and a generic one for all users. If you want to create the new folder for all users, choose Open All Users instead of Open in step 2.

4. In the confirmation box that appears, click Delete Shortcut.

Working with Desktop Shortcuts

Shortcuts are a major feature of Windows XP. The Start menu organizes and presents shortcuts to various programs you can run, but shortcuts can also sit directly on the desktop. You have already seen some examples of this in previous chapters—the Recycle Bin, for instance. The Recycle Bin folder is actually a hidden folder inside the Windows folder on your hard disk, but a shortcut to it appears on your desktop so that you can easily open it without having to wade through several levels of folders in a file management window. •

When you install new programs, they often place shortcuts for themselves on the desktop. If you don't want them there, you can delete them. You can also create your own shortcuts on the desktop for programs you use frequently, and you can arrange the shortcuts on the desktop as you wish.

Arranging Shortcuts

When you first install Windows XP and your applications, most desktop icons align with the left side of the screen (the exception is Recycle Bin, which appears by default in the bottom-right corner). However, you can place the icons anywhere you like on the desktop.

Moving an Icon

To move an icon on the desktop, simply drag it as you have learned to drag any other object:

1. Point to the icon you want to move.

2. Hold down the left mouse button and move the mouse to drag the icon. Release the mouse button when the icon is in the desired location.

If you try to move an icon and it immediately snaps back to the left side of the screen, the Auto Arrange feature is turned on. To turn it off, see "Arranging Icons Automatically" later in this chapter.

Using a Grid to Help Align Icons

It can be difficult to get the desktop icons aligned precisely with one another for a neat appearance. Turning on an invisible alignment grid can help; when you move an icon, it snaps to the grid as you drop it.

To turn the alignment grid for the desktop on or off:

1. Right-click the desktop. A shortcut menu appears.

2. Choose Arrange Icons By ➤ Align to Grid to turn the feature on or off. A check mark next to Align to Grid means that the feature is already on.

Arranging Icons by a Criterion

To tidy up the desktop, you might want to arrange the icons on it by a specific criterion such as alphabetically by name. When you do this, they align in an orderly top-to-bottom column at the left side of the screen. If there are more icons than can fit in a single column, Windows starts another column.

To arrange the icons by a criterion:

1. Right-click the desktop. A shortcut menu appears.

2. Point to Arrange Icons By and then choose the criterion for arrangement: Name, Size, Type, or Modified.

Name arranges alphabetically. *Size* arranges according to the file size in bytes. *Type* arranges according to the type of program the icon represents (program, data file, etc.). *Modified* arranges according to the date on which the icon was last modified.

Arranging Icons Automatically

You can turn on the Auto Arrange feature for the desktop so that icons always align neatly at the left. This feature helps keep the desktop tidy by preventing icons from being scattered haphazardly around the desktop.

> **WARNING** If you turn on Auto Arrange, you will no longer be able to move icons around on the desktop; as soon as you do, they will snap back into automatic arrangement.

To turn Auto Arrange on or off:

1. Right-click the desktop. A shortcut menu appears.

2. Choose Arrange Icons By ➢ Auto Arrange to turn the feature on or off. A check mark next to Auto Arrange means that the feature is already on.

Deleting a Desktop Shortcut

Deleting a desktop shortcut is much like deleting a file in a file management window. There are two ways you can do it:

◆ Click once on the shortcut to select it and then press the Delete key.

You may have noticed another feature on the shortcut menu: Show Desktop Icons. This is new in Windows XP and is turned on by default. If you turn it off by selecting it, all the icons will disappear from your desktop. Turn it back on by selecting it again, and the icons will reappear.

❖ Right-click the shortcut and choose Delete.

Either way, a Confirm File Delete box appears. Click Yes.

Creating a New Desktop Shortcut

If there is a particular program or data file that you access frequently, you might want to place a shortcut for it on the desktop. That way, you can double-click that shortcut to open the file whenever you need it.

There are several ways to create desktop shortcuts. The following sections outline some of the most popular ones.

Creating a Shortcut from a Program on the Start Menu

If you want to create a desktop shortcut to a program (rather than a data file), the easiest way is to copy its shortcut from the Start menu onto the desktop. Here's how to do that:

1. Open the Start menu and locate the program for which you want to create a shortcut. You can create a shortcut for any of the programs or utilities on the top-level Start menu or on the All Programs menu.

2. While holding down the Ctrl key, drag the item to the desktop. The plus sign next to the dragged icon indicates that you are creating a copy.

> **TIP** Instead of holding down Ctrl in step 2, you can right-drag (that is, drag with the right mouse button). When you release the mouse button, a shortcut menu appears. Click Create Shortcuts Here.

Creating a Shortcut from a File Management Window

If you want a desktop shortcut to a data file, your best bet is to locate the data file in a file management window and then create a shortcut for it with drag-and-drop, like this:

1. Open a file management window, and locate the file.

> **WARNING** Don't maximize the window; you must be able to see the desktop in the background.

2. Hold down the Alt key and drag the file to the desktop.

The shortcut that appears has "Shortcut to" in its name, to help you distinguish it from the actual file. You can rename the shortcut if desired, as with any other file. (Press F2 and type a new name.)

> **NOTE** The curved arrow in the corner of the icon indicates that you have created a shortcut.

Customizing Toolbars

In Chapter 2, you learned that by default, Windows XP doesn't show any toolbars in the taskbar. But you also learned that you can easily enable this functionality by right-clicking the taskbar, choosing Toolbars, and then selecting the name of the toolbar you want to use.

In the following sections, you'll learn how to reposition and modify taskbar toolbars to meet your needs. I'll use the Quick Launch toolbar as an example

Why do you hold down Alt here, whereas you used Ctrl in creating a shortcut from the Start menu? Ctrl creates a copy; since the icons on the Start menu are already shortcuts, you are simply copying them. Alt creates a shortcut; the files in the file management window are not already shortcuts, so you must use Alt. If you used Ctrl, you would create a full copy of the file on the desktop.

because it's the most popular toolbar, but you can perform these procedures with any toolbar in Windows.

Adjusting Toolbar Length

If you see a double right arrow  to the right of the Quick Launch toolbar, it means that there are more buttons than can be displayed at the toolbar's current size.

To lengthen the Quick Launch toolbar:

1. Point to the handle (the dots) on the taskbar area to the right of the toolbar. The mouse becomes a double-headed arrow.

2. Drag to the right, shortening the taskbar and allowing the Quick Launch toolbar to grow.

Changing Toolbar Buttons

You will probably want to delete some of the icons on the Quick Launch toolbar, and add others. For example, if you use Microsoft Outlook, you will want to delete the icon for Outlook Express, the free e-mail reader that comes with Windows XP. And you might want to add icons for your favorite programs, such as a game that you play every day.

Deleting a Shortcut from a Toolbar

Deleting from the Quick Launch toolbar is similar to deleting from the Start menu:

1. Right-click the button you want to delete.

2. In the shortcut menu that appears, click Delete.

```
Open
Run as...
Pin to Start menu

Send To             ▶

Cut
Copy

Create Shortcut
Delete
Rename

Properties
```

3. In the confirmation box that appears, click Yes.

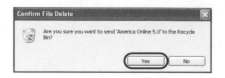

Adding a Shortcut to a Toolbar

Adding a shortcut to the Quick Launch toolbar is, again, very similar to doing the same to the Start menu:

1. Locate an existing shortcut to the program or file. It can be on the Start menu, on the desktop, or in a file management window.

2. While holding down Alt, drag the item to the Quick Launch toolbar. A vertical line shows where the item will appear. When you release the mouse, a button for the item appears on the toolbar.

Remember, Alt creates a shortcut; Ctrl creates a copy. If you are dragging an existing shortcut, you can hold down Ctrl in step 2. However, Alt works regardless of the source type.

TIP   You can also create new toolbars, although it's beyond the scope of this book.

Managing Programs in the System Tray

As you learned in Chapter 1, the system tray is the area immediately to the left of the clock on the taskbar. It contains icons for programs that are running in the background, such as Windows Messenger (see Chapter 17), an antivirus program, or a program that controls a writable CD-ROM drive.

Recall from Chapter 1 that by default, Windows XP hides the less-used system tray icons; so if a double left arrow appears next to your system tray, click it to see the complete array of icons.

Opening a System Tray Program's Window

These programs in the system tray are waiting for your signal to spring into the foreground and open their own window. In many cases, you can simply double-click one of the system tray icons to open its window.

You can also right-click an icon to see a menu of commands for it. If there is a boldfaced command, it's the command that will execute when you double-click the icon. In most cases, the boldfaced command is Open, Start, or something similar that opens a window. For example, in the next figure, it's Start Message Manager.

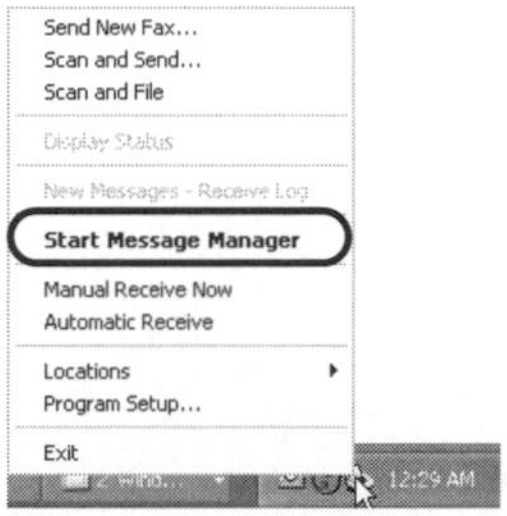

Closing a System Tray Program

To close a system tray program, right-click it and look for a command such as Exit or Close. Each program's menu is a little different. The program will reload the next time you start your computer.

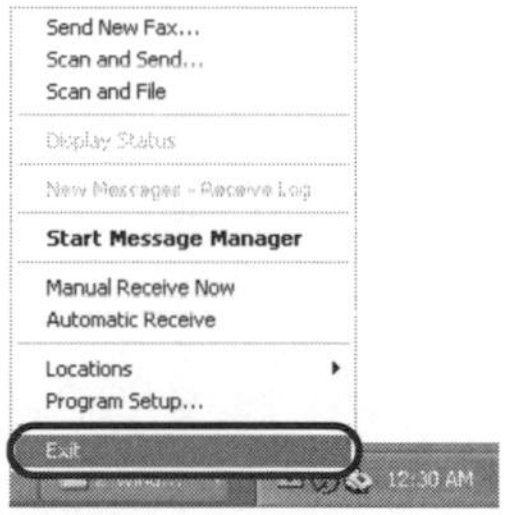

Controlling Which Programs Load at Startup

Some programs, when you close them from the system tray, offer to help you disable them for the future. If you see a message like that, you can respond to the prompt to decide whether you want the program to be automatically started each time Windows starts.

Other programs load automatically at startup because there are shortcuts for them in the Startup folder (on the All Programs menu). To prevent such a program from loading at startup, remove its shortcut from that folder, like this:

1. Click Start and then choose All Programs ➢ Startup. View the list of programs there.

Not all programs that load at startup have icons in the Startup folder. If you are having trouble getting rid of an automatically starting program, try right-clicking the program's icon in the system tray and looking for a Configure or Properties command that might open a dialog box in which you can control the program's startup. If that fails, try running the program's Setup program (through Add or Remove Programs, as in Chapter 6) to see whether there is an option for changing the way the program is installed.

2. If the program you want is listed, right-click it and choose Delete.

3. A confirmation box appears. Click Yes to confirm.

Part 3

Working with Multimedia Content

Many of Windows XP's greatest improvements over earlier Windows versions center around multimedia content. Windows XP makes it easier than ever to import and manage photographs, music, and video clips and combine them to make your own multimedia presentations. In this part, you will learn about Windows XP's scanner and camera tools, about Windows Media Player for playing audio and video content, and about Windows Movie Maker for assembling your own content into video presentations.

Working with Multimedia Content

8

Working with Photographs and Still Images

Windows XP provides unprecedented support for digital images. From setting up your scanner or camera to producing high-quality prints, Windows guides you every step of the way with easy-to-follow wizards. In this chapter, you will find out how to set up scanners and cameras, how to use them to acquire digital images, and how to print those images yourself or use a professional printing service to do it.

Digital
Composed of numbers (digits) that a computer can understand and process.

When selecting a scanner or digital camera for use in Windows XP, you will have best results with a model that's on the Hardware Compatibility List (HCL) for Windows XP. Microsoft publishes this list online at **www.microsoft.com/hcl**. This is a list of devices that various versions of Windows support.

Setting Up a New Scanner or Digital Camera

Setting up a scanner or **digital** camera in Windows XP is very easy. Simply connect your scanner or camera to your computer, as described in the instructions that come with it. Windows automatically detects the device, and a bubble appears over the system tray letting you know. Most scanners and digital cameras come with a Setup CD, but you probably won't need it.

Windows XP will work with almost any brand and model of scanner or camera, but Windows may not directly support it. What's the difference? With directly supported models, Windows uses its own drivers and its own interface, so no matter what brand and model you have, the procedures for using the device are the same. If a model is not supported, Windows can't operate it directly, so you must install the interface software that came with the device. This is not a big hardship; you will simply be using the device in the same way that people with earlier versions of Windows use it, rather than in the Windows XP way.

Does Windows Recognize Your Scanner or Camera?

To check to see whether the needed drivers for your scanner or camera are installed in Windows, do the following:

1. Choose Start ➢ Control Panel.

2. In Control Panel, click Printers and Other Hardware.

3. Click Scanners and Cameras.

4. Look for your scanner or camera on the list that appears. If you see it, Windows sees it, too.

Running the Scanner and Camera Installation Wizard

If Windows doesn't see your scanner or camera immediately, you might try giving it a little shove in the right direction. Scanners and cameras with USB (Universal Serial Bus) interfaces are usually detected right away, but models that use other interfaces such as a parallel port might not be.

1. Start at the Scanners and Cameras window. To get there, perform steps 1–3 of the preceding procedure.

2. Click Add an Imaging Device in the Imaging Tasks pane.

If Control Panel doesn't have a Printers and Other Hardware option, the panel might be in classic view. You can either switch to category view by clicking Switch to Category View and then return to step 2, or simply double-click the Scanners and Cameras icon and skip to step 4. You will learn more about Control Panel in Part 3 of this book.

The Scanner and Camera Installation Wizard works well with models on the HCL, but might not work with unsupported models. If it fails to get your device up and running, try the Setup software that came with the device. You can also check the device manufacturer's Web site to see whether an updated driver or Setup program might be available for Windows XP. See Chapter 17 for help with the Internet.

3. The Scanner and Camera Installation Wizard opens. Click Next to continue.

4. Select the manufacturer and model from the list and then click Next, or, if you have a Setup disk that came with the device, insert it and click Have Disk.

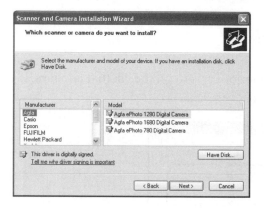

5. Select the port to which the device is connected, or leave Automatic Port Detection chosen if you don't know or if the port doesn't appear on the list. Then click Next.

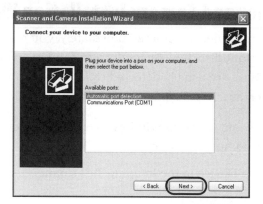

6. Type a name for the device, or leave the default name. Then click Next.

7. Click Finish. Windows installs the drivers for the device and sets it up to appear in the Scanners and Cameras window.

If the preceding steps didn't get your device up and running, try inserting the Setup CD that came with the device and running the Setup program. The disadvantage of that method is that the device will use the manufacturer's drivers, rather than the Windows ones, so the remainder of the steps and procedures outlined in this chapter may not be accurate for your situation. Read the documentation and online help that came with the device.

Scanning from an XP-Compatible Scanner

When Windows recognizes your scanner, you are ready to scan. You can scan photos, drawings, text, or anything else that appears on paper. The only limitation is that the item to be scanned must fit in your scanner.

1. Choose Start ➤ All Programs ➤ Accessories ➤ Scanner and Camera Wizard.

TIP	As an alternative to steps 1 and 2, you can start in the Scanners and Cameras window (from Control Panel) and double-click the device you want.

2. If you have more than one scanner or camera, a box appears, in which you choose which device you want to work with. Click the desired device and then click OK.

3. The Scanner and Camera Wizard opens. Click Next to continue.

4. Place the item to be scanned in the scanner, if you haven't done so yet.

5. On the Choose Scanning Preferences screen, select the type of picture you want to scan: Color Picture, Grayscale Picture, or Custom.

NOTE   If you choose Custom, you can click the Custom Settings button and fine-tune the scanner settings, but most people won't need to do that because the default settings work well in most cases.

6. Click the Preview button. The scanner scans a quick pass over the image and presents a preview of it on-screen.

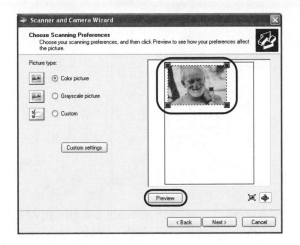

7. The wizard automatically crops based on what it thinks are the image boundaries. If needed, drag the squares in the corners of the image to adjust the area to be scanned.

8. Click Next to continue.

9. Type a name for the picture. The default name is "Picture," or whatever name you last used, but you will probably want a different name.

10. Open the Select a File Format drop-down list and choose a graphics format in which to save. You can choose JPG, BMP, TIF, or PNG.

11. If you want to store the picture somewhere other than the default location (in a subfolder with the name you provided in step 9, inside the My Pictures folder), enter it in the Choose a Place to Save... text box, or click Browse to locate it.

12. Click Next to continue, and wait for the scanning to take place.

JPG is best for use on Web pages, while TIF is popular with commercial print publications. BMP is good for creating images to use as background wallpaper in Windows (see Chapter 11).

13. After the picture has been scanned, you have the option of copying it to the Internet or ordering a print through a photo service. For now, decline both of these; leave the default Nothing chosen and click Next.

Your pictures have been successfully copied to your computer or network.
You can also publish these pictures to a Web site or order prints online.

What do you want to do?

○ Publish these pictures to a Web site

○ Order prints of these pictures from a photo printing Web site

⊙ Nothing. I'm finished working with these pictures

14. On the final screen of the wizard, click Finish.

A file management window opens, showing the subfolder of My Pictures that you created in the wizard. You can use the links in the shortcut pane to rename it, copy it, or perform any other listed activity. If you want to print, see "Printing a Photo" later in this chapter for some guidance.

The view shown here is called Filmstrip view. A special view for displaying pictures, it's available on the View menu in graphics-display windows such as My Pictures.

Transferring Pictures from a Digital Camera

A digital camera is like a regular camera except instead of recording images on film, it records them as computer data. There are two main kinds of digital cameras—those that are permanently connected to your PC and those that you can take out into the world and use, and then hook up to your PC for image transfer.

Depending on the type of camera you have and its features, the procedure for transferring pictures to your PC may be a little different from the steps that follow. These steps are for a connected camera, but they point out where a go-anywhere type of camera would be different.

1. Perform steps 1–3 of the preceding procedure ("Scanning from an XP-Compatible Scanner").

   The next few steps are for connected cameras only. They show how to take pictures. With a go-anywhere camera, the pictures have already been taken, so you might not have this capability. If your pictures have already been taken, skip to step 5.

2. A preview appears, showing what your camera is "seeing" at the moment. Position the camera so that the desired image appears in the preview.

3. Click the Take Picture button.

4. Reposition the camera and take more pictures if desired. Here, three pictures have been taken.

The rest of this procedure applies equally to all types of cameras.

5. The pictures currently stored in the camera appear. By default, all pictures have a check mark in their upper-right corner, indicating that they will be saved. If you don't want to save one of the pictures, click its check mark to toggle it off. In the next figure, the third picture has been deselected.

6. Click Next to continue.

Note the Rotate Clockwise and Rotate Counter-clockwise buttons below the pictures. Click one of these if you need to turn the selected picture 90 degrees.

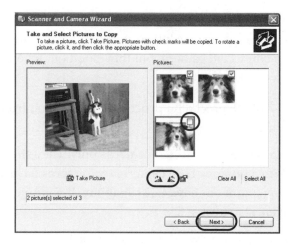

7. In the first text box on the Picture Name and Destination screen, type a name to use as a prefix for the picture names. Each picture will have the name you type plus a number. For example, if you type Camera, the first picture will be named Camera01, the second Camera02, and so on.

8. If desired, select a different save location in the Choose a Place to Save… box. By default, the location is a subfolder with the same name that you typed in step 7, inside the My Pictures folder.

9. (Optional) If you want to remove the pictures from the camera after you save them to your hard disk, mark the Delete Pictures from My Device after Copying Them check box.

10. Click Next to continue.

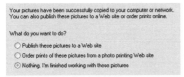

The files are copied to your computer, and deleted from the camera if you chose that option.

11. As with the scanner, you can choose whether to copy the pictures to the Internet, order prints online, or do nothing. Leave Nothing selected and click Next.

12. On the final screen of the wizard, click Finish.

13. The new folder opens with the pictures displayed.

From here, you can use the links in the left-hand pane to rename the pictures, copy them, or perform any other listed activity. The pictures are regular files, just like any others you learned to work with in Chapter 3. If you want to print, see "Printing a Photo" later in this chapter for some guidance.

Viewing Images

Whether you acquire an image from a scanner or from a camera, the end of the procedure leaves you in a file management window in Filmstrip view, with the image displayed in a preview area. If you don't see a preview, choose View ➤ Filmstrip. You can use the buttons below the image preview to manipulate it:

The **Previous Image** and **Next Image** buttons ⓘⓘ let you switch to other images in the same folder, if there are any. You won't use them while working with a single image.

Rotate Clockwise and **Rotate Counterclockwise** ⬆⬆ let you turn the image 90 degrees. This affects your current view of the picture, but not the picture itself.

Printing a Photo

Windows XP includes a Photo Printing Wizard that can help you get the best possible print of your pictures.

1. In the folder containing the pictures, select all the pictures that you want to print. You can print multiple pictures as a batch.

NOTE Notice that when you select multiple pictures, none of them appear in the preview area.

2. Under Picture Tasks, click Print This Picture (or Print the Selected Pictures, if you selected more than one).

If you are interested in editing your pictures, I strongly recommend that you buy a graphics management program such as Paint Shop Pro. Windows XP's default graphics program is Paint, but Paint is very simple, as you saw in Chapter 4, and lacks features such as cropping and converting to grayscale that you might find useful for editing and manipulating images.

If you have a digital video camera, you can also use Windows XP to edit and enhance your home movies. See Chapter 10 for details.

Selecting File ➤ Print prints a single copy of the picture on your default printer with default settings. It bypasses the Photo Printing Wizard.

3. The Photo Printing Wizard opens. Click Next to continue.

4. If you selected more than one picture in step 1, the selected pictures appear. If you have changed your mind about printing a particular picture, clear its check box to deselect it. Then click Next.

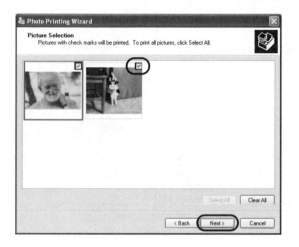

5. If you have more than one printer, open the What Printer Do You Want to Use? drop-down list and select the desired printer. For example, you might have a black-and-white laser printer and a color ink-jet printer.

The Install Printer button is a shortcut to the Printers folder for adding a new printer to your system. You'll learn more about adding printers in Chapter 13.

6. (Optional) You can also click Printing Preferences to set options for your printer. The exact options that appear depend on the printer model. Here are the options for my printer:

Notice that I have the option of choosing a paper type from the Media drop-down list. For best photo printing results, use some photo paper for your ink-jet printer. It's a glossy, nonporous paper that makes for prints that look almost as good as those developed in a real photo lab.

7. On the Printing Options screen, click Next to continue.

8. On the Layout Selection screen, choose a layout. Many layouts are available, with different numbers and sizes of prints. Then click Next.

Remember how in grade school, you used to order a certain number of wallet-sized photos, a certain number of 5×7s, and so on? Well, now you can print all the sheets you want of those various sizes by selecting different layouts.

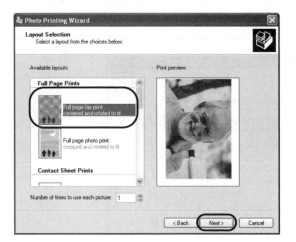

The photos print.

9. Click Finish to close the wizard.

Ordering Photo Prints Online

If your printer doesn't give you the quality of photo printing you want, you might try one of the online printing services. They specialize in printing digital photographs on professional-quality photo printers. Their prices are comparable to those for conventional film developing.

Windows XP has a built-in link to these services. From the file management window for the photos, follow these steps:

1. Select the photos you want to order prints of.

2. In the Picture Tasks pane, click Order Prints Online.

3. The Online Print Ordering Wizard opens. Click Next.

4. Select which pictures you want to order by clearing the check box next to any you don't want. Then click Next.

If you don't see thumbnail images of the available pictures, right-click a blank area in the dialog box and choose View ➤ Thumbnails.

5. Select the company you want to use.

At this writing, only three are available; by the time you read this, there may be others.

6. Click Next to continue.

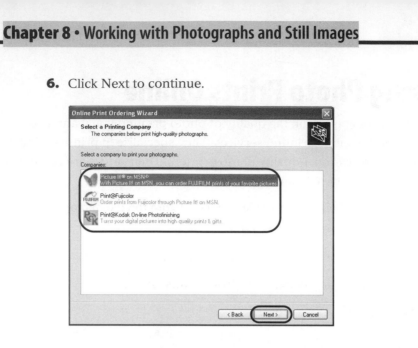

The steps at this point diverge depending on the company you picked. For example, here's what you see if you chose Picture It! On MSN.

7. Continue following the on-screen prompts to create and place your order.

9 Playing Music and Videos

Windows XP has richer, more robust multi-media capabilities than any previous version, including a new and improved version of Windows Media Player for playing sound, music, video clips, and DVD movies. In this chapter, you'll learn the ins and outs of this fun and versatile program.

Introducing Windows Media Player

Windows Media Player is a great multipurpose application for playing audio and video clips, burning audio CDs, ripping (that is, copying) files from audio CDs, listening to Internet radio stations, and more. You'll be amazed at all it can do! You can:

- Play media clips, including videos, music, and sound effects, in any of dozens of different formats.

- With an Internet connection, explore an online Media Guide that provides free sound and video clips that you can download from your favorite artists.

- With an Internet connection, listen to hundreds of Internet radio stations. Some of these are online broadcasts of your favorite stations around the world; others are Internet-only stations.

- Play audio CDs on your computer, using features like track selection, random play, and so on.

- Play DVD movies on your computer (provided you have the right support software installed; I'll explain more about that later).

- Copy songs from your audio CDs to your hard disk so that you can listen to them while you work without inserting the CDs.

- Organize your sound clips from various sources into custom playlists, creating your own "mixes."

To start Media Player, choose Start ➢ All Programs ➢ Windows Media Player.

> **TIP** If you have the Quick Launch toolbar displayed, you can also start Windows Media Player by clicking the player's icon there ▶.

Getting the Latest Version

Windows XP came with Windows Media Player 8. Since Windows XP's original release, two more versions of Media Player have been released (9 and 10), free for downloading from Microsoft, and with new systems the latest Media Player available comes preinstalled. Versions 8 and 9 are similar in their operation, but 10 has a much different interface.

Here is version 9:

And here is version 10:

The biggest difference is that the tabs that move between sections are on the top in 10, whereas they were on the side in 9 and earlier. However, there are many other differences that are not as obvious. Because of this, I strongly recommend that you upgrade to 10 before working through this chapter.

To upgrade, open Windows Media Player (Start ➢ All Programs ➢ Windows Media Player) and choose Help ➢ Check for Player Updates. A wizard will walk you through the process of upgrading if needed. You can also download this update from Windows Update, which is explained in Chapter 6.

NOTE The first time you open Windows Media Player, and also the first time after upgrading it, a wizard will walk you through some configuration settings. Leave the defaults marked unless you have a strong preference otherwise on a particular setting.

Windows Media Player has several tabs across the top of the main work area in version 10, or to the left in earlier versions. You can click a tab to bring a certain page to the front, as you would in a multitabbed dialog box. In this chapter you'll learn about the various tabs and the content and benefits they provide.

Using the Windows Media.com Guide

Assuming you are connected to the Internet, you can click the Guide tab to open the Windows Media.com Web page within Windows Media Player. This page is a treasure chest of hyperlinks to various audio and video content available on the Web.

> **NOTE** It is also possible to work with this Web page from outside of Windows Media Player, just by opening `http://www.windowsmedia.com` in your Web browser.

You can click any of the links on the Guide tab to listen to or watch clips from the featured artists. You can also browse a huge library of material from your favorite artists by clicking Artists A–Z.

The format and content available on the Media Guide tab varies greatly over time—even from day to day—because it's actually a Web site that you're accessing, rather than a fixed program.

Playing Internet Radio Stations

Imagine if you could listen to almost any radio station, anywhere in the world, with no static and no antenna problems. That's what Internet radio is like! You'll be amazed at the quality and variety of programming available.

NOTE	The Radio feature works quite differently in version 10 versus earlier versions. In version 10, you open a separate browser window for the radio tuner, whereas in earlier versions the radio tuner was integrated.

Internet Radio is part of the offerings on the Guide tab in version 10.

1. Click Radio Tuner to open the list of stations from which to select.

2. See the next several sections to learn how to select and play a station.

Playing a Featured Station

Featured stations are ones that have paid a promotional fee to Microsoft for top placement. They appear at the top of the list. Just for the practice, try playing one of these:

1. Click one of the stations on the Featured Stations list. Some details about the station appear below its name.

2. Some stations have a Play link; others have a Visit Website to Play link:

❖ Click a Play link to play the station from Windows Media Player. (Control passes back to that window.)

❖ Click a Visit Website to Play link to open a different Web site that has instructions for playing that station. (The steps vary depending on how the site owner has set it up.)

If you have a slow Internet connection, it might take several minutes before the station begins to play. You might also experience some pauses or choppiness in the play. Broadband Internet users should not experience these problems.

NOTE Why does a station take so long to load? It's because Internet radio is a streaming audio format. The music is transmitted to your PC just in time for it to be played. On a slow PC, the least little delay can result in a choppy playback, so Media Player creates a buffer—a storage area for several seconds of incoming data. That way, if there is a delay in transmission, the music continues to play out of the buffer while your PC catches up, and there is no interruption. The slower your Internet connection, the longer it takes to fill the buffer initially.

If you need some silence, click either Pause or Stop at the bottom of the Media Player window. Pause stops the broadcast temporarily, but picks up where you left off when you click Pause again. Stop stops the station entirely.

To mute the volume while allowing the station to continue to play, click the Mute button. To adjust the volume, drag the Volume slider to the right or left.

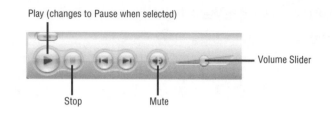

Play (changes to Pause when selected)

Volume Slider

Stop   Mute

 NOTE   What's the difference between Pause and Stop when it comes to radio? It depends on how the station is broadcast. If you're listening to a station that broadcasts "live," there is no difference. But if you're listening to a station that broadcasts from prerecording and you click Stop, the recording will start from the beginning when you click Play to start it again. With Pause, though, it will stop at the current spot and restart from that same spot when you click Pause again to "unpause" the broadcast.

Browsing the Available Stations

You can search for a specific station from a list of hundreds all over the world. If you know the station's call letters or location, you can search by that criterion; you can also browse stations by genre.

To find a station, go back to the My Radio Tuner browser window and do any of the following:

- ❖ Click Find More Stations to open a search page.

- ❖ Click one of the categories listed to view the search page with results preselected for that category.

- ❖ Enter search text in the Search Keyword box, such as the call letters, city, or type of music, to view the search page with results that match.

From the results of your search, you can click a station to open its details and then play it the same as you did the featured station earlier.

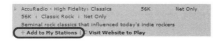

Bookmarking Your Favorite Stations

As on a car radio, you can create presets for your favorite Internet stations. Media Player comes with a list of presets called "Featured Stations," which you saw earlier. You can't edit this list (it contains stations that have paid a fee to Microsoft), but you can create your own list of favorite stations by doing the following:

1. Find a station, as in the preceding section, and click it.

2. Click Add to My Stations.

To play one of the stations on your My Stations list:

1. Click Return to My Stations.

2. If your My Stations list doesn't already appear, click My Stations to see your list.

Playing an Audio CD

When you insert an audio CD in your CD-ROM drive, one of two things will happen:

◇ The CD will start playing automatically in Windows Media Player, or

◇ A prompt will appear asking you what you want to do with the CD. If you get the prompt, click Play Audio CD Using Windows Media Player and click OK.

TIP   To prevent a CD from playing automatically when you insert it, hold down Shift as you insert it.

Some audio CDs have computer programs on them as well as music, and inserting such a CD runs the program rather than playing the music. In that case, Media Player won't start automatically; you must exit from the CD's own program and then start Media Player manually.

The Now Playing tab appears as the CD starts playing. While the CD plays, you can change to any tab in Media Player. The CD will continue to play.

Customizing the Now Playing Tab

Here's what the Now Playing tab looks like when a CD is playing:

In the center is the visualization pane. You can click the right- and left-arrow buttons above the current visualization to change it. Click the Select Now Playing Options button and then choose Visualizations to choose a different visualization category.

TIP Choose Download Visualizations to get more visualizations from the Microsoft Web site.

You can also display an equalizer pane by clicking the Now Playing Options button again and choosing Enhancements ➢ Graphic Equalizer. Its controls help you fine-tune the audio output. The buttons and sliders on it work just like those on a regular stereo. And that's just one of the many enhancement choices you can choose from, as you can see from the menu. Play around with these on your own.

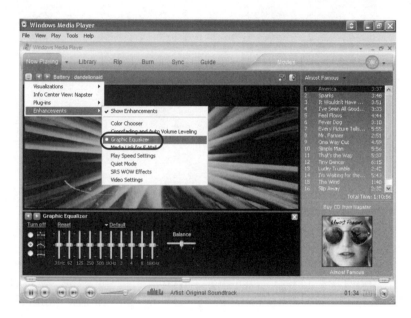

The playlist, if turned on, appears on the right side of the Now Playing tab, reporting the track names and times. You can jump to a particular song on the CD by double-clicking its name on the playlist.

You can turn the playlist display on or off by clicking the Maximize Video and Visualizations Pane button.

Using the Player Controls

The player controls appear at the bottom of the screen. (They appear in all views, not just Now Playing, but this is a good time to discuss them.) They work just like those on a regular CD player or cassette tape deck. You can pause, stop, fast-forward, rewind, and so on. The big slider above the other player control buttons is Seek; you can drag it to skip forward or backward in the track that's currently playing.

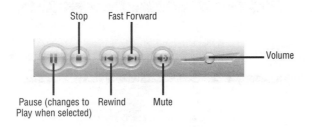

Stop

Fast Forward

Volume

Pause (changes to Play when selected)

Rewind

Mute

Selecting Which Tracks to Play

If there's a particular track you don't want to hear, right-click its name and choose Disable Selected Tracks from the shortcut menu.

To rearrange the order of tracks in the playlist, right-click a track and then choose Move Up or Move Down to change its position in the playlist.

Ripping CD Tracks

Now, let's move on to the Rip tab. *Rip* means to copy audio tracks from an audio CD into a computer-readable digital format such as WMA or MP3. From the Rip tab, you can see detailed information about each track on the CD, and copy tracks to your hard disk for later listening when you no longer have the disc in your drive.

To copy tracks from a CD to your hard disk:

1. On the Rip tab, clear the check box for any tracks that you don't want to copy.

2. Click the Rip Music button.

When the tracks have been copied, they show up on the Media Library tab, which you'll learn about in "Playing a Clip" later in this chapter.

NOTE The first time you use the Rip Music feature, you might see a security dialog box. Mark the Do Not Protect Content check box and then click OK. By choosing not to protect the content, you enable the copied tracks to be played on other computers; that way, you can copy the tracks onto a disk and take them to some other computer for listening. This is legal for the original owner, to retain the tracks in case of an accident, but it's illegal to share copyrighted tracks with others.

Windows Media Player 10 lets you specify what file format you want to rip files into. The most common formats are WMA and MP3. To choose the format you want:

1 Choose Tools ➢ Options.

2. Click the Rip Music tab.

3. Open the Format drop-down list and choose the format you want.

4. Click OK.

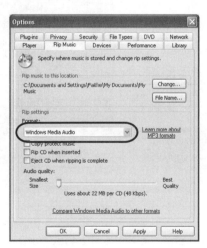

Working with the Library

Now, let's head over to the Library tab, where you can manage all your various types of music clips in one place.

The Library in Windows Media Player 10 has three panes. The leftmost pane is a folder tree, just like the one in Windows Explorer. Clips are broken down in various categories here. In the middle pane are the clips in the currently selected category. The right pane is a playlist. You can drag clips here to queue them up for playing.

Playing a Clip

To play a clip, double-click it, or click it and then click the Play button at the bottom of the window. If it's an audio clip, it simply plays and the Library remains on-screen. If it's a video clip, it switches to the Now Playing tab so that you can see the video as well as hear it.

Play (changes to Pause when selected)

In this chapter, I'll show you mostly audio clips in Library, but you can also add video clips to it, in the same way as audio clips.

Removing a Clip from the Library

To remove a clip from the Library, select it and press Delete, or right-click it and choose Delete from the shortcut menu. Then choose Delete from Library Only or Delete from Library and My Computer.

Adding Clips to the Library

As you saw earlier, copying tracks to your hard disk from a CD is one way to get clips into your Library. Another way is to download clips from the Internet and then add them to the Library like this:

1. Choose File ➢ Add to Library ➢ Add File or Playlist.

2. In the Open dialog box that appears, locate and select the file you want to add.

3. Click Open.

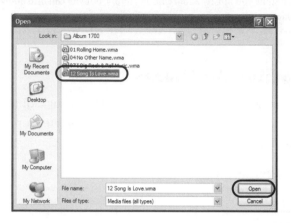

The song is added to your Library.

Depending on how the file was created, it might not have all the information that a CD-copied track contains. For example, both the artist name and the song title might appear together in the Artist column, and there might be no genre or album information. You can edit the entry by right-clicking and choosing Edit, and then tabbing between the columns.

Automatically Adding Many Clips at Once

You're probably thinking that adding all your clips to the Library is going to be a big chore, right? Wrong. Media Player has a feature that searches your hard disk and adds all the clips it finds automatically.

To search your hard disk for clips to add:

1. Choose Tools ➢ Search for Media Files.

2. The Add to Media Library by Searching Computer dialog box opens. Open the Search On drop-down list and choose the drive on which you want to search, or choose All Drives.

WARNING The Search box near the top of the Windows Media Player window is not the same as the Tools ➢ Search for Media Files command. Instead, it searches by keyword among files that are already in the Media Library.

3. If you don't want to search the entire selected drive, fill in a folder name in the Look In box, or click Browse to locate one. This will search the chosen folder and any child folders within it, ignoring the rest of the drive.

4. For fastest results, leave the New Files Only option button marked in the center section.

5. (Optional) Click the Advanced Options button, and enter any additional criteria.

For example, using Volume Leveling will even out the differences between clips recorded at different volumes. However, it slows down the process considerably, so use it only if you know there's a problem with uneven volumes.

6. When you have selected the search options you want, click Search.

7. When the status appears as Completed, click Close. The found clips now appear in your Media Library.

Copying Music to a Portable Digital Audio Player

If you have a portable digital audio device that Windows Media Player supports, you can copy clips to it from within Media Player.

To get started, connect your portable player to your computer using whatever method it needs (mine uses the USB port) and then turn the device on. The first time you connect it, Windows might go through a process of recognizing and configuring the device.

Then do the following:

1. Click the Sync tab, and then open the drop-down list on the left and choose a playlist or other category to copy to your player.

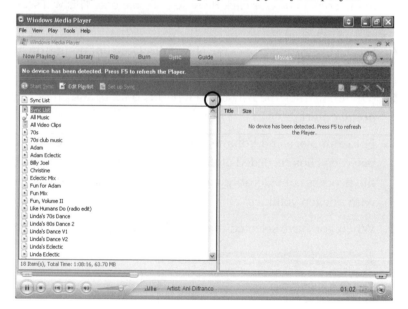

Or, if you want to copy songs from more than one already-organized grouping, display the Library tab and drag and drop the desired files to the rightmost pane. Then click back to the Sync tab when finished.

2. Click the Start Sync button (on the Sync tab). The files are copied to your portable device.

3. (Optional) Afterward, go back to the Library tab, select all the files in the rightmost pane (the Sync List), and press Delete to remove them from the list.

Creating an Audio CD

Creating an audio CD is similar to copying to a portable audio player, thanks to Windows XP's CD-writing technology. Windows Media Player treats a blank, writeable CD like a portable player. The only difference is that each song must go through an extra step of being converted from digital audio to CDA (CD Audio) format.

Here's how to create an audio CD from clips in your Library:

1. Insert a blank, writeable CD in your CD drive.

2. In the Library, open the drop-down list at the top of the right pane, where it currently may read Sync List from the previous section, and choose Burn List.

3. Drag and drop files from the Library to the right pane (now the Burn list).

NOTE   A music CD can hold 70 or 80 minutes of music, depending on the disc. If you have more clips selected than will fit, some of them report "May not fit" next to them. Deselect the check boxes of some clips until all selected clips report "Ready to copy."

4. Click the Burn tab. The selected files appear in the left pane.

5. Click the Start Burn button. Then wait for the CD to be burned.

WARNING   Avoid using your computer for any other activities while a CD is being created, to avoid errors.

Playing a DVD Movie

Windows XP includes a full-featured DVD player capability, which you can use if you have a DVD drive and **MPEG decoding** capability on your PC.

In order to play DVD movies on your PC, you must have two things: a DVD-compatible CD-ROM drive and the capability of decoding MPEG-format data in which DVD movies are stored. This decoding capability can come from a separate circuit board in your PC, from a video card that includes MPEG decoding capability, or from special decoding software. Check your computer's manual to see whether you have this capability. Most PCs that come with DVD drives also come with MPEG decoding, but some bargain PCs might not.

To play a DVD movie, simply put it in your DVD drive. It should start playing automatically in Windows Media Player.

If a dialog box like the following one appears, choose Play DVD Video Using Windows Media Player and then click OK.

If you think your PC has an MPEG decoder, but you see the following message, perhaps you need to install drivers for the decoder. Search the discs that came with your computer and see whether there is a DVD player that you can install. If you install a DVD player, it may not work the same as described here because Windows won't be using Media Player to play the movie, but rather the utility that came with your decoder.

If the movie doesn't start automatically, you can open Windows Media Player, choose Play ➤ DVD, VCD, or CD Audio, and then select the movie to play.

TIP   Some DVDs have special features, such as wide-screen capability. To access the features for the DVD, right-click the display and choose DVD Features; then select a feature from the menu that appears.

Depending on the movie, it may start from the beginning, or you may see an on-screen menu. If you do see a menu, you can explore the menu options or simply click Play to get the movie going.

To see the movie display full-screen, choose View ➤ Full Screen. To return to a windowed view, press Esc.

10

Creating Your Own Sounds and Videos

With Windows XP, you aren't limited to playing other people's music and videos—you can create your own. Many earlier versions included Sound Recorder for recording audio with a micro- phone, but Windows XP also has Windows Movie Maker, which takes audio and video recording and mixing to a new level.

Using Sound Recorder

Let's start by reviewing a venerable Windows accessory: the Sound Recorder. It enables you to record audio, such as your voice or ambient sounds like rainfall or thunder, much like a portable cassette tape recorder. To do this, you must have either a built-in microphone on your PC (which is often the case with laptops) or a microphone attached to the Mic port on your sound card. Sound Recorder will also record any other sounds that your sound card is playing, so you could also use it to record CD music or streaming audio from the Internet—in theory, anyway. (There are better ways to record music from CDs, however, as you saw in Chapter 9.)

Once you have recorded a sound clip, you can attach it to a system event in Windows, you can include it in a Windows Movie Maker show (covered later in this chapter), you can play it as an audio clip in Windows Media Player (Chapter 9), or you can use it in a variety of other ways. You can even attach it to an e-mail and send it to a friend (Chapter 18).

Recording a New Sound Clip

To record a sound clip with Sound Recorder:

1. Choose Start ➢ All Programs ➢ Accessories ➢ Entertainment ➢ Sound Recorder.

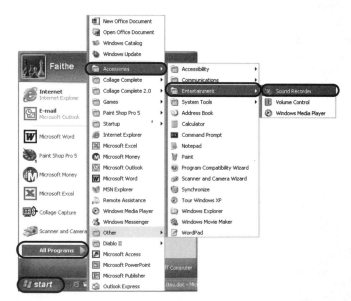

2. Make sure your microphone is plugged into your sound card's Mic port (not applicable on laptops with built-in mikes).

3. Click the Record button in the Sound Recorder window.

4. Speak, sing, or do whatever it is you want to do into the microphone.

5. When you are finished recording, click the Stop button ▣.

Playing Back a Recorded Clip

After recording a clip, you will probably want to test it before you save it, to make sure that your microphone worked okay and that the recording level was appropriate.

To play back a recorded clip:

1. Click the Play button ▶ in the Sound Recorder window.

2. (Optional) To play a different portion of the recording, drag the slider to the left or right, to skip forward or backward.

3. When the clip finishes playing, it stops automatically. To stop it early, click the Stop button ▣.

If you don't like the clip you've recorded, simply re-record. Whatever you recorded already will be discarded.

Saving a Clip as a File

Once you have recorded a clip you like, you can save it as an audio file on your hard disk. Sound Recorder clips are saved in waveform (WAV) format.

1. Choose File ➤ Save.

You can open files to play in Sound Recorder with the File ➤ Open command. You can also double-click sound files in a file management window to play them, but they will play in Windows Media Player rather than in Sound Recorder.

2. In the Save As dialog box, type a name for the clip in the File Name text box.

3. The default save location for sound clips recorded with Sound Recorder is My Documents. Change to a different save location if desired.

4. Click Save. The file is saved.

Sound Recorder is very simple—it only records audio. If you would like to record video or edit existing audio or video, try out Windows Movie Maker, which is the subject of the remainder of this chapter.

Introducing Windows Movie Maker

Windows Movie Maker helps you organize multimedia clips—that is, pictures, videos, soundtracks, voice narrations, and so on—into movies that you can play on your computer monitor, store on your hard disk, and e-mail to friends and family.

Suppose, for example, that you have video footage of little Tommy taking his first steps. You can hook up your video camera or VCR to your computer (with the right equipment, of course) and create a digital video clip from that footage. You can then edit that clip and combine it with a soundtrack and voice-over narration.

In order to use video footage, you need a way of getting it into your PC. One way is to buy a video interface device (Dazzle is one brand) that plugs into an open slot on your motherboard or connects to a port on your computer. Its purpose is to translate analog footage, such as from a video camera or VCR, into a digital file on your PC. Another way is to use a digital video camera to record the video directly. Such cameras typically come with their own interface for importing content into your PC, or they work with a FireWire (IEEE 1394) port that you buy and install separately.

A movie need not include video footage, however. If you have a scanner or digital camera, you can import still images from it, and you can also create a movie out of images you've acquired from other sources such as the Internet. A movie with still photos is somewhat like a slide show, with each image remaining on the screen for a few seconds (5 seconds is the default) and then being replaced by the next image.

The music for your movie soundtrack can come from a music clip stored on your hard disk. You can copy one from a CD-ROM, as you learned in Chapter 9, or use a clip that you have downloaded from a Web site.

If you have a sound card and a microphone, you can record voice narration for your movie. This is different from a soundtrack—it plays "on top of" the soundtrack at the same time. You can record your voice using Sound Recorder, as you learned at the beginning of the chapter, but Windows Movie Maker also has a built-in audio recorder that you might find more useful when trying to synchronize narration with video.

Here's a broad overview of the steps for creating a movie. I'll explain each of them in more detail in the remainder of the chapter.

1. Import the content for the movie into Windows Movie Maker collections. These collections are not movie-specific; they can be drawn from again and again.

2. Start a new movie, and arrange the video clips or still photos in the order in which you want them.

3. Add a soundtrack if desired.

4. Record voice narration if desired.

5. Preview your movie and then save it to your hard disk.

Starting Windows Movie Maker

To start Windows Movie Maker, choose Start ➤ All Programs ➤ Accessories ➤ Windows Movie Maker.

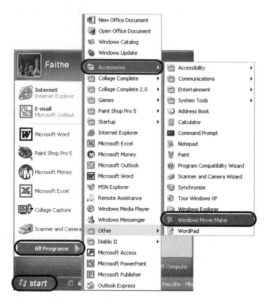

NOTE The latest version of Windows Movie Maker is version 5.1 at this writing, and that's the version shown here in this book. Earlier versions work somewhat differently. Get a free update to Windows Movie Maker through Windows Update (see Chapter 6) or download it directly from Microsoft's Web site. Go to `http://www.microsoft.com/windowsxp/using/moviemaker/default.mspx` and click Downloads.

Creating Collections

You can save all your content in the same **collection**, or you can create different collections for each type of content, or for content on particular subjects. Collections are a lot like folders in a file management window.

To create a collection:

1. Click the New Collection Folder button (or choose Tools ➢ New Collection Folder).

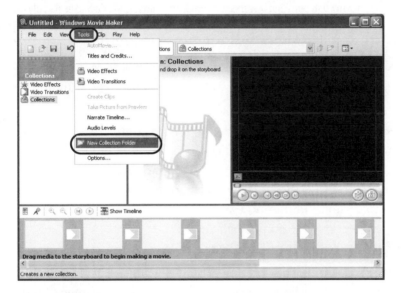

2. Type a name for the new collection and then press Enter.

Now, whenever you are recording or importing content, simply make sure the desired collection is selected before you record or import, and the items will be placed in that collection.

Collection
An organizing folder into which you place media clips in Windows Movie Maker, such as sounds, pictures, or videos. Collections are not movie-specific; you can organize your clips into collections and then make many different movies by pulling clips from them.

Recording New Content

You can record new content for your show right from within Windows Movie Maker. The recording process depends on what input devices you have.

Recording from a Video Camera

> **TIP** Digital video cameras need not be expensive. I'm using a $100 Intel PC Camera Pro that plugs into my USB port, and it works just fine with Windows Movie Maker. Its only drawback is that it must stay attached to the PC in order to function; I can't take it outside to capture footage.

With a digital video camera, you can feed directly into Windows Movie Maker from the camera. You can also take still pictures using your digital video camera, as you saw in Chapter 8.

If you have a regular video camera that records onto tape, you'll need some sort of interface device to connect it to your PC. It might work directly with Movie Maker, or it might require you to use the software that comes with the interface to first save the video to your hard disk. If that's the case, see the upcoming section, "Importing Existing Content."

Configuring Your Video Camera

Before you record for the first time, you will want to select your video and audio source and configure the settings for your video camera. To do that:

1. Ensure that your video camera is connected to your PC and that your PC recognizes it. (See Chapter 8.)

2. In Windows Movie Maker, choose File ➢ Capture Video.

3. In the Video Capture Wizard's Video Capture page, select the camera and adjust its settings if needed (such as volume level).

> **NOTE** If your video camera doesn't have any audio recording capability, as is the case with my Intel PC Camera Pro, Windows Movie Maker will use your computer's microphone to pick up the audio. Make sure your microphone is plugged in and ready.

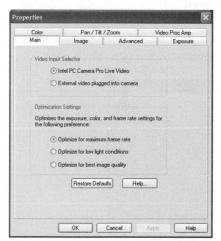

4. (Optional) Click the Configure button to configure the settings for your video camera. The Configure Video Capture Device dialog box appears.

5. Make any adjustments to the camera settings as needed.

For example, click Camera Settings to open the Properties box for your camera. Yours will look different (depending on the camera model), but here is an example. Click OK when done with the Properties box.

You can also click the Video Settings button to open the Properties dialog box that controls the video capture format. Make any changes needed and then click OK.

6. Back in the Configure Video Capture Device dialog box, click Close.

From here, you can click Cancel if you are not ready to record yet, or go on to the next section.

Recording a Video Clip

After you initially set the properties for video recording, as you did in the preceding section, you shouldn't have to reset them every time you want to record a video clip. Instead, just do the following:

1. Make sure the collection to which you want to save is selected in the folder list. If you need to close the Video Capture Wizard dialog box in order to check this, click Cancel.

2. If the Video Capture Wizard dialog box is not already open, choose File ➢ Capture Video to open it.

3. Click Next.

4. Enter a filename for the captured video clip. Then click Next.

5. Leave the default option selected (Best Quality for Playback on My Computer) and click Next.

6. (Optional) If you want to limit the size of the clip being recorded, make sure the Capture Time Limit check box is marked, and enter the time limit in its text box. The default is 2 hours.

7. (Optional) If you want the video feed broken into separate clips every time it detects a different frame (such as when you turn the camera on, or turn off the Pause feature), make sure the Create Clips When Wizard Finishes check box is marked. Otherwise, the entire video feed will be stored in a single clip.

8. When you are ready to record, click the Start Capture button.

9. When you are finished recording, click Stop Capture.

10. Click Finish. The clip is saved, and appears in the collection (in the center pane). Since it is selected, the first frame of it also appears in the preview pane (the right pane).

TIP	You can rename a clip as you would any other file: Right-click it and choose Rename; then type a new name and press Enter.

If you chose Create Clips When Wizard Finishes in step 7, a new collection folder is created for the clip inside the collection. If you didn't use Create Clips, a single new clip is placed directly in the collection. The fact that the video is split isn't a problem, because when you assemble the movie, you can place the clips adjacent to one another so that the movie will appear to be one continuous video piece. Splitting merely adds flexibility to the movie-assembly process.

Playing Back a Video Clip

To check out the video clip you recorded, click it and then click the Play button. It plays in the preview pane to the right. Each clip plays separately, even if all the clips were recorded at once. Use the play controls beneath the preview pane to control the clip, just as in Windows Media Player (Chapter 9). You can drag the slider to skip forward or backward in the clip.

Splitting a Video Clip Manually

In addition to using the automatic splits that Windows Movie Maker creates as it records, you can also manually split a video clip into one or more separate clips. To do so, play the clip, and at the desired split point, click the Split button . You can do this with clips you record and also with imported clips from other sources. (See the next section, "Importing Existing Content.")

Importing Existing Content

You can import existing videos, music, sounds, still images, and music files into your collections.

Importing existing content is the same regardless of the content's format. Windows Movie Maker accepts content in a wide variety of formats, including all popular digital video formats such as MPEG, WMV, and AVI. It also accepts many sound and graphic file formats.

To import content:

1. Select the collection into which you want to import.

2. Choose File ➢ Import into Collections.

3. In the Import File dialog box, locate and select the file you want to import.

4. Click Import to import the file.

If you find that you accidentally imported the file into the wrong collection, you can easily drag it to another collection, just as you do when managing files in Windows Explorer.

Creating a Movie Project

Now that you have imported or recorded the content for your movie, you are ready to start assembling it in a **project**, which you'll save in Windows Movie Maker.

What's the difference between a movie and a project? Well, when you "publish" the project as a movie, you create a read-only copy that you can never edit again; that's why it's important to save the project as well as the movie. Projects continue to be editable, so you can always make changes and republish the movie whenever you are ready to reflect those changes.

You can assemble a project in any order, but I like to start with the visual images (video clips and still photos) and then add the soundtrack. Finally, as the last step, I add the voice narration.

Starting a New Project

A new, blank project starts when you start Movie Maker, but you can create a new project at any time by doing the following:

1. Click the New Project button ⬜ (or choose File ➤ New Project).

2. If prompted to save the changes to the existing project, click Yes or No and save (or not) as appropriate.

Understanding Project Views

There are two views of the project: Storyboard and Timeline. *Storyboard view* shows pictures only; each video clip is represented by a picture of the first frame of the video. Each clip takes up the same one-frame space on the storyboard, regardless of its actual length.

Project
The working file for a movie you are creating in Windows Movie Maker.

You can add audio clips to Timeline view only. If you attempt to drop an audio clip on the storyboard, a message appears, telling you that it is switching to Timeline view; click OK to continue.

Timeline view, in contrast, shows each visual clip's size according to the amount of time it will occupy in the movie. And beneath the pictures runs a soundtrack line indicating what sounds will be heard while the pictures are appearing.

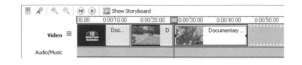

To switch between Storyboard and Timeline views, you can use the View menu, or click the Show Storyboard (or Show Timeline button) above the timeline (or storyboard).

Adding Clips to the Project

Start your project by dragging pictures or video clips from your various collections into the project timeline or storyboard at the bottom of the screen. Simply drag and drop, as you have learned in file management.

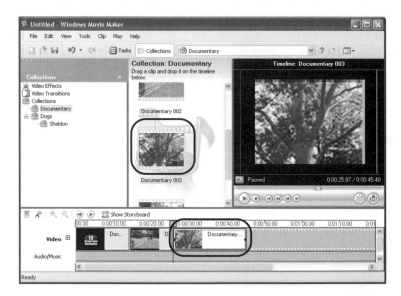

To remove a clip from the project, click it on the timeline or storyboard and then press the Delete key.

To move the clip around on the project, drag it to the left or right.

Changing the Duration of a Still Image

When you import a photo into a collection, it is assigned a default duration. The original setting is 5 seconds, but you can change the default duration by choosing Tools ➢ Options and entering a different value in the Picture Duration box.

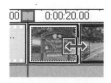

The photo's default duration, however, is always the setting that was in effect when it was imported. So, for example, if you import a photo when the Default Imported Photo Duration is set to 5 seconds, and you later change that setting to 10 seconds, all photos you imported prior to the change will remain with 5-second durations.

You can change a still picture's duration on the timeline in an individual project, however. Do the following:

1. View the project in Timeline view.

2. Click the picture for which you want to change the duration. (Make sure you choose a still photo, not a video clip.) A small black triangle appears on its right edge.

3. Drag that triangle to the left or right to adjust its duration. Drag to the right to make it longer or to the left to make it shorter.

If the picture was not at the end of the project and you increased its duration, the clip to its right automatically moves over.

Applying Video Effects

The newest version of Windows Movie Maker (unlike the one that came with Windows XP initially) provides many transition effects you can apply to move between clips in your project. To apply one:

1. Select a clip in the project (in Timeline or Storyboard view).

2. Choose Clip ➤ Video ➤ Video Effects.

3. Click the effect you want and click Add. You can add more than one effect to a clip, and they will occur in the order in which you choose them on this list.

4. Click OK.

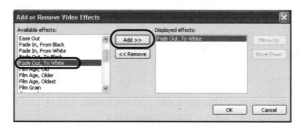

You will probably want to test your movie after applying an effect; double-click the clip in the storyboard or timeline to play it in the Preview window.

Adding Sound and Narration

Now that the visual part of your movie is assembled, it's time to work on music and narration. If the video you recorded included sound, it will automatically be included with the video footage. In the following sections, you'll learn how to add *additional* sounds and music.

Adding a Musical Soundtrack

To include a soundtrack, add a CD or other music clip to a collection and then drag it onto the timeline. If you are not already in Timeline view, the view switches for you automatically.

Recording Narration

After you've finalized the duration of each clip, you're ready to record your narration. You won't want to record it earlier, because if the durations of the clips change, the narration will be off.

To record narration:

1. Prepare your microphone and ensure that it's working.

2. Switch to Timeline view if you aren't already there.

3. Choose Tools ➤ Narrate Timeline. The Narrate Timeline controls appear.

4. Adjust the recording level using the Input Level slider if desired. Speak into the microphone and use the meter next to the slider as your guide.

5. When you are ready, click Start Narration.

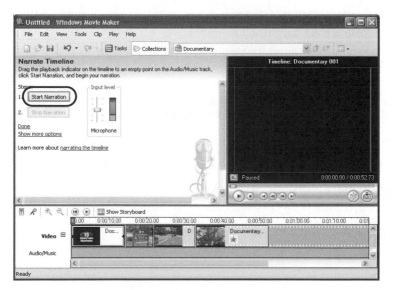

Your movie begins showing in the preview pane, and the Start Narration button becomes a Stop Narration button.

6. Speak into the microphone, narrating as you go along. When you are finished, click Stop.

7. In the Save Windows Media File dialog box that appears, enter a filename for the narration track and then click Save.

The track is saved in WMA format.

If you previously assigned a musical soundtrack, you might find that the narration has forced the soundtrack to move over on the timeline. To have them play simultaneously, drag them so that they overlap.

Previewing the Movie

Before you publish the movie (that is, save the project in movie format), you will want to preview it to make sure everything is as you want it to be.

To preview the movie in the preview pane, simply click the Play button while the first clip of the project is selected in the timeline or storyboard.

To view it full-screen, choose Play ➢ Full Screen.

Saving the Movie

Ready to save your project in movie format? First, save your project as a project. Remember, you can't make changes to a published movie, so if you want to change it, you'll need to make the changes to the project and then republish. To save your project, choose File ➤ Save (or click the Save button on the toolbar), and save as you would any other data file in a program.

Now you're ready to publish your movie! To do so:

1. Choose File ➤ Save Movie File.

2. In the Save Movie Wizard dialog box, choose a location for the saved movie. Then click Next. The most common location is My Computer.

3. Enter a filename for the new movie and click Next.

4. Leave the Best Quality for Playback on My Computer option button marked, and click Next.

5. Wait for the movie to be created and saved.

6. Click Finish. The movie plays in Windows Media Player.

Part 4

Customizing Windows XP

Windows is an amazingly flexible operating system. If there's something you don't like about the way it works, chances are good that it's adjustable. From the screen colors to the mouse pointer size and speed, all the settings you can imagine are there for your adjustments. In this part of the book, you'll learn how to change the appearance and functionality of Windows XP, and how to set things up so that each person in your household can maintain their own individual customization settings.

Customizing Windows XP

11 Adjusting Screen Appearance

• •

Everyone has different tastes, so why should one Windows look-and-feel suffice for all? In this chapter, you will learn how to make the Windows desktop look radically different, with colors, wallpapers, icons, screen-resolution changes, and more. You'll also learn how to customize the taskbar so that it takes up more or less space on-screen and/or appears in a different location.

Changing the Display Mode

The display mode is actually a combination of three distinct settings: resolution, color depth, and refresh rate. The following sections explain those settings and how to adjust them.

Changing the Resolution and Color Depth

Resolution

The number of individual pixels (dots) that make up the screen display in a certain video mode. A common resolution, for example, is 800 pixels wide by 600 pixels tall (800×600).

The **resolution** is the number of pixels that make up the display. The more pixels (dots) per inch, the finer the level of detail, and the smaller everything will appear on-screen. For example, at a high resolution such as 1280×1024, all the icons on the desktop will appear very tiny (see the next figure), while at a low resolution, like 800×600 (second figure), they will appear much larger. Reason? An icon, a menu, a character of text, and so on is a precise number of pixels in size. When the pixels are closer together, the object looks smaller. The Windows desktop, on the other hand, always expands to fill the entire available screen space; it doesn't have a fixed size.

You might want to increase the resolution if you would like to see more detail on-screen at once without scrolling. For example, at a higher resolution, you can see greater portions of Web pages at once, and more cells in a spreadsheet. Or, if you have limited vision, you might want to decrease the resolution so that everything appears larger.

Color depth is the number of colors to choose from for each pixel. The higher the color depth, the more unique colors you can display at once on-screen, and thus the better your photographs and graphics will look.

Color depth is measured in bits. For example, 4-bit color depth provides 16 color choices because 16 combinations are possible with a 4-digit binary number (2 to the 4th power). There are 8 bits in a byte, so 4-bit color requires half a byte for each pixel. In a 600×800 display, that would be 600×800 (480K) divided by 2, or 240K. That's not much—most video cards come with at least 4MB these days. Higher resolutions add up quickly, however. For example, 1024×768 in 32-bit color would require about 2.51MB.

Windows XP's default is to use a high color depth (32-bit), which results in the best-quality display. If, however, you are playing a game that requires some other color depth, or if you are concerned about sluggish system performance, you might decrease the color depth to see if that helps.

In earlier versions of Windows, the lowest resolution was 640×480, but in Windows XP, the lowest resolution for most video cards is 800×600.

Color depth
The number of color choices for each pixel. The more colors to choose from, the better and more realistic photos and other graphics will appear on-screen.

To adjust the resolution and color depth:

1. Right-click the desktop and then choose Properties.

2. Click the Settings tab.

3. Under Screen Resolution, drag the slider to the left or right to change the resolution.

4. Open the Color Quality drop-down list and choose a color depth.

5. Click OK.

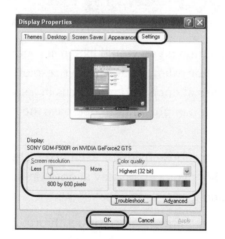

6. If this is the first time you have chosen this resolution or color depth, a dialog box appears asking you to confirm that the new display mode works. Click Yes within 15 seconds, or the display will revert to the previous resolution setting.

Changing the Refresh Rate

The **refresh rate** is the speed at which each pixel's color is refreshed by the laser inside the monitor. Each pixel's color starts decaying immediately after the laser hits it, so the laser must repaint the entire screen many times per second,

Refresh rate

The frequency with which the pixels on the screen are repainted, or refreshed, by the laser inside the monitor. The higher the refresh rate, the less flicker in the display and the easier the display is on your eyes. A common refresh rate is 85Hz.

pixel by pixel. The more times per second this happens, the higher the refresh rate and the less flicker you see in the display. Flicker is caused by pixels starting to decay to black before the laser gets around to hitting them again. The refresh rate is limited by the monitor's capability.

To change the refresh rate, do the following:

1. Right-click the desktop and then choose Properties.

2. In the Display Properties dialog box, click the Settings tab and then click the Advanced button. A properties box for the monitor and video card appears.

3. Click the Monitor tab; then open the Screen Refresh Rate drop-down list and choose a refresh rate. To eliminate noticeable flicker, set the refresh rate to at least 85Hz if your monitor is capable of it.

4. Click OK. Your monitor changes its refresh rate.

> The Hide Modes That This Monitor Cannot Display check box, when active, prevents you from selecting a higher refresh rate than the driver for your monitor thinks it can handle. Leave this marked. An exception might be appropriate if Windows hasn't correctly identified your monitor and you know your monitor is capable of a higher refresh rate than the current driver will allow.

5. If this is the first time you have changed to this refresh rate, a confirmation box appears. Click Yes.

6. Click OK to close the Display Properties box.

Changing the Desktop Appearance

Customizing the Windows desktop is a favorite activity with almost everyone. Windows XP makes it easy to express your own personal flair by the background, font, and color choices you make for the on-screen display. In the following sections, you will learn about several of the adjustments you can make to change how Windows looks.

Working with Desktop Themes

A desktop theme is a combination of font, background image, and color choices, plus, in some cases, sounds and icons. Applying a theme to your desktop is a time-saver because you don't have to adjust individual appearance settings, and you also get the benefit of prechosen color combinations and other choices designed to look good together.

Windows XP has a new look-and-feel compared to earlier Windows versions, and one reason is that it has a new theme called Windows XP applied by default. If you prefer the classic Windows appearance, you can change to the Windows Classic theme. You can also choose any of several other themes.

To change the theme:

> If there's something about a theme you don't like—the colors, the desktop background, and so forth—don't worry. You will learn to change it later in this chapter.

1. Right-click the desktop and then choose Properties.

```
Arrange Icons By   ▶
Refresh
───────────────────
Paste
Paste Shortcut
───────────────────
New                ▶
───────────────────
Properties
```

2. In the Display Properties dialog box, click the Themes tab (if it doesn't already appear).

3. Open the Theme drop-down list and choose the theme you want. A sample of it appears in the Sample pane.

> **TIP** If you have an active Internet connection (see Chapter 16), you can choose More Themes Online to open a Web browser window that enables you to download additional themes from Microsoft's Web site.

4. Click OK.

Notice the Save As button in the dialog box. If you have modified the appearance so that the settings for a particular theme are no longer fully in effect, the word *modified* will appear next to the current theme name. If you see that, you can click Save As to save the modified settings under a new theme name.

The Delete button enables you to delete the themes you have created; it is inactive unless one of your custom themes is selected.

Changing the Desktop Background

The background is the big flat area on which all the icons sit. By default, it contains **wallpaper** of a grassy hill and blue sky. You can choose a different wallpaper, or turn off wallpaper altogether and use a solid color as the background.

Wallpaper
A graphical image placed on the desktop background.

To change the desktop background:

1. Right-click the desktop and then choose Properties.

2. In the Display Properties dialog box, click the Desktop tab.

3. Click the name of a graphic on the Background list. A sample appears. Or click None from the list to remove the wallpaper altogether.

4. Open the Position list and choose Stretch, Tile, or Center.

Stretch enlarges a single copy of the image to fill the available space.

Tile fills the available space with multiple copies of the image at its default size.

Center places a single copy of the image at its default size in the center of the desktop and allows whatever color you select in step 5 to appear around the edges.

5. If you chose None in step 3, or if you chose Center in step 4, click the Color button to open a palette from which to choose a solid background color.

Rather than choose a color from the palette, you can click Other to open a dialog box containing a larger assortment of colors from which to choose.

6. Click OK.

The Customize Desktop button enables you to change what icons appear on the desktop. You'll learn more about it in the upcoming section "Changing Desktop Icon Appearance."

Changing Screen Colors and Window/Button Style

You saw in the preceding section how to change the desktop background color, but there are many other color choices to be made. You can change the color of virtually every screen element you see. You can also switch back and forth between the Windows XP window and button style (the big blue buttons and fat borders) and the classic Windows style.

To change colors and window/button style:

1. Right-click the desktop and then choose Properties.

2. In the Display Properties dialog box, click the Appearance tab.

3. Open the Windows and Buttons list and choose either Windows XP Style or Windows Classic Style.

4. Open the Color Scheme list and choose a different color scheme if desired.

5. Open the Font Size list and select a font size. The available font sizes depend on your choice in step 4. The Windows Standard color scheme, for example, has Normal, Large Fonts, and Extra Large Fonts to choose from; some other color schemes have only Normal.

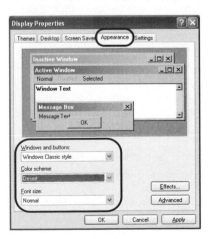

The color schemes are completely different for the Windows XP style and the Windows classic style. Classic style has many more to choose from.

You can click the Effects button to open the Effects dialog box. There you can fine-tune some appearance settings for Windows, such as showing shadows under menus, making menus fade in and out, and enlarging the icons on the desktop.

6. If you are satisfied with the colors you've selected, click OK, and you're done. Otherwise, click Advanced to adjust colors for individual parts of the screen and go on to step 7.

7. In the Advanced Appearance box, open the Item list and select the item you want to recolor or change the settings for. You can also click an item in the sample area above if you don't know its name.

NOTE Depending on what item you choose, different options will become available. For example, here I've selected Active Title Bar, and all the options are available. If you choose an item, such as Desktop, that doesn't contain text, the Font controls won't be available. Different aspects are also customizable depending on whether you are using Windows XP style or Windows classic style buttons and menus.

8. If the Size box next to Item is available, select a size. The measurements are in pixels.

9. Click the Color 1 button and select a different color if desired. You can choose Other for a dialog box that offers more color choices.

10. If the Color 2 button is available, click it and select a second color. Color 2 is mostly for window title bars; it allows a fade effect from one color to the other. It's not available in color depths of less than 16-bit.

11. If the Font list is available, open it and choose a font. Font is available only for items that contain text.

12. If the Size box next to Font is available, enter a font size. Font size is measured in points. A point is $\frac{1}{72}$ of an inch.

13. If the Color box next to Font is available, click it and choose a text color.

14. If the B and I buttons are available, click them to toggle Bold and Italic
on and off if desired.

15. Go back to step 7 to customize some other screen item, or click OK if
you're finished.

16. Click OK to close the Display Properties box.

Changing Desktop Icon Appearance

By default, the Windows desktop is fairly empty; there are very few system
icons on it. One that *does* appear by default is the Recycle Bin.

If you have worked with other versions of Windows, however, you may be
accustomed to extra shortcuts for Internet Explorer, My Computer, My Documents, and My Network Places. You can place these icons back on the desktop
in Windows XP with a few simple mouse clicks. You can also change the icons
used for these shortcuts.

To modify the desktop icon configuration:

1. Right-click the desktop and then choose Properties.

2. In the Display Properties dialog box, click the Desktop tab and then
click Customize Desktop.

3. In the Desktop Items dialog box, under Desktop Icons, mark the check boxes for any shortcuts you want to appear on the desktop.

4. If you want to change the icon used for a particular shortcut, do the following:

   a. Click the icon you want to change and then click Change Icon.

   b. In the Change Icon dialog box, click the alternative icon to use. Or, to browse in a different location for an icon, click Browse and choose a different **icon file**.

   c. After selecting an icon, click OK.

   d. Repeat steps a–c for any other icons you want to change.

5. Click OK to close the Display Properties box.

Choosing a Screensaver

If you often leave your computer turned on and unattended for long periods of time, you might want to use a **screensaver**, or set the monitor to turn itself off completely after a specified period of inactivity. The latter, in particular, can reduce your electric bill, especially if you have a large monitor.

Icon file

A file containing one or more icons. An icon file can be an executable file (`.exe`), a library file (`.dll`), or an icon graphic file (`.ico`). A shortcut in Windows typically uses one of the icons from the file for which it is a shortcut, but it need not do so necessarily; you can assign an icon from any source to any file.

Screensaver

A moving image on the screen that appears after a certain number of minutes of idleness, to prevent burn-in on your monitor. With old monitor technology, screensavers were an important tool, but today they are mostly for fun because power management features in the computer and the monitor can turn the monitor off completely after a specified period of inactivity.

To set up a screensaver, follow these steps:

1. Right-click the desktop and then choose Properties.

2. In the Display Properties dialog box, click the Screen Saver tab. Then open the Screen Saver drop-down list and choose a screensaver. A sample of it appears in the preview area.

3. In the Wait box, enter the number of minutes of idle time before the screensaver activates.

4. (Optional) If you want users to have to type the currently logged-in user's password when the screensaver deactivates, mark the On Resume, Password Protect check box.

> Multiuser systems are covered in Chapter 14.

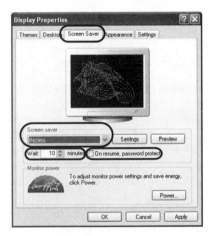

5. (Optional) To change the settings for the chosen screensaver, click the Settings button. Then make any changes in the dialog box that appears and click OK. The settings for each screensaver are different; here are the settings for Bezier, for example:

> The Preview button previews the chosen screensaver in full-screen view, not just in the preview area. To exit from the full-screen preview, move the mouse or press a key.

6. If you don't need to change the monitor's automatic shutoff setting, click OK, and you're done. Otherwise, click the Power button.

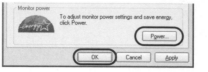

7. In the Power Options Properties dialog box, open the Turn Off Monitor drop-down list and select a number of minutes of idle time that should elapse before the monitor shuts off.

8. (Optional) If you want your hard disks to stop spinning after a certain interval of inactivity, open the Turn Off Hard Disks drop-down list and select a number of minutes. Most people leave this set to Never for a desktop PC.

9. Click OK to close the Power Options Properties box.

10. Click OK to close the Display Properties box.

Changing How the Taskbar Looks and Operates

You have already learned about a few small ways to customize the taskbar, such as adding the Quick Launch toolbar to it. In this final section of the chapter, you'll find out about some other taskbar options that affect the way it looks and/or behaves.

Setting Taskbar Properties

Like most other on-screen items, the taskbar has its own set of properties you can adjust for it. To check them out and make changes if desired, do the following:

1. Right-click the taskbar and then choose Properties.

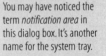

2. In the Taskbar and Start Menu Properties dialog box, mark or clear the check boxes for any of the following settings:

Lock the taskbar.   When this is selected, no changes to the taskbar are allowed. When cleared, you can make changes.

Auto-hide the taskbar.   When selected, the taskbar appears as a very thin line at the bottom of the screen until you move your mouse into its area; then it springs open. This can save screen space.

Keep the taskbar on top of other windows.   When selected, the taskbar is always visible, no matter what other windows are open. When cleared, the taskbar is like other windows, in that a window can be placed on top of it, obscuring it.

You may have noticed the term *notification area* in this dialog box. It's another name for the system tray.

Group similar taskbar buttons.   When marked, if two or more of the same sort of window are open (such as two Word documents or two file management windows), they show up as a single button on the taskbar. Click it to see a menu showing all the open windows in that category. When the check box is cleared, each window has its own taskbar button.

Show Quick Launch. When marked, the Quick Launch toolbar appears on the taskbar. When cleared, it does not. You learned about the Quick Launch toolbar in Chapter 1.

Show the clock. When marked, the clock appears at the right end of the taskbar.

Hide inactive icons. When marked, the system tray displays only recently accessed icons, along with a left-pointing arrow button; you can click the button to see the rest of the icons.

Resizing the Taskbar

By default, the taskbar occupies a single row at the bottom of the screen. If there are more open windows than will fit, up and down arrows appear on the taskbar, and you can scroll through the "pages" of open window icons by clicking the arrows.

You can also enlarge the taskbar so that it has multiple rows. To do so, position the mouse pointer over the top edge of the taskbar and drag upward. To decrease the size, drag the top edge back down.

12

Customizing System Settings

• •

In Chapter 11 you learned some ways to make
Windows XP look different. Now it's time to learn
how to make Windows act and sound different, too.
In this chapter, you will learn how to change the
date and time, adjust keyboard and mouse performance, and change audio and system sounds.

Setting the Date and Time

Have you ever wondered how your computer always seems to know the date and time? It's because of timekeeping circuitry built into the motherboard. There is a small battery on the motherboard that keeps this clock powered even when you turn off the computer.

If you move to a different time zone, or if your computer's clock starts losing time (which can happen if the battery needs changing), you can adjust the date and time setting through Windows.

To change the date or time:

Windows XP comes with a feature that will automatically synchronize the time on your computer with a time server on the Internet once a week. You'll see how to turn it on or off in these steps.

1. Double-click the clock on the taskbar.

The Date and Time Properties dialog box appears.

2. If the date shown on the Date & Time tab is incorrect, click the correct date on the calendar. To see a different month or year, open the Month or Year drop-down list and make another selection.

3. If the time shown is incorrect, enter a new time in the text box below the clock.

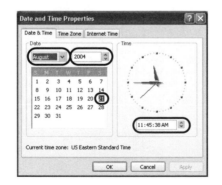

4. If you have changed time zones, click the Time Zone tab. Then select your time zone from the drop-down list.

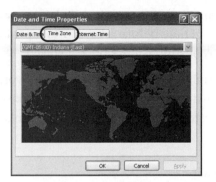

5. To check the time against a **time server** on the Internet, click the Internet Time tab and then click Update Now. If one server doesn't work, try choosing another one from the list of servers and clicking Update Now again.

6. If you don't want to use the time server automatically in the future, clear the "Automatically synchronize with an Internet time server" check box.

7. Click OK.

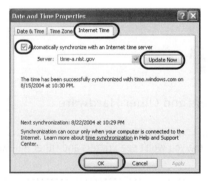

Changing Keyboard Properties

The keyboard works pretty well right out of the box; you don't need to do anything special to make it work. However, you can make a few fine-tuning adjustments to its performance to make typing more convenient.

Time server

An Internet site that's set up to provide the correct date and time to anyone who requests it. It's sort of like those "time and temperature" phone numbers you might have called before.

You might turn off automatic synchronization if your computer isn't connected to the Internet full-time. That way, you can manually use Update Now whenever you happen to be connected instead of worrying about trying to be connected when the next update is scheduled.

Key repeat

When you hold down a key, at first nothing happens. But if you continue to hold down the key, after a second or two, the key's character starts repeating rapidly on the screen, as if you were quickly pressing and releasing the key repeatedly. This is called *repeat,* and it's a convenience in case you want a whole line of a certain character. (For example, some people might create a divider line in a document with a row of periods or plus signs.)

Two of the keyboard settings you can adjust have to do with **key repeat**. You can set the repeat delay (the amount of time before a key starts repeating) and the repeat rate (the speed at which repeating occurs once it starts).

The other keyboard setting is cursor blink rate. When you type in a word processor or other program, the cursor (usually a vertical line) blinks to make it easier for you to locate it. The cursor blink rate controls the speed of the blinking.

To set keyboard properties:

1. Choose Start ➢ Control Panel.

2. In Control Panel, click Printers and Other Hardware.

> **NOTE** If your Control Panel is in classic view, you won't see Printers and Other Hardware. Double-click Keyboard and skip to step 4.

3. In the Printers and Other Hardware window, click Keyboard.

4. In the Keyboard Properties dialog box, click the Speed tab if it isn't already selected.

5. Drag the sliders to adjust repeat delay and repeat rate. To test the settings, click inside the text box and then hold down a key.

6. Drag the Cursor Blink Rate slider to adjust the blink rate.

7. Click OK to close the Keyboard Properties box.

Both the keyboard and the mouse have a Hardware tab in their Properties boxes, but most people won't need to use it. It contains options for installing a different device driver, in case Windows has detected your keyboard or mouse incorrectly (not likely) or in case you have a custom driver that you want to install.

8. Close Control Panel.

Adjusting Mouse Operation

Since you use your mouse for almost all activity in Windows, it's imperative that the mouse operate the way you want it to. Fortunately, almost every aspect of mouse operation is customizable. You can change the range of cursor motion, the size of the cursor, and many other factors.

To explore mouse settings, and possibly make some changes, do the following:

1. Choose Start ➤ Control Panel.

2. Click Printers and Other Hardware.

NOTE　If Control Panel is in classic view, double-click Mouse instead of following steps 2 and 3.

3. In the Printers and Other Hardware window, click Mouse.

4. On the Buttons tab in the Mouse Properties dialog box, adjust any of these settings if desired:

Switch Primary and Secondary Buttons   If you are left-handed and you want to use your strongest finger for the primary mouse button, you might want to switch the button functions.

Double-Click Speed   Drag the slider to adjust the speed at which you must double-click in order for Windows to recognize your intent as a double-click and not two single clicks. Slow it down if you are having trouble double-clicking fast enough; speed it up if you are accidentally double-clicking frequently. Test the new setting by double-clicking the folder to the right of the slider.

ClickLock   This setting turns the mouse button into a toggle, like the Caps Lock key, so that you don't have to hold it down when you want to drag. It's useful for people with limited mobility or dexterity—but irritating for almost everyone else.

5. Click the Pointers tab; then open the Scheme drop-down list and select a different **pointer scheme** if desired.

The bonus chapter, "Using the Accessibility Tools," covers many more accessibility features that are useful to people with physical handicaps, limited vision, or limited hearing. You'll find this chapter at Sybex's Web site, **www.sybex.com**. On the Home page, type the book's ISBN code, 2982, in the Search box and then click Go. On the search results page, click the book's title to go to the page for the book.

Pointer scheme

A collection of mouse pointer graphics designed to look good together. A scheme provides a pointer for each of the dozen or more types of pointers that Windows employs, such as Normal Select, Busy, and Working in Background.

6. To enable or disable the **pointer shadow**, click the Enable Pointer Shadow check box.

7. (Optional) If you want to customize the chosen pointer scheme, click an individual pointer on the list and then click Browse.

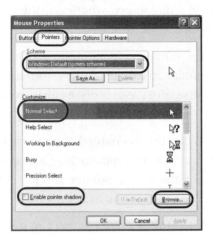

A Browse dialog box opens, showing all the available pointers. Select a different pointer and click Open.

8. Click the Pointer Options tab and then adjust any of these settings as desired:

Pointer Speed   Drag the slider to change the mouse sensitivity—that is, the distance that the mouse pointer moves on-screen in relation to the distance that you physically move the mouse.

Pointer shadow

A shadow that appears behind the mouse pointer on-screen. It's primarily for decoration; turning it off can slightly improve the performance of a slower computer.

Enhance Pointer Precision   Turn this feature on to enable some minor improvements to pointer movement; turn it off on a slower computer to improve performance.

Snap To   Turn on to make the mouse pointer automatically jump to the default command button in a dialog box whenever one is open, making it easier for you to click that button.

Display Pointer Trails   Turn on to make a "trail" appear behind the pointer when you move it—similar to exhaust fumes from a car. The trail can help you find the mouse on-screen more easily if you have limited vision.

Hide Pointer While Typing   When this is enabled, the mouse pointer disappears when you are typing in a program such as a word processor, to avoid confusion between the mouse pointer and the cursor. When you move the mouse, the cursor pops back into view.

Show Location of Pointer   When this is enabled, you can press the Ctrl key to make a radiating circle flash around the pointer. This is good for people with limited vision or those who tend to "lose" the pointer on-screen, but who don't like the pointer trails feature.

9. Click OK to accept your new settings.

Setting Sound and Audio Properties

Sound and audio properties control how sound comes out of your PC. Most PCs have a sound card, or sound support built into the motherboard. You plug speakers into the sound card or into a built-in speaker jack on the PC, and Windows sends forth sounds and music from the sound card. It's all pretty straightforward, unless you have more than one sound card or some special speaker configuration. In that case, you might need to adjust the sound and audio properties for best performance with your system.

Even though you probably won't need to adjust your sound and audio settings, it's a good idea to check them out anyway just for your own education. There are also a few little tweaks and secrets hidden in these properties that everyone can benefit from, such as the ability to show or hide the speaker icon in the system tray for quick volume adjustments.

Here's how to adjust the settings:

1. Choose Start ➢ Control Panel.

2. In Control Panel, click Sounds, Speech, and Audio Devices.

3. In the Sounds, Speech, and Audio Devices window, click Sounds and Audio Devices.

4. On the Volume tab of the Properties dialog box, change any of the following settings as desired:

Device Volume   Drag the slider to adjust the overall system volume.

Why might someone have more than one sound card? Primarily so that they can have more than one set of speakers plugged in simultaneously, each doing its own thing. People who use a computer to record their own music might find this especially useful. For example, with two sound cards, you could have external speakers playing an audio CD while an electronic keyboard plugged into another sound card feeds music into some headphones and records only the keyboard track to disk.

Mute   Mark this check box to temporarily disable all sounds from the speakers.

Place Volume Icon in the Taskbar   Select or deselect to add or remove a shortcut for adjusting the volume in the system tray (next to the clock).

Double-clicking that icon  in the system tray will open the full Play Control dialog box; single-clicking it will open a single Volume slider like this:

Advanced (in Device Volume Section)   Click this button to open the Play Control dialog box, through which you can adjust the volume for individual devices such as the microphone, speakers, and line in. This is the same dialog box that you get when you double-click the speaker icon in the system tray.

Speaker Volume   Click to open a dialog box in which you can adjust the volume for right and left speakers separately.

Advanced (in Speaker Settings section)　Click to open an Advanced Audio Properties dialog box, where you can choose a speaker configuration that takes advantage of any extra speaker features you have, such as a woofer or Surround Sound.

5. Click the Audio tab and then make any changes needed to the following controls:

In the **Sound Playback** section, if you have more than one sound card, choose the one you want to use as the default. The Volume

MIDI music

MIDI stands for Musical Instrument Digital Interface. It's the interface through which digital instruments like keyboards are attached to your sound card for input.

and Advanced buttons in this section are the same as those on the Volume tab.

In the **Sound Recording** section, if you have more than one sound recording device, select the default one. Normally, this would be the same as your default playback device—your sound card. However, if you have more than one sound card, you might use one for playback and another for recording.

In the **MIDI Music Playback** section, select the default device to use for **MIDI music**. If you aren't sure, leave it set for the default.

6. Click OK to close the Sounds and Audio Devices Properties box.

7. Close Control Panel.

You will learn in the next section how to select system sounds on the Sounds tab of this dialog box.

Sound scheme

A named group of sound-file assignments for various system events. Not every sound scheme provides a sound for every system event, but almost all schemes provide sounds for at least the most popular dozen or so events.

Program event

Anything that happens in Windows is technically a program event. This can include a menu opening or closing, a dialog box opening or closing, a program opening or closing, an error occurring, and so on. Another name for this is *system event*.

Assigning Sounds to Events

You may have noticed that in your day-to-day Windows activities, sounds play at certain times. For example, there's a startup sound, a shutdown sound, a sound when an error occurs, a sound when you receive new e-mail, and so on. You can control these sounds, either by selecting a different **sound scheme** or by assigning individual sounds to **program events**.

To change your system sounds:

1. Repeat steps 1–3 of the preceding procedure to reopen the Sounds and Audio Devices Properties dialog box.

2. Click the Sounds tab; then open the Sound Scheme drop-down list and select a scheme. (Or, to turn off all sounds, choose No Sounds. This removes sound assignments for all system events.)

3. If any sound changes have been made since you last selected a scheme, a warning box appears. Click No to decline to save your current settings, or click Yes to save them. (If you choose Yes, enter a name for the new scheme and then click OK.)

4. To change an individual program event's sound, select the event in the Program Events section and then choose a sound from the Sounds drop-down list.

Or, to assign a sound that isn't on that list, click Browse, locate and select the sound file, and click OK.

To preview a sound, click the Play button ▶.

5. Repeat step 4 for each program event you want to change.

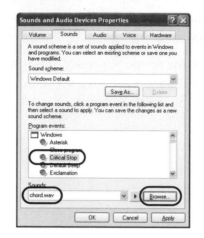

6. (Optional) If you want to save your changes as a new scheme, click Save As. The Save Scheme As dialog box opens.

7. Type a name for the new scheme and then click OK.

8. Click OK to close the Sounds and Audio Devices Properties box.

9. Close Control Panel.

There are many more Windows settings you can change than this chapter has explored. You might want to go through Control Panel on your own, icon-by-icon, and see what's available. For example, if you have a game controller, you can calibrate it using the Game Controllers Properties in Control Panel.

13 Managing Fonts and Printers

● ●

Printing is one of the most common activities on a computer, because people often need to share hard copy with others. It's a lot easier than lugging your computer around to show people what's on the screen! In this chapter, you will learn how to set up a printer in Windows XP, and how to adjust the properties for the printer and to control its print queue. You will also learn how to add and remove fonts from your system, and how to print a sample of each installed font.

Setting Up a New Printer

Almost all printers these days come with their own Setup disk, and you should use it if it's available. These Setup programs often install extra utilities that can help the printer work at its best. See Chapter 6 for help running a Setup program.

If you don't have the Setup disk for a printer, try downloading a Setup program for the printer from the printer manufacturer's Web site. Chapter 17 covers using Internet Explorer to visit Web sites.

Sources of Printer Drivers

If you have difficulty finding a Windows XP driver for your printer, one might be available online at the printer manufacturer's Web site. Here are some Web addresses of popular printer manufacturers:

- ◆ Lexmark: `www.lexmark.com/drivers/index.html`
- ◆ Hewlett-Packard: `www.hp.com/cposupport/software.html`
- ◆ Epson: `support.epson.com/filelibrary.html`

There is also a company called GRC that provides, as part of its Web site, a very comprehensive list of printer manufacturers and direct links to their driver download sites. The Web address is `www.printgrc.com/drivers.cfm`.

You might also try `www.windrivers.com`.

Local printer

A printer that is physically attached to your own PC, usually with a parallel cable or USB cable.

Network printer

A printer that is connected to some other PC on your local area network (LAN), or connected directly to the LAN. For example, if you have a network, you can print from any computer, using the printer attached to any other computer. However, you must set up the printer (as a network printer) on each PC from which you want to print.

If neither of the above is a viable option, you can possibly set up the printer to work in Windows XP using the Add Printer Wizard. Windows supports many printer brands and models, and perhaps it has support for yours.

Starting the Add Printer Wizard

Regardless of whether you are setting up a **local printer** or a **network printer**, the beginning steps are the same. Follow these steps to start the Add Printer Wizard:

1. Choose Start ➢ Control Panel.

2. In Control Panel, click Printers and Other Hardware.

3. If you are not sure whether the printer is already installed in Windows, click View Installed Printers or Fax Printers.

Or, if you know it's not installed yet, click Add a Printer and skip to step 5.

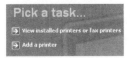

4. If, in the Printers and Faxes window, you don't see your printer's icon among the installed printers and fax machines, click Add a Printer to start the Add Printer Wizard.

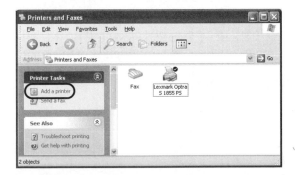

5. On the Welcome screen, click Next.

Here's where the procedure splits. If you are installing a local printer, see the following section. To install a network printer (that is, one not directly connected to your computer), see the section "Setting Up a Network Printer."

Setting Up a Local Printer

If the printer is directly connected to the computer, continue the Add Printer Wizard from the preceding section by doing the following:

1. On the Local or Network Printer screen, leave the default settings selected ("Local printer attached to this computer" and "Automatically detect and install my Plug and Play printer") and click Next.

| NOTE | When Windows automatically detects a printer, it bypasses the options for setting up network sharing of the printer. If you want to set up the printer to be shared, you can clear the "Automatically detect..." check box in step 1, or you can go ahead and set up the printer as unshared and then refer to "Sharing a Printer" later in this chapter. |

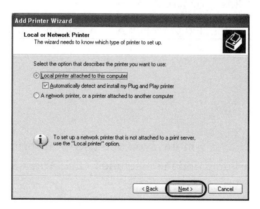

2. Wait for Windows to try to detect your printer. If it succeeds, the following message appears. Click Next and then skip to step 9.

If Windows does not find the printer, this message appears instead. Click Next.

> ⚠ The wizard was unable to detect any Plug and Play printers. To install the printer manually, click Next.

3. On the Select a Printer Port screen, select the printer's port if it doesn't appear correctly. Then click Next.

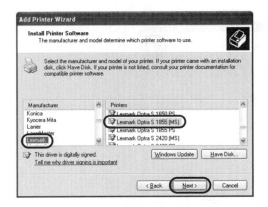

Most printers use the built-in parallel port on the computer (LPT1), while some newer printers use USB or infrared. However, USB and infrared printers are always detected automatically.

4. On the Install Printer Software screen, select the printer's manufacturer and model from the lists provided. Then click Next.

Some printers can use more than one driver. For example, a PostScript-capable computer can use a regular driver (identified by MS in this figure) or a PostScript driver (identified by PS). You can install each driver as a separate "printer" and then choose between them for individual print jobs.

NOTE
If your printer doesn't appear on the list, you can try to get a driver from the manufacturer's Web site. Then click Have Disk in step 4 instead of selecting from the list, and enter the path to the driver file.

5. On the Name Your Printer screen, type a name for the printer. This name will appear under its icon in the Printers and Faxes window and in Print dialog boxes in individual programs.

6. Click Yes or No to choose whether this printer should be the default printer. Then click Next.

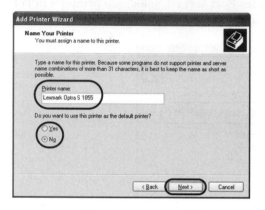

7. If you want to share the printer on your LAN, on the Printer Sharing screen, click Share Name and type a name by which the printer should be known on the network. Otherwise, leave Do Not Share This Printer selected. Then click Next.

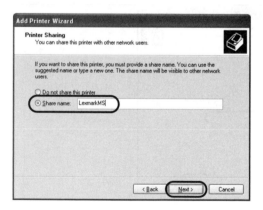

8. If you chose to share the printer in step 7, on the Location and Comment screen, enter extra information in the Location and Comment boxes if desired. Then click Next.

9. On the Print Test Page screen, click Yes or No to print a test page or not. You should print a test page if you have any doubts as to whether the printer is functioning correctly. Then click Next.

10. On the Completing screen, click Finish to end the wizard and install the needed drivers. You may be prompted to insert your Windows XP CD.

Now the printer is set up and ready for use.

Setting Up a Network Printer

If you want access to a printer that some other computer on your network has made available for sharing, you must install its driver on your own PC. To do

You will learn in Chapter 15 how to set up a simple network to connect computers together for sharing resources.

so, first follow the steps under "Starting the Add Printer Wizard" earlier in the chapter, and then do the following:

1. On the Local or Network Printer screen, choose "A network printer, or a printer attached to another computer." Then click Next.

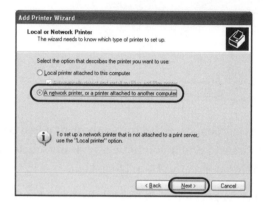

2. On the Specify a Printer screen, leave the default, Browse for a Printer, selected and click Next.

> **TIP** If you happen to know the complete path to the printer, you can enter it in step 2 instead of browsing. Network paths must follow the Universal Naming Convention (UNC), like this: \\computername\printername.

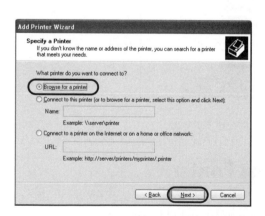

3. Windows checks your network and displays a list of all shared printers that are available. Click the one you want and then click Next.

4. On the Default Printer screen, choose Yes or No to set this printer as the default or not. Then click Next.

5. On the Completing screen, click Finish. Windows goes out to the network and downloads the driver for the printer from its local PC, and transfers that driver to your computer.

You can now use the printer just as though it were connected directly to your own computer.

Setting Printer Properties

Each printer's driver has a Properties dialog box built into it. The tabs and settings in this box vary depending on the printer type and model, but some settings are common to all.

To display a printer's properties, start in the Printers and Faxes window, which you worked with earlier in the chapter. To get there, choose Start ➢ Control Panel ➢ Printers and Other Hardware ➢ Printers and Faxes. Then right-click the printer's icon and choose Properties.

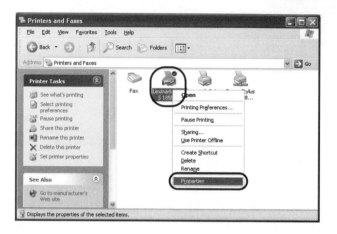

The printer's Properties dialog box appears. All such boxes have multiple tabs, with dozens of settings you can adjust. The one for my Lexmark laser printer looks like this:

Dithering

A method of representing shades of gray using only black ink by creating very fine patterns of black dots interspersed with white space. It can also be done with colors to form shades for which you don't have ink. For example, yellow and red dots can be interspersed to approximate orange.

Most printers' Properties boxes include some way of adjusting the print quality. This can include dots-per-inch (dpi) resolution, color versus black and white, or graphics **dithering**.

Here are a few common settings for a black-and-white laser printer, for example. You'll find them on various tabs.

Print quality   A dpi rating, such as 600×600 or 1200×1200. The higher the quality setting, the crisper the output and the slower the printing.

Print quality enhancement (on/off)   Some printers have a resolution enhancement technology that you can enable or disable to get crisper results from a lower dpi.

Halftoning   The method for dithering graphics. If available, Auto Select is usually the best setting.

Fonts   If available, choose to use the printer's built-in fonts whenever possible. This saves the time needed to download TrueType fonts to the printer when the printer already has those fonts built in.

Paper size   Choose Letter or Legal, whichever size is loaded most often in the printer.

Copies   Usually 1, but if you always need multiple copies of every-thing you print, you might set this higher. You can also increase the number of copies for individual print jobs in a program's Print dialog box.

Print density   Choose Light, Medium, or Dark. This controls how much toner the printer uses. Start with Light. As a laser printer's drum ages, you might need to reset this to Medium or Dark to get good-quality printouts.

Sharing a Printer

One of the tabs in the printer's Properties box is Sharing; you can use it to set up the printer to be shared on your network, if you didn't do that when you installed the printer initially.

From the Sharing tab, do the following:

1. Click Share This Printer.

Sharing works by default only if the other people also have Windows XP; if they have other Windows versions, you must make drivers for those Windows versions available, too. To do so, on the Sharing tab, click Additional Drivers and then select the other operating systems you need to support.

2. Enter a share name in the Share Name box. This name will appear on listings from which others can choose. The name doesn't need to be the same as the name on your own PC.

3. Click OK to close the Properties box.

Now other people can select your printer and install its driver on their own PCs, as covered in "Setting Up a Network Printer" earlier in the chapter.

Controlling a Print Queue

Each printer has its own queue in which documents wait to be printed. Most home users print only one document at a time and have only one PC and printer, so the queue will not be a big issue. However, if several people share a printer on a network, there sometimes might be a list of several documents waiting for their turns to be printed. You can view this list and—if you have the appropriate network permissions—rearrange and even delete print jobs on it.

To display and manage a printer's queue, do the following:

1. Choose Start ➤ Control Panel ➤ Printers and Other Hardware ➤ Printers and Faxes, and then double-click the printer. The queue for the printer appears. If the window is empty, there are no documents waiting to be printed. The queue shown here contains three documents.

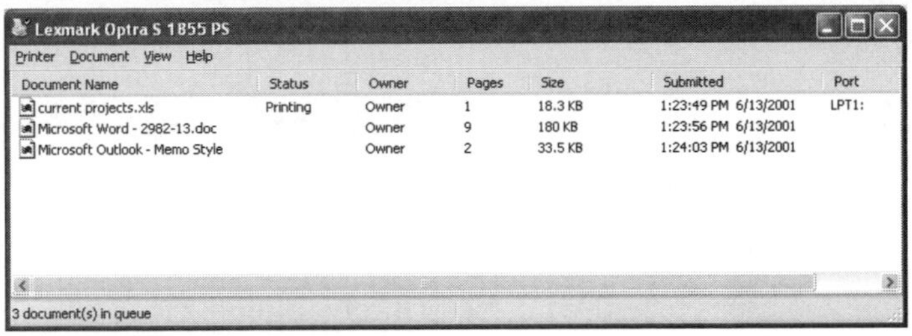

2. Do any of the following:

- ❖ To move a certain job higher or lower in the queue, drag it up or down. This lets you prioritize jobs differently from the order in which they were submitted.

- ❖ To pause a particular print job, select it and choose Document ➢ Pause. To resume it, repeat. You might do this to allow another print job to go ahead of it if you're in a hurry for a certain printout.

- ❖ To delete a particular print job, select it and choose Document ➢ Cancel or press Delete. A confirmation box appears; click Yes. If you accidentally print a document with many pages, you could cancel it here so that it doesn't waste your paper.

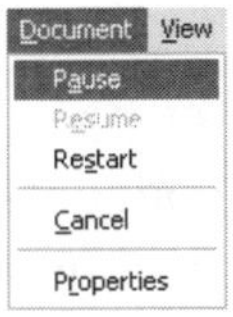

- ❖ To pause the entire printer, choose Printer ➢ Pause Printing. To restart it, repeat. This might be useful if the printer is spitting out garbage and you need to stop it to see what's wrong with it, but you don't want to lose all the jobs in the queue.

- ❖ To delete all print jobs in the queue, choose Printer ➢ Cancel All Documents. This is a quick way to delete all the jobs at once, instead of canceling each one individually.

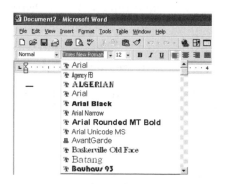

3. When you are finished with the printer's queue, close its window.

Managing Fonts

Fonts are typefaces that you can use on-screen and in printed documents. The more fonts you have, the more flexibility you have in creating documents with exactly the look you want. For example, you might create a newsletter that uses Arial for the headings, Times New Roman for the body text, Arial Black for the page numbers, and so on. (Too many fonts, however, can be difficult to manage and can cause some programs that use fonts to operate more slowly.)

Windows XP comes with several fonts, including Courier New, Times New Roman, Arial, and Symbol. You might also have other fonts installed, depending on what other software you have. For example, Microsoft Office comes with many fonts.

Viewing Installed Fonts

One way to see a list of the installed fonts is to open the Font drop-down list or the Font dialog box in a word processing program. For example, here's the Font list in Word 2000:

From within a program, you can choose the font you want to apply to selected text or to text you are about to type. In some programs, like the one shown above, the fonts appear in their actual typeface on the list, so you can scan for a font that meets your needs.

Another way to view the installed fonts is to open the Fonts listing from the Control Panel, as shown in the following steps. From there, you not only can view the installed fonts, but also can add and remove fonts.

1. Choose Start ➤ Control Panel.

2. In Control Panel, click Appearance and Themes.

The Appearance and Themes window appears.

3. In the See Also pane on the left side, click Fonts.

The fonts that appear in the Fonts window show up as icons rather than actual samples of the individual fonts.

Notice that not all the font icons are the same. The ones with **TT** on them are TrueType fonts. These are fonts designed for use in Windows (or on a Macintosh). They are advantageous because they are scalable to any size. The icons with *O* on them are OpenType fonts. OpenType is an improved version of True-Type that's new to Windows XP.

Fonts with an **A** on their icon are fixed-size fonts. You may not have any of these. They have various purposes; some of them are system fonts for use in a command-line interface, and others are specific to a particular printer or program.

You should try to use OpenType or TrueType fonts whenever you can in your work. They offer several advantages over other fonts. For starters, they are scalable—that is, you can use them in any size you want. They also can be embedded in word processing documents in some programs, so that a person working with the document on another PC can see and print it correctly even if that person's computer doesn't have the same fonts installed.

Previewing a Font

It can be difficult to tell from a font's name what the typeface actually looks like. To see a sample of a font, double-click its icon, and a preview window opens for it. This window shows information about the font such as its type and file size, and then shows a sample sentence in several sizes.

To print this sample page, click Print. To close the window, click Done.

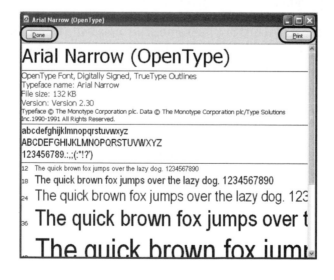

Deleting a Font

If you have a lot of fonts, it can be difficult to find the font you want in an application; you must scroll through a long list. Fonts also take up space on your hard disk—anywhere from 100K on up per font. Therefore, you might want to delete some of the fonts that you never use.

To delete a font from your system:

1. Select the font in the Fonts window.

2. Press Delete. A confirmation box appears.

3. Click Yes.

Adding a Font

Most of the sources of new fonts provide their own installation utility, so you will seldom need to install fonts manually. For example, if you buy a CD full of fonts, it probably contains a font browse and installation utility. Or, if you buy a new word processing program that comes with fonts, the same Setup program that installs the word processing program probably installs the fonts, too.

However, you might occasionally need to install fonts through Windows. For example, if a colleague provides a font to you on a disk (or e-mails it to you), you might need to install it. Or, if you bought an inexpensive disk full of fonts, or downloaded free fonts from the Internet, an installation utility may not be provided.

When you install a font, you can choose whether or not to copy it to the Fonts folder. If you choose not to, the font will not take up any space on your hard disk. (For a single font, this isn't an issue, but if you're dealing with dozens or hundreds of fonts, the used space can add up.) However, the font won't be available unless the disk from which it came is available. For example, if you

The Internet is a rich source of additional fonts, usually free for the downloading. Try `www.font.net/downloads.htm`, for example, or `www.microsoft.com/typography/free.htm`.

leave the font on another PC on your LAN, and your network isn't working, you won't be able to use the font.

To install a new font (or multiple new fonts), follow these steps:

1. From the Fonts window, choose File ➢ Install New Font.

2. In the Add Fonts dialog box, navigate to the drive and folder containing the font.

3. In the List of Fonts pane, select the font you want to install. To select more than one, hold down the Ctrl key as you click on multiple fonts. Click Select All if you want to select all the fonts in the folder.

4. (Optional) If you don't want the font to be copied to your Fonts folder, clear the Copy Fonts to Fonts Folder check box.

5. Click OK. The font is installed.

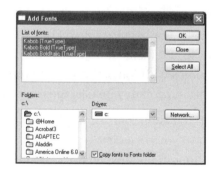

14 Sharing a PC with Multiple Users

In many households, there is only one computer and several people who need to use it. Each person has their own ideas about what constitutes attractive screen colors and important shortcuts to place on the desktop, but everyone can have separate settings in Windows XP with the User Accounts feature. Each person simply logs in as him- or herself, and Windows remembers all the settings and preferences. In this chapter, you will learn how to create and delete user profiles and how to switch between users without rebooting.

Introducing User Accounts

User accounts allow individual users to have their own settings in Windows. These settings include screen appearance choices, Start menu customizations, Favorites lists in Internet Explorer, and other individual options.

Depending on the way your PC is currently set up, you may or may not be prompted to select a user account when you start up your PC. If only one user is set up, Windows won't ask who you are—it will simply start up.

If there are multiple users, however, Windows will display a Welcome screen, from which you click your name to indicate who you are.

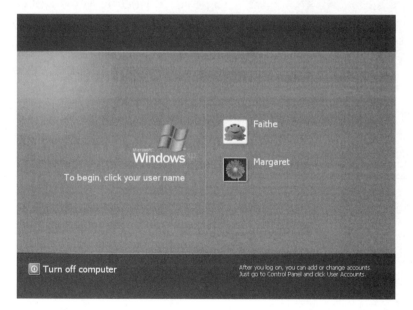

With the Welcome screen shown above, a password is not required to log on as a particular user. In most homes, password security is not needed. However, if you would like each person to enter a password in order to log on, you can set a password for each account. You'll learn how to do that later in the chapter in "Managing Account Passwords."

If you prefer, you can also set up Windows to display the same type of login dialog box used in earlier versions of Windows:

See "Changing the Login Screen" later in this chapter.

When different users are logged in, several parts of Windows are different as well. For example, a different My Documents folder is accessible for each user, and different shortcuts appear on the Start menu. The Favorites and History lists in Internet Explorer are different, and different desktop shortcuts and appearance settings might appear as well.

Logging Off

When you are finished using the computer, you can shut it down as you learned in Chapter 1, or you can simply log off. Logging off closes all your open programs and files and returns to the Welcome screen, so that someone else can log on.

To log off:

1. Click Start ➤ Log Off.

A user account in Windows XP Home Edition can have one of two statuses: Administrator or Limited. An Administrator account can install and remove programs, read and change existing data files, and make changes to its own and other user accounts. A Limited account can only run programs and change its own user account password. Most adult household members will probably need an Administrator account, but you might want to assign children a Limited account to prevent them from making changes that will cause problems.

2. Depending on how your PC is set up for user accounts, you might see a dialog box like this:

Or it might look like this:

Either way, click Log Off. All open programs close, and the Welcome screen returns.

Switching between Users

When you log off, all your programs and files are closed. Windows XP, however, also includes the ability to switch users while leaving the first user's programs and settings active. This enables you to quickly switch to your own settings and perform a few tasks with minimal disturbance to someone else who is also working on the computer.

NOTE Fast User Switching must be turned on in order for the following procedure to work. See "Changing the Login Screen" later in this chapter if Switch User does not appear as an option for you.

To switch users, do the following:

1. Click Start ➢ Log Off.

2. In the Log Off Windows dialog box, click Switch User.

The Welcome screen returns, with an indicator showing that the previous user still has programs running:

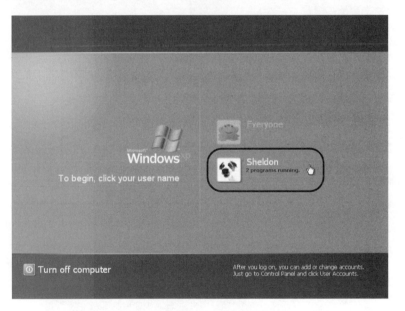

3. Click some other user's name to switch to.

Managing User Accounts

When you first installed Windows XP, you were probably prompted to enter your name and the names of anyone else who would be using the PC. Windows created user accounts for each of those names at that time. You can set up more accounts any time you like.

Opening the User Accounts Window

Most of the activities in the remainder of this chapter will start from the User Accounts window, so let's open it now.

1. Choose Start ➤ Control Panel.

2. In Control Panel, click User Accounts.

The User Accounts window opens. From here, you can create new accounts, delete or change existing ones, and choose between the normal Welcome screen and the more secure "classic" login.

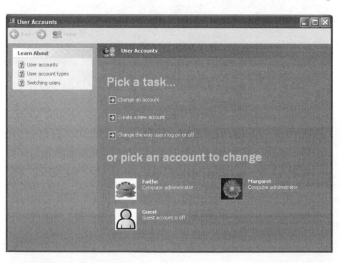

Adding an Account

You can add new accounts at any time, whenever someone in your household would like to use the computer with their own settings. To do so, start at the User Accounts window and then do the following:

1. Click Create a New Account.

2. Type the name of the person for whom you are creating the account, and then click Next.

Name the new account

Type a name for the new account:

Sheldon

This name will appear on the Welcome screen and on the Start menu.

Next >   Cancel

3. Choose the type of account you want: Computer Administrator or Limited. Users with Computer Administrator privileges have free access to change anything about the computer's configuration; those with Limited privileges can only run programs and change their own password.

4. Click Create Account. The account is created.

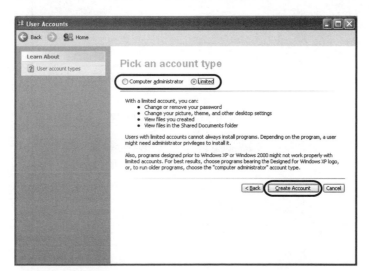

Creating Limited accounts for children, teens, and novice users can ensure that they don't delete important files.

Deleting an Account

If you decide you don't need an account you have set up, you can delete it. To do so, start at the User Accounts window and then do the following:

1. Click the account you want to delete.

2. Click Delete the Account.

→ Delete the account

3. If you plan to move this user's settings to another computer, choose Keep Files. This will create a folder on the desktop with that user's name, containing the user's documents and desktop shortcuts. If you won't need that user's documents and settings, click Delete Files.

> **WARNING** Each user has their own My Documents folder, separate from other users' folders. If you choose Delete Files in step 3, any documents that were in that user's My Documents folder will be deleted. If you have any doubts about whether to keep any of the files, choose Keep Files. You can then sort through them later and copy anything worth keeping to your own My Documents folder.

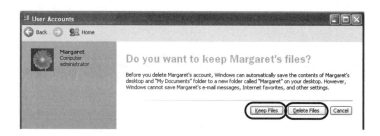

4. A confirmation message appears. Click Delete Account.

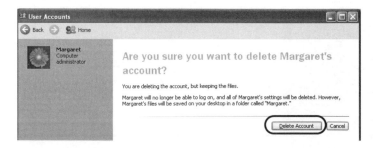

Renaming an Account

You might sometimes need to rename an account. For example, perhaps when you initially set up your user accounts, you included each person's first and last name in the account names. But now you realize that because everyone in your family has the same last name, you would prefer that the account names be first-name only. Or perhaps you want everyone in the whole household to use a single account, so you plan to rename one of the accounts "Everyone" and delete all the others.

To rename an account, start at the User Accounts window and then do the following:

1. Click the account you want to change.

2. Click Change My Name.

➜ Change my name

3. Type the new name and then click Change Name.

![User Accounts window showing "Provide a new name for your account" with the name "Everyone" typed in a text box and a circled Change Name button with a Cancel button beside it.]

4. Click Back ⬅ Back to return to the User Accounts window.

Changing an Account's Privileges

As mentioned earlier, an account can have one of two privilege sets: Computer Administrator or Limited. To switch between the two for an account, do the following from the User Accounts window:

1. Click the account you want to change.

> **WARNING** To use this procedure, you must be logged in with a Computer Administrator account (not a Limited account).

2. Click Change the Account Type.

 Change the account type

3. Click the account type you want: Computer Administrator or Limited. Then click Change Account Type.

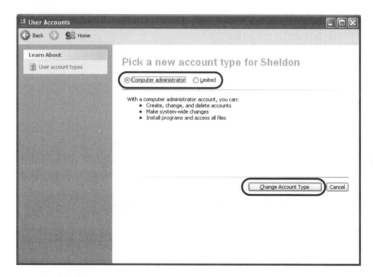

4. Click Back  to return to the User Accounts window.

Changing an Account's Picture

When you create a new account, it is assigned a picture at random. You can choose a different picture from the several pictures that come with Windows XP, or you can assign a picture from a file.

To change an account's picture, do the following:

1. From the User Accounts window, click the account you want to change.

![Sheldon Computer Administrator account icon]

You can take digital photos of each person in your household and then assign those picture files to the user accounts.

2. Click Change the Picture.

➔ Change the picture

3. Click the picture you want and then click Change Picture.

Or, to choose your own picture, click Browse for More Pictures. Then navigate to the picture you want to use, click it, and click Open.

NOTE If the picture needs to be scanned or acquired from a digital camera, click Get a Picture from a Camera or Scanner and then refer to Chapter 8.

The new picture now appears for the account, replacing the previously used picture.

Managing Account Passwords

If you don't want everyone to have free access to every account, you must specify a password—that is, enable *password protection*—for each account. Then, every time someone tries to log on or switch accounts, a password prompt will appear.

Setting a Password

To set a password for an account, do the following from the User Accounts window:

1. Click the account for which you want to set a password.

2. Click Create a Password.

    → Create a password

3. Type the password in the "Type a new password" text box, and then again in the "Type the new password again to confirm" box.

4. (Optional) If you want to provide a password hint, enter it in the "Type a word or phrase to use as a password hint" box.

5. Click Create Password.

6. Click Back to return to the User Accounts window.

When you turn on password protection for an account, all stored passwords, cookies, and security certificates for that account are wiped out. This might affect your Web surfing. For example, if you automatically log on to a certain Web site because your username and password are stored in Internet Explorer, the next time you visit that site, you might need to reenter that information.

Password hints make it easier for users to remember their passwords, but also make it easier for someone to guess the password, decreasing the security of your system.

Now, whenever someone chooses that user account, a password box appears, prompting for the password. You can click the **?** button to get the hint, as shown here.

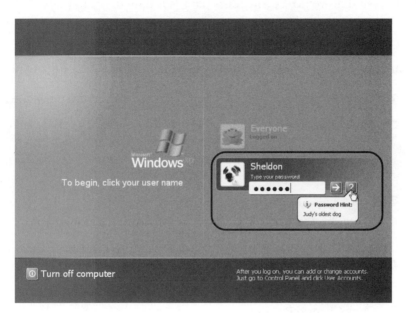

Removing a Password

Removing a password disables the password protection for the account, so that it is once again freely accessible by anyone. To remove a password, do the following from the User Accounts window:

1. Click the account for which you want to remove the password. Notice that password-protected accounts are marked as such on-screen.

2. Click Remove the Password.

   ⇨ Remove the password

3. Some information appears about losing personal certificates and stored passwords for the account. Read it and then click Remove Password.

Removing the password is not the same as setting the password to be blank; if you do that, Windows will prompt you for a password and you must press Enter without typing anything as your password.

Changing a Password

Security experts recommend changing a password occasionally for added security, so that would-be intruders have less time to try to guess it. You might want to change your password every month or so if you are worried about others accessing your sensitive documents.

To change a password, do the following from the User Accounts window:

1. Click the account for which you want to change the password.

2. Click Change the Password.

   → Change the password

3. Enter a new password in the "Type a new password" text box; then type it again in the "Type the new password again to confirm" box.

4. (Optional) Enter a password hint in the "Type a word or phrase to use as a password hint" box.

5. Click Change Password.

Changing the Login Screen

By default, Windows XP Home Edition uses the Welcome screen you've already seen. If you prefer, you can make Windows use a regular Log On To Windows dialog box, as in earlier versions of Windows:

If you haven't assigned a password to the user account, you can leave the Password box empty.

NOTE   If you click the Options button in this Log On To Windows box, a Shut Down button appears, enabling you to shut down the computer rather than logging on.

To set up this type of login box instead of the Welcome screen, do the following from the User Accounts window:

1. Click Change the Way Users Log On or Off.

2. Clear the Use the Welcome Screen check box to use the classic Log On dialog box, or ensure that the check box is marked if you want the Welcome screen.

3. If you are using the Welcome screen, the Use Fast User Switching check box is marked by default. Clear this check box if you don't want **Fast User Switching**.

Fast User Switching
A feature that enables another user to log on without the first user logging off. For example, suppose you are working with Excel, and your daughter wants to check her e-mail. She can log on and do so without your having to exit Excel. Then you can switch back to your own user account and resume your work.

4. Click Apply Options.

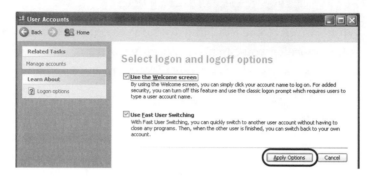

5. Click Back to return to the User Accounts window.

Turning the Guest Account On

The Guest account allows visitors and other people not specifically authorized to use your computer to have access to it. If you set passwords for all of the "real" user accounts, you might want to enable the Guest account in case someone wants to use the computer but doesn't know any of the passwords.

By default, the Guest account is off. It has Limited privileges, so anyone using it can only run programs; they cannot make changes to system settings that could affect performance or ruin anyone else's documents or programs.

To enable the Guest account, do the following from the User Accounts window:

1. Click the Guest account.

2. Click Turn On the Guest Account.

Now the Guest account will appear along with the other accounts on the Welcome screen.

Part 5

Online and Network Connectivity

This part of the book explains how to connect your computer to other computers, either in your own home or across the globe. You'll learn about home networking and Internet access, as well as how to send and receive e-mail and how to customize the settings in your Web and e-mail programs.

Online and Network Connectivity

15

Setting Up a Home Network

● ●

More and more people these days have multiple computers in their homes. In many cases, it's advantageous to connect them into a network so that they can share resources like printers, hard disks, and even Internet connections. In this chapter, you will learn how to set up a simple home network and how to choose which resources should be made available to other PCs on your network.

Understanding Networks

A *network* is a group of computers that have been connected together. It can be as small as two computers or as large as the whole Internet itself, and the computers can be connected with cables, with infrared signal, through phone lines, or through some other method. Any method of sending data from place to place can serve as a network conduit.

There are two main types of networks: those with a **server** and those without one. On a server-based network, all data passes through the server on the way to its final destination. The server acts as a traffic cop and, in many cases, also serves as a repository for shared data. A serverless network, also called a **peer-to-peer network**, exists when several computers are connected without any of them being "in charge." Because a server-based network requires a dedicated PC to be the server, and most home users don't have a spare computer they can devote to that purpose, almost all home networks are of the peer-to-peer type.

A trip to your local computer store will show you that many network technologies are available for small peer-to-peer networks.

The traditional network type is wired Ethernet. It requires a network card in each computer, plus cables that connect to a hub or switch. This type of network is fast and reliable, but the cables can be somewhat unwieldy.

You can also buy networking kits for networks that connect through the telephone jacks or AC power outlets in your home. These networks work well in buildings where the computers are physically far apart, even on separate floors, because you don't have to run cabling through hallways or drill holes for it in floors.

Wireless networking kits are also available. These are more expensive, and don't work well when the PCs are on different floors. However, since there are no cables, they are very convenient. There are three standards for wireless networking: 802.11a, 802.11b, and 802.11g. When possible, buy equipment that supports 802.11g. (Standard 802.11b would be a fallback, but avoid 802.11a because of limited popularity and compatibility. It is destined to be the Betamax of wireless networking.)

Server

A computer that exists on a network in order to assist the other computers in communicating with one another, or to hold and "serve up" data that multiple users might want. The server typically runs a special version of Windows (such as Windows 2003 Server) and is not used for applications.

Peer-to-peer network

A network in which all computer are equal, with no computer serving as a server. Such networks are good for homes and small offices because they don't require an extra computer to function as a server; but as more computers are added to the network, its overhead—shared by all computers equally—can become a performance drain on individual computers.

Regardless of the type of network kit (or individual networking components) you buy, the basic installation process is the same:

1. Physically install the hardware in the PCs using the directions that came with the kit. This usually involves installing a circuit board in a desktop PC or inserting a PC Card in a slot in a laptop.

2. Establish the connection between the PCs, either by running cables, connecting phone lines, or setting up wireless access. Again, the directions will explain the specifics.

3. Run the Network Setup Wizard on each PC to set it up. (Or run the software that came with the kit on each PC, if applicable.) Or, if you have wireless networking equipment and Windows XP Service Pack 2, run the Wireless Network Setup Wizard.

Setting Up Windows for Networking

There are two steps in setting up a home network: making Windows identify the networking hardware, and making Windows use that hardware to communicate with other computers. The first step will probably occur automatically when you turn on your PC after installing the networking hardware. The second step might happen automatically, too; but if it doesn't, you can run the Network Setup Wizard to set the network up.

Checking for Existing Network Connectivity

Your home network might already be working, with no special setup needed; Windows XP is very intelligent about guessing at the proper settings and configuring network devices automatically.

If you aren't sure whether your PC is already set up for networking, do the following:

1. Open the Start menu and look for My Network Places. Computers that have *not* been set up for networking usually don't have this command on the top-level Start menu.

2. Click My Network Places.

3. In the Network Tasks pane of the My Network Places window, click View Workgroup Computers.

Workgroup

Windows XP's name for a peer-to-peer network.

If your computer has been set up to be part of a peer-to-peer network, your computer will appear as an icon in the **workgroup**. If any other computers have already been set up as well, they will also appear. In the following figure, there are three computers on the existing network.

If you can't browse the network as described above, you will need to run the Network Setup Wizard. See the next section.

Running the Network Setup Wizard

The Network Setup Wizard accomplishes several things. It installs the needed network drivers and **protocols**, it configures your computer for Internet connection sharing if desired, and it enables file and printer sharing. To run the Network Setup Wizard, follow these steps:

1. Choose Start ➤ All Programs ➤ Accessories ➤ Communications ➤ Network Setup Wizard.

2. The Network Setup Wizard opens. Click Next to begin.

3. Read the information about network setup, and confirm that you have taken all the listed steps already to prepare your network hardware. Then click Next.

Protocols
Languages that network components use to speak to one another. One of the most popular protocols is TCP/IP, which is used on the Internet and on most home and business networks.

4. On the Select a Connection Method screen, choose the statement that best matches your computer's situation. Then click Next.

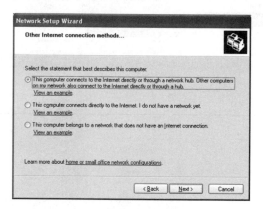

5. If you chose Other in step 4, additional choices appear. Click the one you want and then click Next.

6. If you have more than one network card in your PC—for example, one for your Internet connection (cable or DSL) and one for your home network—you will be asked which card is for the Internet. Select it and then click Next.

NOTE If you don't know which network card is which, leave the default one selected. You can always rerun this wizard later if you were wrong.

The most common way to name a computer is to assign the name of the person to whom the computer belongs. If several people use each computer, you might want to name the computers according to their brand or model or according to the room they are in.

7. Enter a name and description for the computer. These will appear when other computers are browsing the network to find this one. Then click Next.

WARNING If you already have a high-speed Internet connection up and running on the computer, don't change the computer's name. Some cable and DSL Internet connections require your computer name to be a specific string of numbers and letters provided by the Internet service provider. If you change the computer's name, the Internet connection might not work.

8. Specify a workgroup name, or leave the default MSHOME. You can use any name, but all the computers must use the same workgroup name in order to see one another. Then click Next.

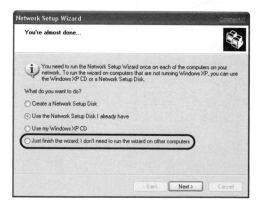

9. If you have Service Pack 2 installed, the Wizard asks whether you want to turn on File and Printer Sharing. This is required if you want other PCs to be able to access this computer's files and printers. Make your selection and click Next.

10. Depending on your network, you might be asked whether you want to create a Setup disk for other computers in your network. Any computers that don't run Windows XP will need to be set up. If you have other non-XP computers, follow the prompts to create a Setup disk; otherwise, choose Just Finish the Wizard and then click Next.

11. Check the settings to confirm, and then click Next to apply them.

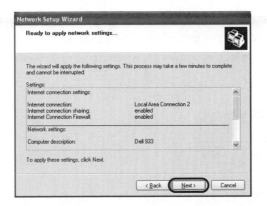

12. Wait for Windows to apply your new settings; then click Finish.

You might be prompted to restart your computer; if so, click Yes to do so. When Windows restarts, your network will be ready to go!

NOTE If you have a wireless network and Service Pack 2, you might want to run the Wireless Network Setup Wizard. It walks you through the process of enabling wireless networking security. If you have a flash RAM device and if each PC and access point has a USB port, the wizard can configure them all automatically using that flash RAM device to transfer the needed settings to each one.

Sharing Folders

Each Windows XP computer has a separate My Documents folder for each user account, plus a Shared Documents folder that all user accounts on that PC can access. When you set up a PC for networking through the Network Setup Wizard, this Shared Documents folder is automatically made available to other computers on the network; it is shared not only among users on that single PC, but also within your network.

In the following sections, you'll learn how to place files into your own computer's shared folder, how to access the shared folder on other PCs, and how to share additional folders.

Accessing Your Shared Documents Folder

Turn back to Chapter 14 for more information about user accounts.

The **path** to the Shared Documents folder is C:\Documents and Settings\All Users\Documents\Shared Documents (assuming your main hard disk is C:), but you don't have to wade through all those levels to get to it. Here's an easy way:

1. Choose Start ➢ My Documents.

Path

The complete address of a file, including its storage location. A path typically begins with the drive letter, a colon, and a backward slash, followed by the folders, separated by slashes, and finally the file-name—for example, C:\ Windows\System\ run32.dll.

If you don't see Shared Documents, click Shared Pictures to change to the Shared Pictures folder. From there, click Shared Documents in the Other Places list.

2. In the Other Places pane of the My Documents window, click Shared Documents.

If you don't want to store the file in Shared Documents but you still would like to share it, place a shortcut to the file in Shared Documents, or share additional folders, as explained later in this chapter.

To share a file or folder, move or copy it into this Shared Documents folder. The Shared Documents folder contains My Music and My Pictures folders, just like your own My Documents folder. You can also create additional folders within it if desired, as you learned in Chapter 3.

Accessing Shared Files on Another PC

You can browse the shared files on other PCs in your network almost as easily as files on your own PC. Start from the My Network Places window, as in the following steps:

1. Choose Start ➤ My Network Places.

2. If a shortcut for the folder you want to browse appears, double-click it to open that folder. By default, shortcuts to the Shared Documents folders of all other PCs in your workgroup, including your own, appear.

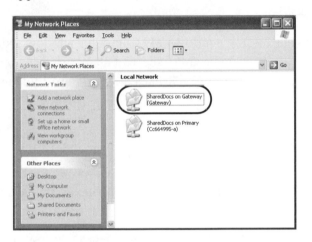

The files in the Shared Documents folder on that PC appear. From here, you can work with the file listing as you would in any other file management window.

If a shortcut did not appear for the folder you wanted to browse on another PC, do the following to look for it:

1. In the Network Tasks pane of the My Network Places window, click View Workgroup Computers.

2. Icons for each of the computers in your workgroup appear. Double-click the one you want to browse.

From here, it's just like browsing your own My Computer window. Double-click the shared folder or drive you want to see. Not all folders will appear— only the ones that have been shared. You'll learn how to share a folder later in this chapter.

Creating a New Network Place

If, in the preceding section, you had to browse the workgroup for the computer and folder you wanted to see, you might want to set up that location as a **network place**.

To create a network place, start in the My Network Places window and do the following:

1. In the Network Tasks pane, click Add a Network Place.

2. The Add Network Place Wizard runs. Click Next to begin.

Network place

A network-based shortcut. Just as you create shortcuts on your desktop to avoid having to wade through the Start menu for a favorite program, you can create a network place to avoid having to browse the network for a shared folder you use often.

3. Make sure that Choose Another Network Location is selected; then click Next.

4. Click Browse to open the Browse for Folder dialog box.

5. Locate and select the computer, drive, or folder for which you want to create a shortcut; then click OK.

6. Back in the Add Network Place Wizard, click Next to continue.

7. On the What Do You Want... screen, type a descriptive name for the shortcut you are creating. (It need not be the same as the name of the original.) Then click Next.

8. Click Finish to end the wizard.

From now on, whenever you open the My Network Places window, the shortcut (a.k.a. network place) you just created will appear there.

Sharing Other Folders on Your PC

To protect your privacy, only the Shared Documents folder on your PC is shared by default. You can choose to share additional folders, though, or even entire drives. For example, if I had a folder called Books on my hard drive that I wanted to be able to use from any PC in my home, I would set it up to be shared, using the following steps.

To share a folder on the network:

1. Open a file management window and locate that folder's icon. For this procedure, you don't want to display the folder's contents—you want to be able to see the folder as an icon.

Windows XP Home Edition is quite limited in its folder security features. In Windows XP Professional, you can assign passwords and various usage permissions to folders and drives, but the Home Edition is limited to the sharing options outlined in this chapter.

2. Right-click the folder and choose Sharing and Security.

3. Mark the Share This Folder on the Network check box.

4. Enter a share name for the folder. By default, it's the same as the folder name, but you can change it if you like. For example, you might want to give it a descriptive name like Project Files.

5. If you don't want people at other computers to be able to make changes to the contents of the folder, clear the Allow Network Users to Change My Files check box.

6. Click OK.

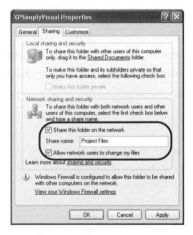

Now the shared folder will appear when other users are browsing the network. It will not be automatically set up with a network place shortcut, but you can create one, as you learned in the preceding section.

Sharing Other Resources

Windows XP makes resource sharing very simple, so many of the extra steps involved in setting up networking and sharing in earlier versions of Windows no longer apply. You learned in Chapter 13 how to share a printer; turn back there now if you need help with that.

The Network Setup Wizard configures Internet connection sharing for you, so you shouldn't need any additional setup. If connection sharing is not working, try running the Network Setup Wizard again, or check Help and Support for troubleshooting assistance.

In a workgroup situation such as a small peer-to-peer network, user accounts are stored on the individual PCs, so you cannot access private resources on one PC using another, even if the same account name exists on both PCs. On large corporate networks with servers, however, user accounts can be portable, so that you can log in as the same user on any PC in the network.

Making a Folder Private

A private folder is just what it sounds like—it's protected from other people's view. It's primarily for protecting files from other users on your local PC rather than from users on other network PCs, since, if you don't want something to be available on the network, you can simply not share it. When you make a folder private, only the user account that owns it can view it.

Not all folders can be made private—only the ones that are part of an individual user profile can be private. In other words, you can make your My Documents folder private, and/or any of the folders within it, but you cannot make a folder private that other local user accounts need access to, such as the Windows folder.

To make a folder private, do the following:

1. In a file management window, locate the folder and right-click it. Choose Sharing and Security from the shortcut menu.

2. Mark the Make This Folder Private check box.

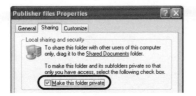

3. Click OK.

4. If you don't have a password for your user account, a box appears, asking whether you want to set one. If you click Yes, the User Accounts window will open. Refer back to Chapter 14 for details about passwords.

When logged in as the user account that owns the private folder, you will not notice any difference between a private folder and a normal one. However, if you try to access a private folder from a different user account, an error message will appear.

16 Connecting to the Internet

I f you already have an Internet connection up and running, good for you! You can skip this chapter. But if you don't have an Internet account yet, or you have one but it isn't currently set up on your com puter, stick around; in this chapter, you'll learn how to get connected.

Understanding Internet Service Providers

The Internet is a vast network of interconnected computers. Most of these computers aren't the ordinary desktop PCs that you have in your home; they're big, powerful servers with permanent connections to the Internet.

Ordinary people like you and me can't afford one of these big computers with full-time Internet connectivity, so we pay a monthly fee to subscribe to a service that owns one of the big computers and leases the use of it. Such companies are called **Internet service providers**, or ISPs. When you sign up with an ISP, you get a username and password and the right to connect to the server by phone, cable modem, or other method. That connection serves as your on-ramp to the rest of the Internet.

Internet service provider (ISP)
A company that offers Internet access for a monthly fee. Some ISPs also offer a small amount of Web server space, on which you can post your own Web pages for others to view.

If you have cable Internet access, you don't have a choice of ISPs; you must use the cable company as your provider. With DSL service, you might have a choice, depending on what is available in your area.

You can choose a regular ISP—either national or local—or an online service like America Online (AOL) that also provides Internet access as part of its service. There are literally thousands of ISPs out there, with dozens to choose from in most metropolitan areas.

Through the Internet Connection Wizard in Windows XP, you can view a list of service providers in your area, choose one, and sign up, all in one convenient procedure. Or, if you already have an ISP account, you can set it up to work with your PC.

Signing Up for a New Internet Account

If you don't yet have an Internet account, you can go any of three ways:

- ◇ You can research all the providers in your area, talk to friends, and make a decision on your own. Then you call the ISP and ask them to send you a startup kit including your username and password. They might also send you a CD with Setup software. If you get a Setup CD, use it to set up your connection; you don't need the rest of this chapter.

If the ISP provides only a username, password, and phone number to dial, set up the connection using the directions under "Setting Up a Connection Manually" later in this chapter.

❖ You can sign up with MSN (Microsoft Network), the Microsoft-owned ISP. This is very easy and painless, and MSN offers good service at an average monthly rate.

❖ You can select a provider from a list of ISPs that Microsoft recommends. Depending on where you live, there might be several to choose from, or there might be none.

Checking the Microsoft Referral Service for ISPs

Before you decide on MSN or a particular local provider, you might want to check out the Microsoft referral service to see what offers are available in your area. Here's how:

1. Open a file management window and navigate to `Program Files\Online Services` on the hard drive on which Windows XP is installed. (It's D: in the following figure, but it's probably C: on your PC.)

2. Double-click Refer Me to More Internet Service Providers.

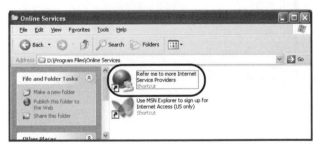

To open the Online Services folder, start in My Computer and double-click the drive on which Windows is installed. Then double-click the Program Files folder, and then double-click the Online Services folder.

3. Wait while the Internet Connection Wizard dials a toll-free number and connects to Microsoft. After a short wait, you will see one of two things.

❖ If any providers in your area have signed up for the Microsoft referral service, you will see them listed; click the one you want and then complete the wizard by filling in the blanks provided. (The exact steps depend on the provider chosen.)

❖ If there are no providers in your area that are part of the Microsoft referral service, a message will appear to that effect. Click Finish.

Signing Up with MSN as an ISP

The name MSN refers to several separate services, all owned by Microsoft:

⬦ MSN is the name of the news service that appears by default when you start Internet Explorer (see Chapter 17). Anyone can browse this Web site at www.msn.com.

⬦ There's also a program called MSN Explorer that you can use instead of Internet Explorer to browse Web content. You can access it from within Windows XP by choosing Start ➢ All Programs ➢ MSN Explorer. You'll learn about MSN Explorer in Chapter 17.

⬦ MSN is also the name of Microsoft's ISP service. Microsoft recommends that you use MSN Explorer with an MSN ISP account, but it's not required.

To sign up with MSN as your ISP, do the following:

1. Choose Start ➢ All Programs ➢ MSN Explorer.

2. A confirmation box appears. If you want to use MSN Explorer for Web browsing and e-mail, click Yes. You probably haven't made up your mind yet, though, so I recommend choosing No. (It will ask again next time.) Either way, a Welcome screen appears.

3. Click Continue.

4. If prompted for your location, open the Country/Region drop-down list and select your country; then click Continue.

5. Leave the default option selected: "Yes, I would like to sign up for MSN Internet Access and get a new MSN e-mail address." Click Continue.

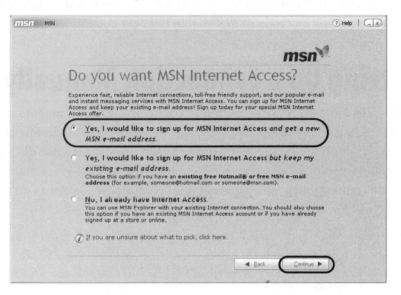

6. Mark any of the dialing options that apply to your situation and then click Continue.

7. Wait while your modem dials a toll-free number and connects to MSN.

8. Complete the remainder of the sign-up process by filling in the blanks provided. In each case, click Continue to move to the next blank.

The remainder of the sign-up process is easy and self-explanatory. After completing it, you will be ready to move on to the next chapter.

Setting Up a Connection Manually

If you already have an ISP account that connects through a modem, or if you just signed up for one with a service provider other than Microsoft, you must set up the connection yourself. Don't panic—it's not difficult. (If you have cable or DSL service, different directions apply; see your ISP for help. In most cases, an installer comes to your home and sets up the connection for you.)

When you sign up with an ISP, you should receive an information sheet containing this information:

> **Username and password**   Required to identify yourself when logging on
>
> **Phone number(s) to dial**   Required to connect to the ISP's computer
>
> **Incoming and outgoing mail server**   Required to send and receive e-mail (see Chapter 18)
>
> **Newsgroup server**   Required to read and participate in newsgroups

Armed with that information, do the following to set up your Internet connection:

1. Choose Start ➤ All Programs ➤ Accessories ➤ Communications ➤ New Connection Wizard.

If you signed up with an ISP that provides a Setup disk, insert it in your CD-ROM drive and follow the prompts. You don't need the following steps.

Newsgroup
A public forum where people can read and post messages on specific topics. A newsgroup is like a public bulletin board on which anyone can tack up notes and read notes posted there.

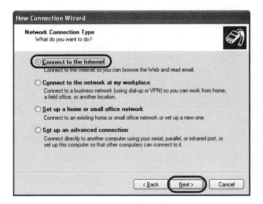

2. At the wizard's Welcome window, click Next.

3. Leave Connect to the Internet selected and click Next.

4. Choose Set Up My Connection Manually and then click Next.

New Connection Wizard

Getting Ready
The wizard is preparing to set up your Internet connection.

How do you want to connect to the Internet?

○ Choose from a list of Internet service providers (ISPs)

⊙ Set up my connection manually

    For a dial-up connection, you will need your account name, password, and a phone number for your ISP. For a broadband account, you won't need a phone number.

○ Use the CD I got from an ISP

         < Back   Next >   Cancel

5. Leave Connect Using a Dial-up Modem selected and click Next. (If one of the other options applies better to your situation, choose it instead and then go on your own for the rest of this procedure.)

New Connection Wizard

Internet Connection
How do you want to connect to the Internet?

⊙ Connect using a dial-up modem
    This type of connection uses a modem and a regular or ISDN phone line.

○ Connect using a broadband connection that requires a user name and password
    This is a high-speed connection using either a DSL or cable modem. Your ISP may refer to this type of connection as PPPoE.

○ Connect using a broadband connection that is always on
    This is a high-speed connection using either a cable modem, DSL or LAN connection. It is always active, and doesn't require you to sign in.

         < Back   Next >   Cancel

6. Type the ISP's name. This is for your own use; it will be the name for the connection's icon. Then click Next.

New Connection Wizard

Connection Name
What is the name of the service that provides your Internet connection?

Type the name of your ISP in the following box.

ISP Name

Iquest

The name you type here will be the name of the connection you are creating.

         < Back   Next >   Cancel

7. Type the ISP's phone number; then click Next.

8. Enter your username and password. Then retype the password for confirmation.

9. All check boxes are marked by default; clear any of them as needed:

- ❖ *Use this account name and password when anyone connects to the Internet from this computer.* If you clear this check box, only the current user account will have access to the connection. Leave this marked unless other people using other user accounts have their own Internet accounts.

- ❖ *Make this the default Internet connection.* If you clear this check box, this connection will not be the one that is automatically used when an application needs Internet access. Leave this marked unless you have more than one Internet connection.

10. Click Next to continue.

11. Mark the "Add a shortcut to this connection to my desktop" check box if desired. Then click Finish. Your connection is now set up.

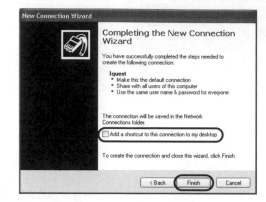

Dialing a Connection

If you added a shortcut to the desktop, just double-click that icon to make the connection. If you did not, you can choose Start ➢ Connect To and then click the connection name.

You might want to put a shortcut to the connection in the Quick Launch toolbar for quick access to it.

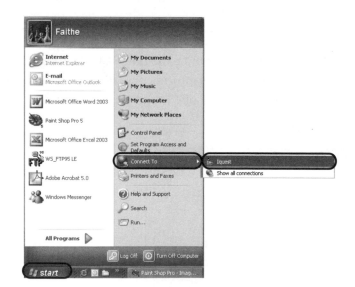

When you double-click the connection icon, a Connect dialog box opens. Your username and password are already stored, as well as the phone number to dial. Click Dial, and the connection is established.

Configuring Dialing Rules

The first time you use your modem or some other device that employs the telephone line, you are prompted to enter your area code and other information about dialing from your current location.

You can change that information at any time, and even set up other dialing locations. For example, on a laptop you might want different dialing locations for each city in which you connect to the Internet. The dialing location information includes the local area code, whether to dial any special numbers to get an outside line, whether to use a credit card or calling card for long-distance calls, and more.

To access the dialing properties, do the following:

1. Choose Start ➤ Control Panel.

2. Click Printers and Other Hardware.

3. Click Phone and Modem Options.

4. Click the Dialing Rules tab if it's not already displayed.

5. To edit an existing location, select it and click Edit (or just double-click it). Or, to create a new location, click the New button.

6. In the Edit Location (or New Location) dialog box, enter information about the connection. Give it a name, enter the area code, and specify any dialing rules as needed.

7. If you need to set any area code rules, click the Area Code Rules tab. Then click New, create a new rule in the New Area Code Rule dialog box, and click OK.

An area code rule would be necessary, for example, in a metropolitan area in which local calls can be placed between area codes.

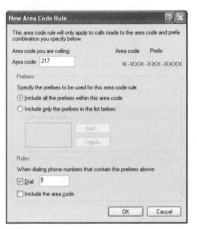

8. If you need to place calls via a calling card when in this location, click the Calling Card tab. Then select the card type from the list and enter the card information. If your brand of card doesn't appear, you can click New to add it.

9. When you are finished with all properties for the location, click OK.

By default, a dial-up connection doesn't use any dialing rules; it simply dials the number exactly as entered. To assign a dialing location to a dial-up connection, follow these steps:

1. Choose Start ➤ My Network Places and click View Network Connections.

2. In the Network Connections window, right-click the dial-up connection and choose Properties.

3. On the General tab of the Properties dialog box, mark the Use Dialing Rules check box and then click the Dialing Rules button.

4. The Phone and Modem Options dialog box appears. Select the location to use for this connection and then click OK.

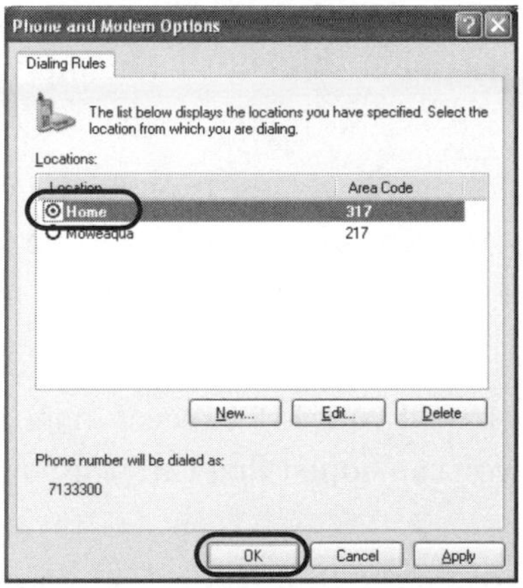

5. Click OK to close the Properties box for the connection.

Troubleshooting Dial-up Problems

Are you having some trouble with your modem, or with connecting to a particular ISP? Here are some ideas for troubleshooting:

Is the modem okay? To find out, open Phone and Modem Options from Control Panel. On the Modems tab, select your modem, and then click Properties. On the Diagnostics tab, click Query Modem. If there's a problem with the modem, an error message will appear. Otherwise, you can assume that your modem is installed and functioning correctly.

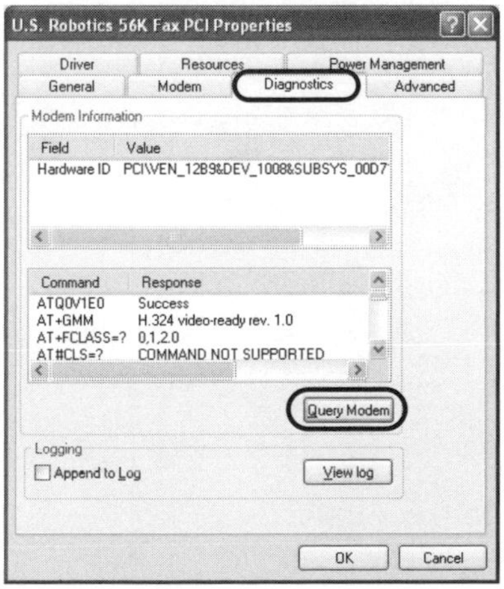

No dial tone? Make sure the phone cable is connected from the wall to the modem. Try hooking up a phone directly to that line and listening for a dial tone.

Static or line noise? Make sure the phone line is plugged into the correct jack on the modem. Most modems have two jacks: one for the line and one for a phone. If you get them switched, the modem might still work, but with lots of static.

Frequent disconnects? Check with your ISP to see if there are any advanced Windows settings you can adjust that can help improve the stability of the connection.

Frequent busy signals? Check with your ISP to find out if there are any alternate phone numbers you can dial.

17

Exploring the Web

Internet Explorer is the Web browser program that comes with Windows XP Home Edition. You can use it to view Web pages posted by companies and individuals all over the world. In this chapter, you will learn how to display a Web page, how to navigate between pages, and how to locate pages containing specific information. You will also learn how to "bookmark" favorite sites for later revisiting, and how to configure and use the built-in pop-up blocker.

Viewing Web Pages

There are several ways to start Internet Explorer (IE). Here are two quick ways:

❖ Choose Start ➣ Internet Explorer.

❖ Click the Internet Explorer icon in the Quick Launch toolbar (if displayed).

When you start IE, your **Home page** loads. The default Home page for IE is the MSN (Microsoft Network) Home page, shown in the next figure.

Home page

The Web page that IE is configured to begin with each time you start the program. It can also refer to the top-level page of a multipage Web site.

NOTE To change your Home page, from IE, choose Tools ➢ Internet Options and then enter a new **Web page** address in the Home Page box in the General tab.

In the preceding figure, all the underlined text and most of the graphics are **hyperlinks**. You can click on any of them to display a different Web page. You can tell that something is a hyperlink because when you move your mouse over it, the pointer turns into a hand, like this: 🖑.

This process of jumping from page to page by clicking hyperlinks is called *browsing*. Browsing is one way to use the Web; you'll learn other ways later in this chapter.

Using the Internet Explorer Toolbar

Use these buttons on the Internet Explorer toolbar to help you explore the Web:

The **Back button** ⬅ Back ▾ returns you to the previously viewed page. You can click the down arrow to its right to open a menu of previously viewed pages.

The **Forward button** ➡ ▾ takes you forward again after using the Back button; if you haven't gone Back, Forward isn't available. If you've gone back multiple pages, the down arrow to the right opens a menu of pages to go forward to.

The **Stop button** ✖ stops a page from loading. It's not available if a page is not currently loading. This is useful when a page is taking too long to load and you don't want to wait.

The **Refresh button** 🗘 reloads the current page. This is useful when an error occurs in loading or when the page contains information you want to update, such as stock quotes.

The **Home button** 🏠 returns you to your Home page.

Web page

A document in HTML (Hyper-Text Markup Language) made available on a public server on the Internet. Companies post Web pages to advertise their products and build goodwill, for example, and individuals post pages about their hobbies and interests.

Hyperlink

An underlined text string, or a graphic, that takes you to some other Web page or document when you click on it. Hyperlinks are also used in the Windows XP help system and can be used in Microsoft Office documents as well. *Hyperlink* can refer to any documents with an address, either on your hard disk or on any Web server in the world. However, on a Web page, *hyperlink* almost always refers to another Web page.

Sometimes when you click a hyperlink, it opens a new browser window. If your Back button is suddenly unavailable, that's probably what happened. Simply close the new IE window, and you'll be back where you were.

Viewing a Specific Page

How many times have you been watching TV and have seen a Web site address flash across the screen? Whether it's Pepsi or Pepcid AC, it seems as though every product and movie has its own Web address these days.

Web site addresses typically begin with `http://`. After that, many, but not all, addresses have www (which stands for World Wide Web, by the way). For example, you will find information about computer books at `http://www.sybex.com`.

If you know the address of the site you want to view, type it in the Address text box, replacing whatever is there, and then press Enter.

Address	http://www.sybex.com

> **TIP** As a typing shortcut, you can leave out the `http://` part, and IE will assume it's there, as long as the address starts with www. Or you can leave out the www part and IE will assume it, as long as you type `http://`. This book doesn't spell out `http://` every time, since you generally don't need to type it. There is a built-in search functionality in Internet Explorer that runs a keyword search if you enter less than a whole address. So, for example, if you just type a word in the Address box and press Enter, IE will try to find Web sites that have that word in them.

Locating Information on the Web

One of the first questions people ask when they start using the Web is "How do I find X?" X can be anything: a person, a bit of information, a Web site for a particular company, and so on. The answer, unfortunately, is "Well, it depends." No single directory exists that lets you find everything. However, many very good partial directories are available, and by visiting several of them, you are likely to find your answer.

Using a Web Search Site

Search sites (sometimes called search engines) are Web sites organized around giant databases of Web page links. They are free (that is, supported by advertisers). You type in certain words, and they spit back to you a list of Web pages that match.

The default Home page, MSN (www.msn.com), provides a Search the Web text box at the top of the page. It's a pretty good search site to start with, and it's easy because you are already there.

Here are some addresses of other popular search sites:

www.yahoo.com

www.google.com

www.lycos.com

www.excite.com

www.webcrawler.com

www.infoseek.com

www.hotbot.com

The basic process for using a search site is simple. Type the keyword(s) you are looking for, and then press Enter or click the button that activates the search (Find, Go Seek, Search, and so on—it depends on the site).

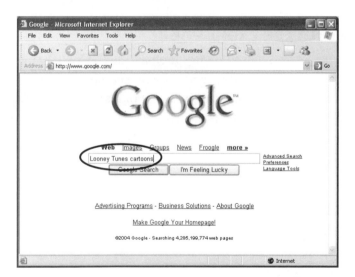

The search site presents you with a list of addresses, usually with some descriptive text above or below each one, as shown in the next figure. Each of the addresses is a hyperlink, and you can click any hyperlink to visit its page. Use the Back button to return to the list and try another address.

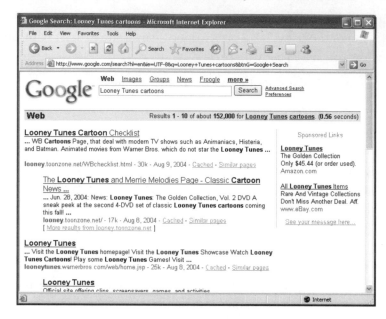

Searching with the Explorer Bar

When you click the Search button on IE's toolbar, the Explorer bar opens to the left of the main browser window and displays search controls. You can search using an animated character, or with just plain-text boxes. By default, the animated character is turned on, like this:

To turn it off, click Change Preferences and then click Without an Animated Character.

Either way, you type the words you want to search for in the text box, and then press Enter or click Search.

> **TIP** The Search pane uses MSN as the search site. You can change to a different search site by changing the search preferences. To do so, click Change Preferences and then click Change Internet Search Behavior. You can then choose from a list of alternate search sites.

If you want the animated character back, click Change Preferences and then click With an Animated Screen Character.

Finding People

Finding a person can be more difficult than finding information. A certain fact might be found on hundreds of pages; you need only to locate one page that happens to contain it. But a person is unique.

To find a person, you can visit one of the popular people directories, such as these:

        www.bigfoot.com
        people.yahoo.com
        www.worldpages.com

Then fill in the blanks provided to search for the person, based on what you know. For example, here's a search in progress at Yahoo!. You can use this site to search for either e-mail addresses or real-world contact information (street addresses and phone numbers).

Favorite
A shortcut to a Web page or other document, either on your own hard disk or on the Internet.

Working with Favorites

The **Favorites** menu stores the addresses of your favorite Web sites for easy access later. The Favorites menu comes with a few pre-created shortcuts that point to Microsoft sites, and you can easily add your own Favorites as well.

To try out the Favorites menu, do the following:

1. Open the Favorites menu.

> **WARNING** Don't confuse the Favorites menu with the Favorites button. IE has both. The Favorites button opens the Favorites list in the Explorer bar.

2. Point to the category you want to see, if the page you want isn't on the top-level menu.

3. Click the link to the page you want to visit.

Adding a Web Page to the Favorites Menu

To add a Web page to your Favorites list, first display the page in IE. Then do the following:

1. Choose Favorites ➤ Add to Favorites.

2. The Add Favorite dialog box opens, and the page title appears in the Name text box. If you want it to appear differently on your menu, change the name in the box.

3. (Optional) To place the favorite in a submenu of the Favorites menu, click Create In. The dialog box expands, as shown. Click the folder in which you want the favorite stored, or click New Folder to create a new folder.

4. Click OK to add the page to your Favorites menu.

Modifying the Favorites Menu

You can modify the Favorites menu later by renaming, deleting, and/or moving entries on it. If you try to visit a page and find that it no longer exists, for example, you would want to remove it from your Favorites menu.

To open the Favorites menu for editing, do the following:

1. Choose Favorites ➤ Organize Favorites.

2. The Organize Favorites dialog box opens. Do any of the following:

◆ To delete an item, select it and then click Delete. Click Yes to confirm.

◆ To rename an item, select it and click Rename. The name becomes editable; type the new name and then press Enter.

◆ To create a new folder, click Create Folder. A new folder appears at the bottom of the list. Type a name for it and then press Enter.

◆ To move an item to a different folder, select it and then click Move to Folder. A list of all the folders on the Favorites menu appears. Click the folder to move the item to and then click OK.

3. When you are finished modifying the Favorites menu, click Close.

Printing a Web Page

You can print any Web page easily. For a quick printout of the entire page (a single copy on the default printer), click the Print button ⬚. To print with more options, use this procedure instead:

1. Display the page to print.

2. Choose File ➢ Print.

3. Select the printer, the page range, and the number of copies, just as in any program.

4. Click Print. The page prints.

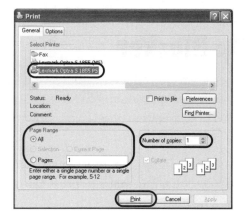

Frames
Multiple panes separated by divider bars. Frames used to be very popular in Web development, but nowadays you will seldom see them in use.

The Options tab in the Print dialog box contains a few special-purpose printing features. If the page you are printing has multiple **frames**, for example, you can choose which frame(s) to print.

There are also two check boxes on the Options tab:

Print All Linked Documents   Prints not only the current Web page, but all the pages that are hyperlinked to it. Beware: This feature uses a lot of paper!

Print Table of Links   Prints a listing of all the hyperlinks on the page.

Using the Pop-Up Blocker

The Internet Explorer pop-up blocker was introduced with Service Pack 2. It prevents those annoying pop-up windows that you might have experienced when viewing Web pages, and also prevents Web pages from downloading software to your PC without your permission.

When you visit a Web site that contains pop-ups, an information bar appears across the top of the Web page letting you know that a pop-up has been blocked. You can click that bar for a menu of options:

If you temporarily allow pop-ups for this site, the setting is active only as long as the Web browser window is open. If you permanently allow pop-ups for this site, the site is added a list. To see that list, and edit it if desired, do the following:

1. From Internet Explorer, choose Tools ➤ Internet Options.

2. Click the Privacy tab. At the bottom of this tab is a check box that turns the pop-up blocker on/off as a whole.

3. Click the Settings button.

4. In the Pop-Up Blocker Settings dialog box, do any of the following:

◆ Click a site that's already on the list and click Remove to remove it from the list of sites from which pop-ups are allowed.

◆ Type a site's address in the Address of Web Site to Allow box and click Add to add it to the list.

◆ Click the Remove All button to clear the list of allowed sites.

◆ Mark or clear the Play a Sound When a Pop-Up Is Blocked check box.

◇ Mark or clear the Show Information Bar When a Pop-Up Is Blocked check box.

◇ Open the Filter Level list and choose a different setting. The default is Medium, which blocks most pop-ups.

5. Click Close, and then click OK.

18 Communicating Online

The Internet is not only a rich source of information, as you saw in Chapter 17, but also a conduit for communication. You can send private e-mail to friends and associates using a program such as Outlook Express, and you can also participate in more public forums such as newsgroups. And for instant message delivery to someone else who is online at the same time as you, you can use a program such as Windows Messenger. In this chapter, you will learn about all three of these communication methods.

POP

Stands for Post Office Protocol. POP is a type of mail server. When you send e-mail to someone, the mail doesn't go directly to their Inbox; it goes to a mail server, which is like a post office. Then the recipient connects to that server using their e-mail program and retrieves their incoming mail. The server that holds this incoming mail is the POP server. In contrast, the server that holds the outgoing mail is usually an SMTP (Simple Mail Transfer Protocol) server. (Don't worry about memorizing this stuff.)

If you have Microsoft Office, you have Outlook, a program that not only manages e-mail but also keeps track of addresses, to-do lists, and calendar items. You're free to use Outlook if you want, but you cannot follow the steps in this chapter with it.

Understanding E-Mail

There are a lot of different e-mail systems out there. They can be broken down roughly into four categories:

POP-based e-mail   This is the kind of e-mail account you get with a regular ISP (see Chapter 16). Its mail can be read using any generic e-mail program such as Outlook Express or Outlook. You need an e-mail program in order to access it. It is sometimes called POP3.

IMAP e-mail   This type is similar to **POP**, but the mail is stored on a central server rather than transferred directly to your PC. It is useful for people who access their e-mail from several different computers. You need an e-mail program to access it, but some providers offer an alternative interface via the Web.

Online service e-mail   This is an e-mail address that's part of an online service. America Online, for example, has its own proprietary e-mail system. You use the AOL software to read and write e-mail. You can't use any other e-mail program with it.

Web-based e-mail   This is e-mail that doesn't require an e-mail program; you read and write it from a Web site. Examples are Yahoo! Mail and Hotmail. These mail accounts are usually free and are not connected with your ISP. Microsoft has built support for Hotmail accounts into Outlook Express, so if you have a Hotmail account, you can check it along with your regular e-mail account using Outlook Express. Other Web-based e-mail can be checked only from the Web.

In this chapter, I'll assume that you have an e-mail account that can be used with Outlook Express, and that you want to use Outlook Express as your e-mail software. Outlook Express comes free with Windows XP.

Getting Started with Outlook Express

To start Outlook Express, do any of the following:

◇ Choose Start ➤ E-Mail.

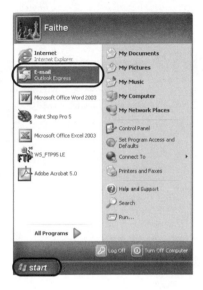

If Outlook Express doesn't appear below E-Mail on the Start menu, perhaps another program such as MSN Explorer or Outlook has taken over as the default e-mail program. To reset the shortcut on the Start menu to point to Outlook Express, right-click the taskbar and choose Properties. Click the Start menu tab and choose Customize. Open the E-Mail drop-down list and choose Outlook Express. Then click OK twice.

◇ Choose Start ➤ All Programs ➤ Outlook Express.

◇ Click the Outlook Express icon in the Quick Launch toolbar (if displayed).

If you haven't set up an Internet connection yet for your PC (Chapter 16), the New Connection Wizard runs and prompts you to set one up.

Then Outlook Express starts. If you haven't yet set up any e-mail accounts, the internet Connection Wizard runs and prompts you to set one up. See the next section for details.

Every time Outlook Express starts, it begins at a Welcome screen, as shown here. You can click one of the folders in the folder list to display the contents of a mail folder, as you would to browse folders in a file management window (Chapter 3).

> **NOTE** If you want to display the Inbox folder for your default mail account when Outlook Express starts, mark the check box at the bottom of the Welcome screen.

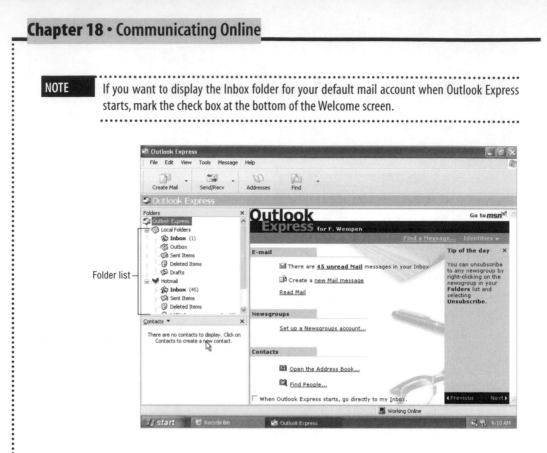

Folder list

Setting Up a Mail Account

You must set up at least one e-mail account in order to use Outlook Express. The Internet Connection Wizard prompts you for setup information the first time you start Outlook Express if you haven't done it yet:

1. In the Display Name text box on the Your Name screen, type the name that should appear on the messages you send. Then click Next.

   The display name need not be the same as your e-mail address. You might put your nickname here, for example.

Display name:	F. Wempen
	For example: John Smith

2. Enter your e-mail address and then click Next. If you have more than one e-mail address, just enter one of them for now; you can set up additional accounts after this initial setup.

You must use a regular e-mail account with Outlook Express rather than a Web-based one, unless your Web-based account is from Hotmail.

E-mail address:	fwempen@hotmail.com
	For example: someone@microsoft.com

3. Choose what kind of mail server handles your incoming mail. If you're setting up a Hotmail account, it's HTTP, which is a Web-based server. Otherwise, it's probably a POP3 server. (The third kind, IMAP, is less common.) Your ISP can tell you which type of mail server to choose, but POP3 is a good guess.

4. If you chose HTTP, make sure Hotmail is selected in the second text box.

If you chose POP3 or some other server type, enter the incoming and outgoing mail server addresses. You will need to get this information from your ISP.

If you don't have the e-mail server names from your ISP, you can guess. The incoming mail server is probably pop. or mail. followed by whatever comes after the @ in your e-mail address. For example, if your e-mail address is mailto:dwayne@mysite.com, your incoming mail server might be mail.mysite.com or pop.mysite.com. The outgoing mail server is probably either smtp. or mail..

Either way, click Next to continue.

5. Confirm your account name and enter the password for it. If you are setting up the primary e-mail address provided by your ISP, the account name and password are probably the same as the ones you use to connect to the Internet in general. If setting up an alternate e-mail address, they will be different.

If you leave Remember Password marked, you won't need to enter your password each time you check e-mail. Clear this check box if privacy is an issue.

Click Next to continue.

6. At the Congratulations screen, click Finish.

7. If you add an HTTP-type mail account, you'll see a message asking whether you want to download folders from the mail server you added. Click Yes to do so.

   You now have an e-mail account set up in Outlook Express, and the main Outlook Express window opens.

Skip down to the section "Managing E-Mail with Outlook Express" if you're ready to get started, or set up additional e-mail accounts as explained next.

Setting Up Additional E-Mail Accounts

You can set up more e-mail accounts at any time in Outlook Express. It can be very handy to have all of your e-mail accounts managed from within a single program such as Outlook Express, because you can send and receive from all accounts in a single operation.

To set up another e-mail account after the first one, do the following in Outlook Express:

1. Choose Tools ➢ Accounts.

2. In the Internet Accounts dialog box, click the Mail tab. Then choose Add ➢ Mail.

3. Complete the Internet Connection Wizard, as in the preceding section.

4. After clicking Finish, you return to the Internet Accounts dialog box. Select whichever account you want to be the default, and click Set as Default.

The default e-mail account will be used whenever you compose a new e-mail message.

5. Click Close to close the dialog box.

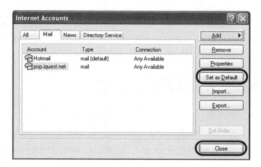

If you have both HTTP and other types of accounts set up in Outlook Express, they will appear in different parts of the folder list in Outlook Express. POP3 and IMAP accounts will appear under Local Folders, and Hotmail accounts will appear under Hotmail, like this:

Managing E-Mail with Outlook Express

Now comes the fun part—receiving and sending mail. In the following sections, you will learn the basic skills required to communicate via e-mail with others.

Receiving E-Mail

When you start Outlook Express, it automatically connects to your mail server(s) and retrieves your new mail. You can also ask it to send and receive at any time by doing any of the following:

◆ Click the Send/Recv button.

◆ Press Ctrl+M.

◆ Choose Tools ➢ Send and Receive ➢ Send and Receive All.

To send and receive for a specific account only, choose Tools ➢ Send and Receive and then select that particular account. Or click the down arrow to the right of the Send/Recv button to open the same menu that you get with Tools ➢ Send and Receive.

Reading E-Mail

The Inbox is divided into four panes. The top-left pane lists the available folders, just as in a file management window. The bottom-left pane lists e-mail addresses you have saved in your Contacts list (if any). The top-right pane lists the e-mail messages in the selected folder, and the bottom-right pane previews the selected e-mail. New messages appear in boldface, so you can distinguish them from those you've already read. You can read an e-mail by selecting it and then scrolling through the preview pane.

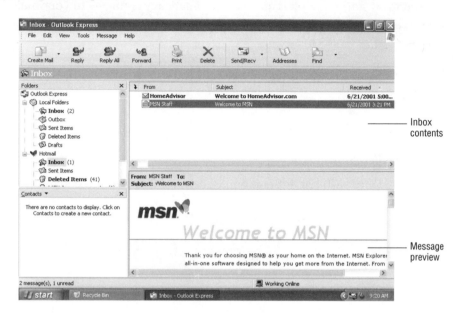

Inbox contents

Message preview

You can also open an e-mail in a separate window by double-clicking it. Here's an example of an e-mail in its own window. Notice that the toolbar buttons change to those appropriate for dealing with the displayed message, rather than the general-purpose Outlook Express buttons.

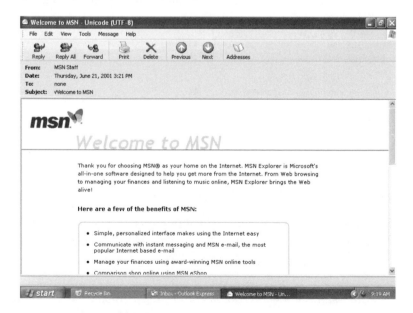

Printing a Message

To print a message, follow these steps:

1. Either display it in its own window, or simply select it in the Inbox. Then click the Print button on the toolbar, or choose File ➤ Print.

2. The Print dialog box opens. Change any print settings as needed and then click Print.

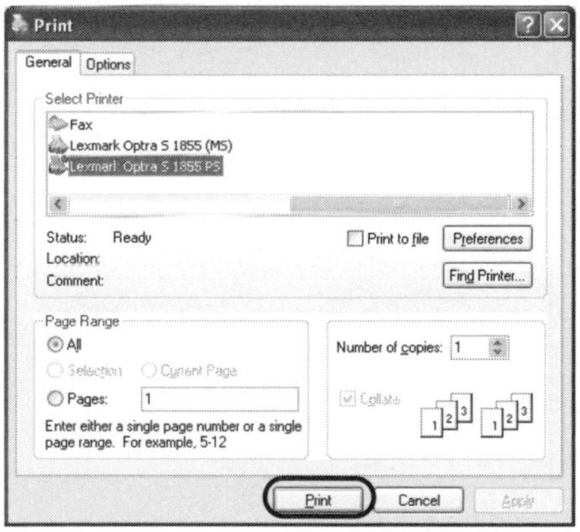

Reading and Saving an Attachment

Some messages you receive have attachments—that is, other files sent along with the message. An attachment can be a forwarded message, a picture, a compressed archive, a document, or any other file type. If a message has an attachment, a paper clip icon ⓤ appears next to it in the Inbox. When you open the message in its own window, the attachment appears on the Attach line.

Attach: ⓦ 2982-17.DOC (63.6 KB)

To save an e-mail attachment to your hard disk, do the following:

1. Select the message in the Inbox, or double-click it to open it in its own window.

2. Choose File ➢ Save Attachments.

3. Type a location in the Save To text box, or click the Browse button to browse for a location.

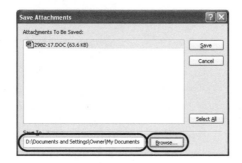

If you chose Browse, select the folder and drive in which to save the attachment, and then click OK.

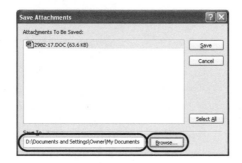

4. Back in the Save Attachments dialog box, click Save.

You don't have to save an attachment to view it. Just do either of the following to open the attachment in whatever program its filename extension is associated with:

◆ When the message is open in its own window, double-click the attachment name on the Attach line.

◇ In the preview pane, click the large paper clip in the top-right corner. A menu opens, showing the attachments. Click the attachment to open it.

NOTE Service Pack 2 for Windows XP added a feature in Outlook Express that blocks potentially unsafe attachments (such as executable files). If you are blocked from sending or receiving an attachment that you know is virus-free, you can turn off the protection. Choose Tools ≻ Options, and on the Security tab, clear the Do Not Allow Attachments to Be Saved or Opened That Could Potentially Be a Virus check box.

Deleting a Message

To delete a message, select it in the Inbox and press Delete, or click the Delete button on the toolbar. This moves the message to the Deleted Items folder, just as deleting a file in Windows moves it to the Recycle Bin.

If you change your mind, you can "undelete" the message by viewing the Deleted Items folder and dragging the message back to the Inbox icon on the folder list.

You can also right-click the Deleted Items folder in the folder list and choose Empty Deleted Items Folder from the shortcut menu.

Just as you can empty the Recycle Bin in Windows, you can clear the Deleted Items folder. Just display that folder, select the message(s) you want to delete from it, and press the Delete key.

Replying to a Message

You can reply to any message you receive simply by clicking Reply and typing your response. Or, to reply to the original sender plus all other recipients, click Reply All. Then click Send to mail your message.

When you reply, the original message appears quoted in the message pane. Each line of it is preceded by a symbol (the default is a solid vertical bar) that indicates that the text is quoted and not original. You can type your reply above the quoted block, or you can insert the lines of your reply between the quoted lines to respond individually to certain points that the writer made.

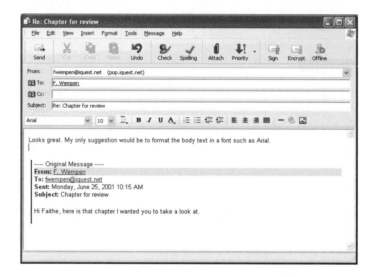

When you click Send to send your reply, the message moves to the Outbox folder. It will be sent the next time Outlook Express sends and receives. To send it immediately, click the Send/Recv button.

After you have replied to a message, its icon in the Inbox changes to an envelope with a left arrow in its corner: 🖼️. In contrast, when you forward a message, covered later in the chapter, the icon changes to an envelope with a right arrow.

Adding a Sender to Your Contacts List

When you reply to a message, the sender's e-mail address is automatically added to your Contacts list (in the bottom-left pane), to make it easier to send more mail to that person later.

> **Contacts** ▼   ×
> ☐ F. Wempen

If you don't want to reply to the sender's message right now, but nevertheless want to add the address to your Contacts list, right-click the message in the Inbox and then choose Add Sender to Address Book.

> **Open**
> Print
>
> Reply to Sender
> Reply to All
> Forward
> Forward As Attachment
>
> Mark as Read
> Mark as Unread
>
> Move to Folder...
> Copy to Folder...
> Delete
>
> Add Sender to Address Book
>
> Properties

Forwarding a Message

Forwarding mail is just like replying to it, except that instead of the message going back to the original writer, it goes "forward" to someone else. To forward a message:

1. Select the message in your Inbox and then click the Forward button on the toolbar.

Forward

2. Address the message to a new recipient by entering an e-mail address in the To box. (See the following section for more help with recipients.)

3. Type any comments you want to make at the top of the message.

4. Click Send.

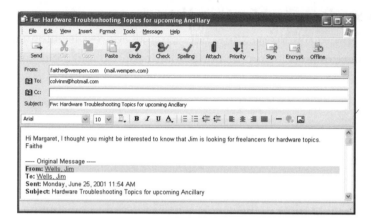

Composing a New E-Mail Message

Composing a new message is just like replying except that you specify a recipient and a subject. You can look up the recipient in your Contacts list or type the address manually.

There are several ways to start a new message:

❖ Double-click a name in the Contacts list (in the bottom-left pane) to start a new message and address it to that person.

◆ Choose File ➣ New ➣ Mail Message.

If you click the down arrow to the right of the Create Mail button, a list of available *stationeries* appears. Stationeries are e-mail templates that add attractive formatting to your messages. They are fun to play with, but are beyond the scope of this chapter; feel free to experiment with them on your own.

◆ Click the Create Mail button.

◆ Click the Addresses button.

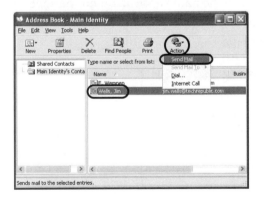

Select a person's name and then click the Action button. Then select Send Mail on the menu that opens.

Any way you do it, a new message window opens. From there, just fill in the recipient's e-mail address (if it's not already there), the subject, and your message text, as shown here:

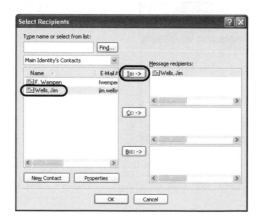

Use the Bcc field whenever you don't want the multiple recipients of a message to have one another's e-mail addresses. For example, if you send out e-mail to a group of customers, using Bcc would preserve each customer's privacy.

If you have more than one e-mail account set up, you can choose which account to use by opening the From box's drop-down list and choosing a different account.

If you are typing the addresses of more than one recipient, separate the addresses with semicolons.

You can look up recipients in your Contacts list while composing a message by clicking the To button 🕮 To: . This opens the Select Recipients window.

Click a name and then click the To, Cc, or Bcc button. The To button copies the name to the To list. The Cc and Bcc fields are for informational copies for other people. Cc is a regular copy, with the name appearing on the sent message. Bcc is a blind copy, where the Bcc recipient's name is hidden. Then click OK to return to composing the message.

Adding an Attachment

You can send pictures, documents, and other files to your friends and family through the Attachment feature of Outlook Express. To attach a file to a message, do the following as you are composing it:

1. Click the Attach button.

2. In the Insert Attachment dialog box, select the file to attach. (Navigate to another folder or drive if needed.) To select more than one file, hold down Ctrl as you click each one.

3. Click Attach.

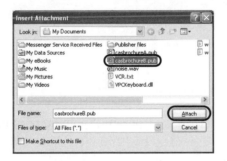

Then finish sending the e-mail normally.

Working with the Contacts List (Address Book)

The Contacts list in Outlook Express pulls its information from an address book. This address book is integrated with Outlook Express but also available as a stand-alone utility (Start ➢ All Programs ➢ Accessories ➢ Address Book).

You can add someone to the address book in several ways. You have already seen how entries are added automatically whenever you send e-mail to someone or reply to a message. You have also already seen that you can right-click a message and choose Add Sender to Address Book.

Here is a way to enter someone in the address book who hasn't sent you a message yet:

1. Click the Addresses button in the toolbar.

2. In the Address Book window that appears, click New. A menu opens; click New Contact.

3. A Properties box appears for the new person. Type the person's e-mail address in the E-Mail Addresses text box and then click Add.

4. Enter the person's first, middle, and last names if desired. You may omit any or all of those fields if you prefer to list the person by e-mail address only.

5. Enter any other information for the person on any of the other tabs. It's all optional.

> **NOTE**   If the person's e-mail address contains @ao1.com, mark the Send E-Mail Using Plain Text Only check box. AOL's proprietary e-mail program sometimes has problems displaying formatted messages from outside AOL.

6. Click OK, adding the person to the address book.

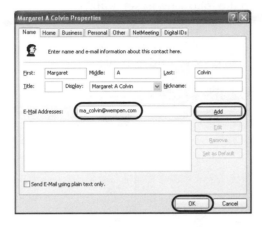

7. Close the Address Book window.

Discussing Topics Publicly in Newsgroups

Newsgroups are like public bulletin boards where anybody can post a message. One person leaves a message, someone else posts a reply (again, which everyone can read), and so on. It's like e-mail en masse. You'll be amazed at the number and variety of newsgroups and the zeal with which some people participate in them!

Outlook Express has a newsreader feature that you can use to read and post to newsgroups. Some people who spend all day reading newsgroups prefer a more sophisticated newsreader, but for most people, Outlook Express's capability is ample.

Setting Up a News Account in Outlook Express

Your ISP likely provides a **news server** as well as a mail server, and its name is probably news. plus whatever comes after the @ sign in your e-mail address, like this: news.myisp.com.

You can also access newsgroups using Internet Explorer instead of Outlook Express; go to www.deja.com. The interface is much more limited, but it's handy when you want to read newsgroups and don't have access to Outlook Express at the moment (such as when browsing at a public library or on a friend's PC).

News server
A computer that stores messages from a variety of newsgroups and provides those messages on demand to any users who request them through a newsreader program such as Outlook Express.

If the news server is already set up in Outlook Express, it will appear at the bottom of the folder list. If not, do the following to set it up:

1. Choose Tools ➤ Accounts.

2. Click the News tab. Then choose Add ➤ News.

3. The Internet Connection Wizard starts. In the Display Name text box on the Your Name screen, type the name by which you want to be known in the newsgroup postings; then click Next.

WARNING You may not want to use your real full name, for privacy reasons.

> When you post a message to a newsgroup or send an e-mail message, your display name will appear in the From field. Type your name as you would like it to appear.
>
> Display name: Faithe
>   For example: John Smith

4. Enter your e-mail address in the E-Mail Address text box and then click Next.

WARNING Again, for privacy reasons (and to avoid receiving junk mail), you might not want to enter your real address. Or you might want to get an extra e-mail account with a Web-based service such as Hotmail and use it only for newsgroup postings.

> People can reply to your news messages by sending you an e-mail message at the address below–or they may post another news message.
>
> E-mail address: nobody@hotmail.com
>   For example: someone@microsoft.com

5. Type the news server name. Ask your ISP for this if you are not sure.

6. Some news servers are restricted, so that only certain people can use them. If you need to access a restricted news server, mark the My News Server Requires Me to Log On check box.

> Type the name of the Internet news (NNTP) server your Internet service provider has given you.
>
> News (NNTP) server:
>
> news.home.com
>
> If your Internet service provider has informed you that you must log on to your news (NNTP) server and has provided you with an NNTP account name and password, then select the check box below.
>
> ☐ My news server requires me to log on

7. Click Next.

8. If you marked the check box in step 6, prompts appear for username and password. Enter them and then click Next.

> **Internet Connection Wizard**
>
> **Internet News Server Logon**
>
> Type the account name and password your Internet service provider has given you.
>
> Account name: [wempen]
>
> Password: ••••••••••••
> ☑ Remember password
>
> If your Internet service provider requires you to use Secure Password Authentication (SPA) to access your news account, select the 'Log On Using Secure Password Authentication (SPA)' check box.
> ☐ Log on using Secure Password Authentication (SPA)
>
> < Back   Next >   Cancel

9. At the Congratulations screen, click Finish.

10. The news account now appears on the News tab of the Internet Accounts dialog box. Click Close.

11. A prompt asks whether you would like to download the newsgroups. Click Yes.

> **Outlook Express**
>
> ⚠ Would you like to download newsgroups from the news account you added?
>
> Yes   No

You don't necessarily have to use the news server provided by your ISP; you can use any public news server. News servers vary as to the groups they carry, so if your ISP's news server doesn't carry a group you want to read, shop around.

12. Wait for the group names to be downloaded. It might take several
minutes. When all the names have been downloaded, they appear in
the Newsgroup Subscriptions dialog box.

13. If you want to subscribe to newsgroups now, see the following section.
Otherwise, click OK to close the Newsgroup Subscriptions box.

Subscribing to Newsgroups

The list of newsgroups can be overwhelming; my news server carries more
than 35,000 of them, and yours is probably similar in volume. Fortunately, Outlook Express allows you to search the list by word, so you can quickly identify
groups that contain a certain word.

To subscribe to newsgroups, do the following:

1. If the Newsgroup Subscriptions dialog box is not already open, click
the news account in the folder list.

If the dialog box is already open, skip to step 3.

2. If you haven't subscribed to any groups yet, a message appears, offering to open the Newsgroup Subscriptions box. Click Yes.

Or, if you don't see that prompt, click the Newsgroups button to open the Newsgroup Subscriptions box.

3. In the Display Newsgroups Which Contain text box, type a word you want to search for. The list is narrowed to only the groups that include that word.

4. Click the name of a group you want to subscribe to and then click Subscribe.

5. Repeat steps 3 and 4 for other topics as desired.

6. Click OK to close the Newsgroup Subscriptions box.

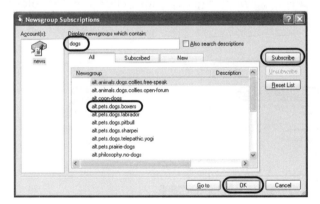

The newsgroups you selected now appear in the folder list, beneath your news server. To view the messages in a group, click its name on the list.

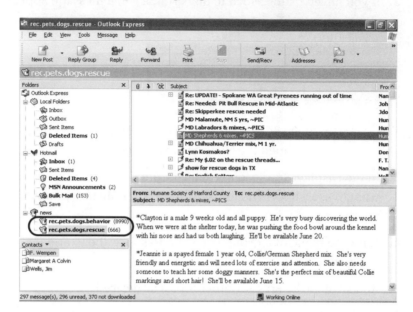

If you ever want to unsubscribe to a group, right-click it on the folder list and then choose Unsubscribe.

Reading Newsgroup Messages

To view a group's messages, click the group name in the folder list. To read an individual message, click it to make it appear in the preview pane, or double-click it to open it in a separate window, just as with e-mail.

Some messages have a plus sign next to them; click the plus sign to expand a list of replies to that message.

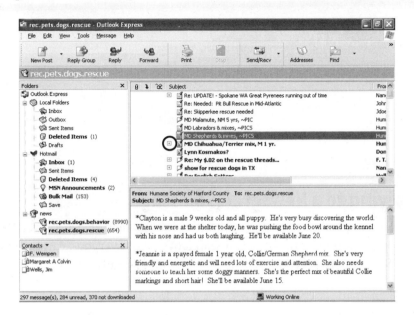

When you read a message (or when it has been selected for a few seconds), it becomes marked as read and is no longer boldfaced. If you want to mark a lot of messages as "read" at once, select them and choose Edit ➤ Mark as Read. Or, to mark the entire list of messages as read, choose Edit ➤ Mark All Read.

One good reason to mark messages as read is to prevent them from showing up the next time you view the newsgroup. To choose whether or not read

messages will show up next time you open this group, choose View ➤ Current
View and then either Hide Read Messages or Show All Messages.

Replying to a Newsgroup Message

You can reply to a newsgroup message either publicly or privately. Usually, it's
considered good manners to reply publicly so that everyone can benefit from
the discussion. However, if you have something negative or personal to say,
reply to the individual instead.

♦ *To reply publicly,* click the Reply Group button in the toolbar.

A message composition window appears, with the complete text of the
message quoted. You might want to delete some of the lines, to avoid
making your reply overly long, but retain any lines that are relevant to
your reply. Then compose your reply and click Send.

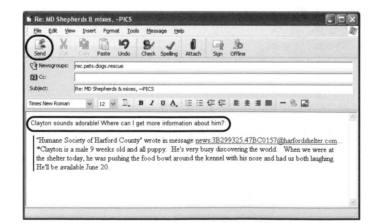

❖ *To reply privately* using e-mail, click the Reply button in the toolbar. Compose your e-mail and then click Send.

Posting a New Message

To post a new message to a newsgroup, first display that newsgroup and then click the New Post button.

Then simply fill in the subject and message, as you do with an e-mail, and click Send. You don't specify a recipient; that information is already filled in, based on the newsgroup that was active when you clicked New Post.

Chatting with Windows Messenger

Windows Messenger is a totally free instant-messaging program that you can use to communicate with friends all over the world one-on-one. Windows Messenger is a real-time chat program, which means that both parties must be online and signed on to Windows Messenger at the same time. The Windows Messenger window keeps track of the members you have entered into its database, and it tells you who is online and available for chat at the moment, and who is not.

.NET Passport
An identification system that Microsoft is promoting for all Microsoft-related Web sites. You enter your contact information once, and then log into a site with your Passport ID rather than registering separately at each site.

Setting Up Windows Messenger

If you haven't yet signed up for a **.NET Passport**, you will need to do so before you can use Windows Messenger. It's easy, and it's free. Then you can simply log into Windows Messenger with your Passport ID and password, and you're ready to go.

There are two ways to get a Passport ID. You can use Internet Explorer to go to www.passport.com and sign up through the Web site, or you can sign up as part of Windows Messenger's configuration.

Follow these steps to set up Windows Messenger and to get a .NET Passport if you don't already have one:

1. Choose Start ➢ All Programs ➢ Windows Messenger.

The .NET Passport Wizard may open automatically at this point. If it does, skip to step 4. Otherwise, continue to step 2.

2. Click the Click Here to Sign In hyperlink.

3. In the .NET Messenger Service dialog box, click the Get a .NET Passport hyperlink.

4. At the .NET Passport Wizard's opening screen, click Next.

5. Because you already have an e-mail account, leave "Yes" selected. Then click Next.

If you want a new, free, additional e-mail account, choose "No. I would like to open an MSN Hotmail e-mail account" and then fill in a sign-up form. When you have finished signing up, return to the wizard.

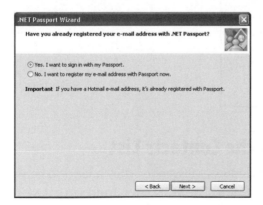

6. If your e-mail is already registered with the .NET Passport service, click Yes. Otherwise click No and then follow the prompts to register it. During that process, you will choose a password for your .NET Passport. This does not have to be the same as your regular e-mail password. (In fact, it is better if it is not the same.)

Then click Next to go on.

7. Type your e-mail address and password for the .NET Passport service, and then click Next.

8. At the You're Done! screen, click Finish.

At this point, the wizard will attempt to sign you on to Windows Messenger. If sign-on is successful, the Windows Messenger screen will appear.

If you continually get an error instead of the You're Done! screen in step 8, try using a Hotmail or MSN e-mail address instead of your regular e-mail address. Sign up for one if needed.

If sign-on fails for some reason, or if you chose not to sign on automatically, a sign-on dialog box will appear. Type your Passport e-mail address and password and then click OK.

Adding Contacts to the Contacts List

To chat with someone with Windows Messenger, they must also be signed up for the service. If you know their Hotmail or MSN e-mail address or .NET Passport ID, you can add them to your Contacts list. You can also search the Windows Messenger directory. People can opt out of the directory, so it's possible the person you are seeking isn't listed; but it's worth a try if you don't know the exact ID.

To add a contact, do the following:

1. From the Windows Messenger window, click Add a Contact or choose
Tools ➤ Add a Contact. The following screen appears:

When asking around to
see who among your
friends and relatives has
Windows Messenger, keep
in mind that until very
recently, the program was
called MSN Messenger; so
anyone who doesn't have
Windows XP will probably
know it by the older name.

2. Type the person's e-mail address in the box provided, if you know it.

The wizard looks up that e-mail address or ID in its database. If the
person has a Hotmail account or a .NET Passport, you see a Success!
message. Continue to step 3.

If the person does not have a .NET Passport ID, a message appears to
that effect. Click Next to go on.

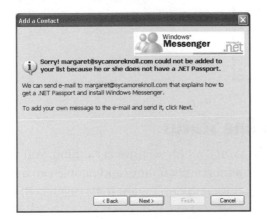

3. The wizard offers to send an e-mail to the person, explaining how to install Windows Messenger. Click Next if you want to send this.

4. Click Next to add another contact, or click Finish if you are done.

Now the people you entered appear on your Contacts list. There are two separate listings: people currently online and people currently not online. The following figure shows one of each.

Controlling Your Online Status

Whenever you are online and Windows Messenger is running, you will appear on other people's Contacts list as currently online, and people can initiate conversations with you. If you are busy and don't want to be disturbed, you can shut down Windows Messenger, or you can simply set your status to indicate that you don't want to talk.

To change your status, choose File ➤ My Status and then select a status on the submenu.

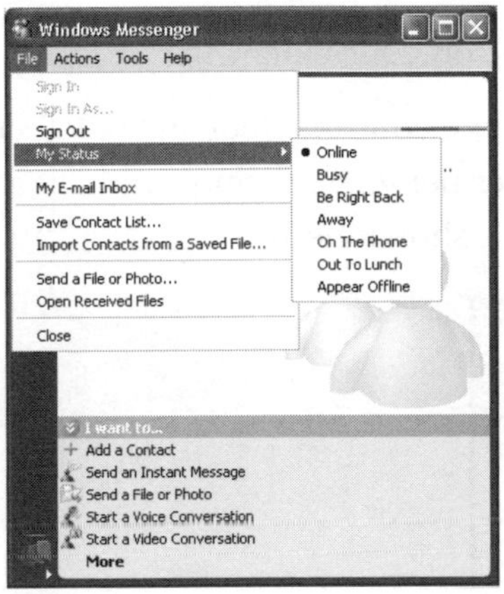

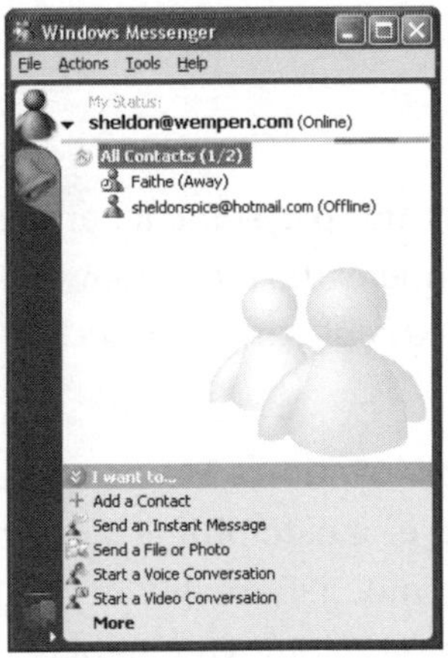

Windows Messenger automatically converts your status to Away whenever you are inactive for more than a specified number of minutes. The default is 15 minutes. To set or change this setting, choose Tools ➤ Options and enter the number of minutes on the Preferences tab, or turn the setting off by deselecting the "Show me as 'Away' when I'm inactive for ___ minutes" check box.

Your status choice will appear next to your name on other people's screens. For example, in the following figure, Faithe has set her status to Away. To allow messages again, set your status to Online.

Chatting with a Contact

You can initiate a conversation with anyone on your Online list (except those who have set a status, as you learned in the preceding section).

To initiate a conversation:

1. Double-click the person's name on your Online list.

2. In the Conversation window, type your message in the lower pane and then click Send. When the other person is typing a message, you will see an indicator to that effect as shown here.

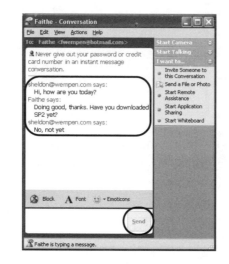

When the person receives your message, a sound plays and a bar flashes on the taskbar of their PC. Clicking that bar opens the message window, just like the one on your PC. The person can type a reply to you and click Send. That's all there is to it!

This chapter has only scratched the surface of Windows Messenger's capabilities. You can manage your Contacts list, send e-mail to offline contacts, share applications, use video cameras in chats, and much more. If you have time, and a friend who also has Windows Messenger, you might want to play with the features on your own.

Chatting can be more than just a two-person affair. You might want to have a "conference call" chat with many participants at once. To invite more people to an existing chat, click the Invite button. Then select To Join This Conversation, and select another online contact. If there is nobody on the list except Other, then none of your other contacts are currently online.

19 Customizing Your Online Experience

The last several chapters have helped you get online and perform some basic tasks, such as viewing Web pages and sending and receiving e-mail. This chapter builds on those skills by explaining some customizations and adjustments you can make to your Web-browsing and e-mail activities. You will learn how to customize Internet Explorer, how to protect yourself and your family from online dangers, and how to set up e-mail message filtering to minimize the amount of junk mail you receive.

Customizing Internet Explorer

Like most good programs, Internet Explorer (IE) is fully customizable. You can change everything, from which toolbars appear to how security is handled.

Rather than going into exhaustive detail about the available settings, let's look at the settings in some general categories. This will give you an idea of what you can change and where you might start looking for the setting that changes it.

Changing the IE Window

On the View menu, you'll find some commands that affect how the Internet Explorer window appears and how content looks within it:

> **Toolbars and Status Bar**   These are the same as in a file management window; refer to Chapter 4 if you need help.

> **Explorer Bar**   From this submenu, you can choose what, if anything, appears in a separate pane to the left of the main window.

Text Size   This controls the size of the text that appears by default on the Web pages you display. In most cases, Web content doesn't specify its own font size; it relies on the browser to choose the font. The default is Medium.

Here's what a Web page looks like when Text Size is set to Largest. This can be useful for someone with limited vision, for example.

Full Screen   Choose this to get rid of the toolbars and other nonpage items temporarily, so that you can see more of a Web page at once. Full Screen view looks like this:

To exit from Full Screen view, click the Restore button 🗗 in the top-right corner.

Changing Internet Options

Most of the remaining settings for Internet Explorer are controlled from within the Internet Properties (or Internet Options) dialog box. The name differs depending on how you get there, but the settings are all the same.

You can get to it in either of two ways:

◆ Within Internet Explorer, choose Tools ➤ Internet Options. If you do this, the dialog box's name will be Internet Options.

◆ Choose Start ➤ Control Panel and then choose Network and Internet Connections ➤ Internet Options. If you do this, the dialog box's name will be Internet Properties.

Let's look at some of the settings in this dialog box. (I'll skip the Content tab in this section, because it's covered in greater detail later in the chapter. And I'll skip Advanced, because there are no settings there that a beginner needs to change.)

General Options

On the General tab (shown in the preceding figure), you'll find the following settings:

Home Page Specify a different Home page (that is, starting page) in the Address box if you like. You can use a Web address here (http://*something*), a network path (*computername**drive**folder*), or a file on your hard disk (C:*something*).

Temporary Internet Files IE caches the pages you visit in a temporary folder on your hard disk so that pages will load more quickly when you revisit them. Click Settings to set up this feature, or click Delete Files to clear the current cache. The Delete Cookies button deletes any **cookies** that have been stored on your hard disk by the Web pages you have visited. (See the Privacy tab, covered later, to choose whether to accept cookies in the future.)

Cookies

Small text files containing settings or personal data that are automatically created and stored on your hard disk when you visit certain Web sites. This data is used to help the site reidentify you if you visit again later, remembering any settings you have entered, such as name, address, and payment information. If you delete cookies, you will lose all automatic logins for Web sites.

TIP Clearing the cache can free up a surprising amount of hard-disk space; so if you're short on space, try that out.

History   IE saves links to pages you have visited in the History folder so that you can call up the pages again later. If you don't clear the History list regularly, anyone who sits down at your PC can see what Web sites you've been visiting. (The History button on the toolbar opens the History list in the Explorer pane.) Specify an amount of time a link should remain in History, or clear the current list with Clear History.

Colors   Click here to open a dialog box where you can set default colors for Web page display.

Fonts   Click here to open a box to choose a default font for text. (To choose a default size, see the preceding section, "Changing the IE Window.")

Languages   Click here to open a box to select a language. (This is not necessary unless you plan to view pages in different languages.)

Accessibility   Click here to open a box to set features that allow you to bypass a page's formatting, to make it easier to see what's on the screen.

[Colors...]   [Fonts...]   [Languages...]   [Accessibility...]

Security Options

When browsing the Web, you must decide how secure you want to be and balance that with how many of the fancy Web features you want to take advantage of. The highest security levels in IE let you explore completely anonymously, with no fear of anything. However, these settings also prevent you from, for example, ordering items online, viewing multimedia content, and playing Java-based games.

The Security tab shows four content zones: Internet, Local Intranet, Trusted Sites, and Restricted Sites. (In the following figure, I have selected Local

Intranet.) You can set a security level for each zone individually and specify which sites are part of that zone. (Click the Sites button to manage the list for a particular zone.) Any sites that are not on the list for the Local Intranet, Trusted Sites, or Restricted Sites are automatically assumed to be in the Internet zone.

Each zone has a slider that you can drag to control the security level. The default for the Internet zone is Medium, which offers a good compromise between safety and capability. It lets you do almost anything, but provides prompts telling you what a page has requested and letting you make the call on whether to allow it.

You can also customize the security level for a zone. If a custom level is already selected, the Security tab looks like this instead:

When you click the Custom Level button, a Security Settings dialog box opens, containing an exhaustive list of security settings you can change for the zone.

Privacy Options

As you learned earlier in the chapter, cookies are little bits of information stored on your hard disk that certain Web pages use to reidentify you when you visit them again. They are generally harmless, but if you prefer more anonymity when Web browsing, you can adjust the cookie-acceptance setting on the Privacy tab. Drag the slider up or down to change the setting.

You can also click the Advanced button to fine-tune the settings for cookies, or click Edit to set a custom cookie setting for a particular Web site.

As you learned in Chapter 17, if you have Service Pack 2 installed, you'll see the pop-up blocker configuration settings at the bottom of this tab, as shown in the preceding figure. Chapter 17 explained how to use it.

Connection Options

The Connections tab helps you manage your means of connecting to the Internet. If you have an always-on connection such as cable or DSL, you will probably never need this tab.

If you need to rerun the Internet Connection Wizard at some point, you can do so by clicking the Setup button here.

If you have more than one dial-up connection, you can select the one you want as the default in the Dial-Up and Virtual Private Network Settings box. Advanced users might also want to set the properties for a connection here, by clicking the Settings button.

Program Options

IE does a lot of stuff behind the scenes for you, without your even realizing it. One of those functions is to load external programs to handle content that IE can't process itself.

The Programs tab lets you specify what external program should run when a particular type of content presents itself. For example, when you click a hyperlink that sends e-mail, your e-mail program opens in a separate window from

IE, and you can select which e-mail program to use on the Programs tab, as shown here:

If you have Service Pack 2 installed, you can also manage your add-ons from here. Click the Manage Add-Ons button to display a list of extensions that have been set up for Internet Explorer. Most of these are probably legitimate and helpful, but annoying adware and spyware utilities can also set up housekeeping here. Open the Show menu and choose Add-Ons Currently Loaded in Internet Explorer to see what is being loaded. You can individually select each add-on and enable or disable it.

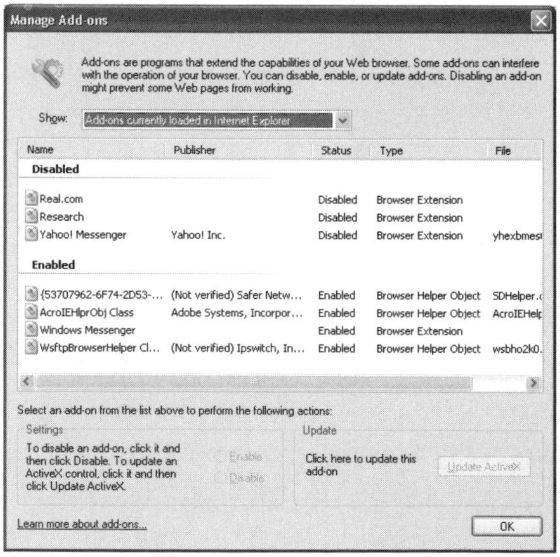

Enabling or Disabling the Windows Firewall

One of the issues with having an always-on Internet connection such as cable or DSL is that because the computer's IP address stays the same from day to day, it becomes easier for hackers to view and potentially modify hard-disk content. A *firewall* program has been the traditional solution to this problem.

Windows XP comes with a firewall feature built in, eliminating the need for a firewall program or device for most home users. It is enabled by default, so you need not do anything special to turn it on. It's available for both network and dial-up connections. It was originally called Internet Connection Firewall, but as of Service Pack 2, its name has changed to Windows Firewall (to reflect the fact that it is for all kinds of connections, not just Internet ones).

> **WARNING** In some cases, having a firewall in place can interfere with your ability to connect to a particular site. This problem doesn't usually occur, however, with publicly available Web sites.

The firewall feature is controlled from the connection's properties. To enable or disable the firewall for a network connection, do the following:

1. Choose Start ➢ My Network Places.

Firewall
A program or device that prevents other users on the Internet from browsing or altering the contents of your hard drive through your Internet connection.

2. Under Network Tasks, click View Network Connections.

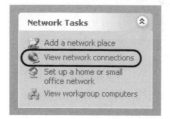

3. Right-click your Internet connection and then choose Properties.

4. In the Properties dialog box, click the Advanced tab.

5. Do one of the following:

❖ If there is a simple check box, mark or clear the check box under Internet Connection Firewall. This is what you'll see if you don't have Service Pack 2 installed:

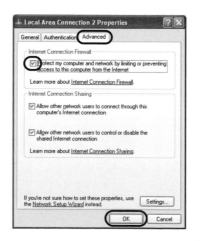

❖ If there is a Settings button, click it to open the Windows Firewall dialog box. This is what you'll see if Service Pack 2 is installed.

Then mark the On or Off option button. You can also explore the other tabs in this dialog box to fine-tune firewall operation if desired. Click OK when finished.

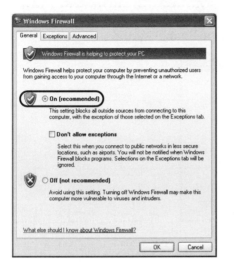

6. Click OK to close the Properties box for the network connection.

Enabling Content Ratings

If you are a parent of minor children who use your PC, you might be concerned about your kids being exposed to adult content online. Internet Explorer provides a content rating feature that can help prevent some of the more obvious smut from reaching your desktop. However, it's not perfect and can't be relied on to filter out 100 percent of the material that you might find objectionable.

Content Advisor works by comparing the settings you choose to the ratings for a particular site. Not all sites have ratings, so you can choose whether you want sites that have no rating to be viewable on your PC. You can also specify a password that can be typed to override the block (so that adults in the household might view sites that the children, who don't know the password, cannot view).

To set up content restrictions:

1. Start in the Internet Options dialog box. You worked with this dialog box earlier in the chapter; open it by choosing Tools ➤ Internet Options from within Internet Explorer or from Control Panel.

NOTE　If you open Internet Options from Control Panel, the dialog box name is different—Internet Properties—but it's the same set of controls.

---

2. On the Content tab, click the Enable button.

3. On the Ratings tab of Content Advisor, set a rating for Language, Nudity, Sex, and Violence. Click a category and then drag the slider bar to choose an acceptable level for it. For example, in the following figure, the Language level is set to Level 2. A description of what that means appears below the slider bar.

4. To block or allow a certain site, type the site's address on the Approved Sites tab and then click Always or Never to set its status. For example, in the next figure, the site www.wempen.com is always viewable, regardless of content, but www.hardcore.com is set to never be visible.

5. On the General tab, do any of the following:

◇ Select or deselect "Users can see sites that have no rating." If this is not marked, all sites without a rating are assumed to be objectionable.

◇ Select or deselect "Supervisor can type a password to allow users to view restricted content."

◇ Set a password by clicking Create Password. (The button becomes Change Password thereafter.)

◇ Find and use other rating systems by clicking Find Rating Systems. (Some systems are free; others require payment.)

6. Click OK to accept the new settings.

7. A box appears, saying that the Content Advisor feature has been enabled. Click OK.

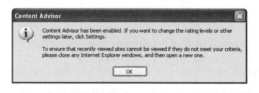

8. Click OK to close the Internet Options box.

Now try to visit some of the sites that are objectionable, to see whether Content Advisor blocks them successfully. If you need to make changes to the settings, reopen the Internet Options dialog box and click the Settings button on the Content tab. To stop using content ratings, click the Disable button on the Content tab.

Setting Mail Controls and Options

Now let's return to Outlook Express, which you learned about in Chapter 18. This e-mail program has several features and options that can make your e-mail management experience easier and more productive. For example, you can create additional folders in which to organize your incoming mail, and create message-handling rules that automatically place incoming messages in these folders. You can also create rules that prevent junk mail from arriving at all.

Organizing Incoming Mail in Folders

You can leave your received e-mail in your Inbox for as long as you like, but the Inbox will eventually become crowded. You therefore might want to create subfolders within your Inbox in which to organize messages that you want to keep around for a while. For example, you could create a folder for each organization you're involved in, a folder for correspondence from family, and a folder for advertisements that you might be interested in looking at when you have time.

To create a new mail folder from Outlook Express:

1. Choose File ➢ New ➢ Folder.

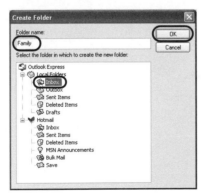

2. In the Create Folder dialog box, type the name for the new folder.

3. Click the Inbox on the dialog box's folder list, assuming you want to create the new folder as a subfolder of the Inbox. Then click OK.

The new folder now appears on the folder list, subordinate to the Inbox. You can move messages to it by dragging them from the Inbox. You can also employ the new folders when creating message handling rules, described in the following section.

Creating Message-Handling Rules

Rules let you specify what should be done to a particular message based on one or more facts about it. Those facts could include who the sender is, what the subject line contains, what size the attachment(s) are, and so on. For example, suppose you belong to an e-mail mailing list called Clean Jokes. You could create a rule that automatically moves any messages addressed to the list into a special folder you have created called Clean Jokes. (See the preceding section to create new mail folders.)

> **NOTE** Rules work only with POP3-type mail accounts. (See Chapter 18 if you need a refresher on mail account types.) They don't work with IMAP or HTTP (Web-based) mail accounts.

To create a message handling rule:

1. Choose Tools ➢ Message Rules ➢ Mail.

2. If the Message Rules dialog box appears, click New.

The New Mail Rule dialog box appears.

If you don't have any rules set up yet, you can skip step 2 because the New Mail Rule dialog box will appear automatically.

3. In the New Mail Rule dialog box, click a check box in the Select the Conditions for Your Rule list to indicate the type of condition you want to set. For example, to base the rule on a particular e-mail address in the Sender field, choose "Where the From line contains people."

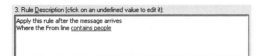

4. In the Rule Description section, click the hyperlink to open a box in which you can specify the condition. For example, here the hyperlink is *contains people*.

5. Clicking the hyperlink in step 4 opens a dialog box. Its exact name depends on the name of the hyperlink you clicked. For example, here it is Select People. Type each value you want to include and then click Add. When you are finished, click OK.

6. Repeat steps 3–5 if needed to place additional criteria in the rule.

7. In the Select the Actions for Your Rule section, click a check box (or more than one) to define what should happen to messages that meet your criteria.

8. Another hyperlink has been added to the Rule Description section, this one for the action you chose. Click that hyperlink. For example, here the new hyperlink is the word *specified*.

9. Click the new hyperlink, and make your selection in the dialog box that appears.

The dialog box content varies depending on the action you chose in step 7. For example, here it is a Move box that enables you to select a folder to move messages to, because I chose Move It to the Specified Folder in step 7. However, if I had chosen something involving people, such as Forward It to People, this hyperlink would open a very differ-ent box.

10. Type a name for the rule in the Name of the Rule text box. For exam-ple, I'll call this one Family Messages.

11. Click OK to create the new rule.

12. The new rule appears in the Message Rules dialog box. Click New to create another rule and return to step 3, click Apply Now to apply the rule to existing messages in the Inbox, or click OK to close the dia-log box.

The rule will be applied automatically to all new incoming messages. To modify or delete a rule later, return to the Message Rules dialog box and use the Remove or Modify buttons there.

Blocking Certain Senders

You can create rules that filter out some of the mail you don't want, as you learned in the preceding section. For example, you could create a rule that would delete all messages with the letters *XXX* in the subject line without having these messages ever appear in your Inbox.

To block the receipt of messages from certain senders, you can create a rule, but you might find it easier to use the Blocked Senders list instead. This list is a bit easier to set up than a rule, and you can quickly add senders to it on the fly. When you block a sender, any mail received from that sender is immediately moved to the Deleted Items folder. The sender doesn't receive any notification of having been blocked.

If the person you want to block has sent you a message already, you can use that message as a basis for blocking further messages, like this:

1. Select the sender's message in your Inbox or any other mail folder.

2. Choose Message ➤ Block Sender.

3. A confirmation appears, asking whether you want to remove all messages from the sender now. Click Yes or No.

Outlook Express

'bernd_heiler@atlas.cz' has been added to your blocked senders list. Subsequent messages from this sender will be blocked.

Would you like to remove all messages from this sender from the current folder now?

[Yes]   [No]

You cannot use Outlook Express to block senders from Web-based (HTTP) e-mail accounts like Hotmail. However, Hotmail offers its own message-blocking service. Go to **www.hotmail.com** to set it up.

4. If you chose Yes, another confirmation box appears. Click OK.

You can also block senders who have not sent you anything yet. When you do it this way, you can block e-mail, newsgroup messages, or both from a sender.

To block any sender:

1. Choose Tools ➢ Message Rules ➢ Blocked Senders List.

2. In the Message Rules dialog box, click Add to open the Add Sender dialog box.

3. In the Add Sender dialog box, type the address in the Address box. You can type either a full address (*something@something*.com) or just a domain name (*something*.com). If you do the latter, Outlook Express will block all messages originating from that domain.

4. Click the option button for the blocking you want: Mail Messages, News Messages, or Mail and News Messages. Then click OK.

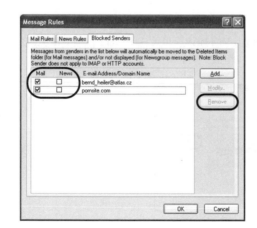

5. Repeat steps 2–4 to block other senders. When you're finished, click OK to close the Message Rules dialog box.

You can make changes to the list of blocked senders at any time. Just display the dialog box again and then select or deselect the check boxes next to each address. To remove an address from the list completely, click it and then click Remove.

Changing the Delivery Schedule

Delivery Schedule
The interval at which Outlook Express connects automatically to your mail server to send and receive e-mail.

The default setting for the **delivery schedule** is 30 minutes, which means that Outlook Express will send and receive mail automatically every 30 minutes as long as you are connected to the Internet. You can change this to any interval you like. You can also specify whether Outlook Express should ask Windows to establish your Internet connection automatically when you are not connected and it's time for a send/receive operation.

To change the delivery schedule, do the following:

1. Choose Tools ➤ Options.

2. On the General tab of the Options dialog box, set the following options:

Play sound when new messages arrive. When enabled, this plays whatever sound is associated with new messages in the Sound scheme. (See Chapter 12.)

Send and receive messages at startup. When enabled, this sends and receives messages each time you start Outlook Express.

Check for new messages every ____ minutes. When enabled, this sends and receives e-mail at the specified interval.

If my computer is not connected at this time. Choose what action to take from this drop-down list. Your choices are "Do not connect," "Connect only when not working **offline**," and "Connect even when working offline."

3. Click OK.

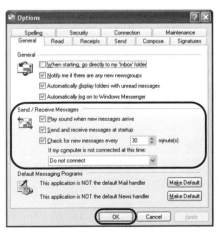

There are many more mail options available in the Options dialog box shown above; explore them on your own whenever you have time.

Offline

Not connected to the Internet. In some programs, including Outlook Express, "working offline" has a specific meaning; it means that you have chosen File ➤ Work Offline to set the program to an offline mode that doesn't prompt you to connect to the Internet.

Part 6

System Maintenance

In this final part of the book, you'll learn how to improve and maintain your Windows XP Home Edition computer. You'll discover some easy-to-use utility programs that can enhance performance and repair errors, and you'll find out how to help Windows recognize new hardware that you install.

System Maintenance

20 Optimizing System Performance

Windows XP includes several utilities that can help make modest improvements in system performance. In this chapter, you will learn about some tools for checking and improving disk operation and for eliminating unwanted files and desktop items.

Checking a Disk for Errors

Disks can sometimes develop errors in the way the files are stored, and those errors can affect system performance. Disk errors sometimes manifest themselves in odd ways. I have seen disk errors cause everything from missing files to out-of-memory errors.

The primary cause of these errors is abnormal program shutdown—in other words, shutting off the computer's power or restarting the system while a program is in use. Unexpected shutdowns aren't always your fault, of course; sometimes a power outage occurs or Windows locks up.

There are two types of errors a disk can have: physical and logical. A *physical error* is a bad spot on the disk, usually caused by physical trauma such as dropping the computer while it's running. A *logical error,* which is much more common, is an error in the **file allocation table (FAT)**. The Check Disk utility in Windows XP can fix both types.

If you are having problems with your PC, it's a good idea to run Check Disk to make sure a disk error is not the root of the problem. You might also run Check Disk every month or so as routine preventive maintenance.

To check a disk for errors, you start from the disk's properties, like this:

1. Choose Start ➤ My Computer.

Earlier versions of Windows included a utility called ScanDisk that performed the same function as Check Disk; it was accessible from the Start ➤ Programs ➤ Accessories ➤ System Tools menu.

File allocation table (FAT)

The organizing table that keeps track of which files are stored in which physical locations on a disk. The term *FAT* has two meanings. Generically, it refers to the organizing table for any disk. FAT16 and FAT32 are also specific file systems for Windows-based computers. The default file system for Windows XP is NTFS.

2. Right-click the disk you want to check, and then choose Properties.

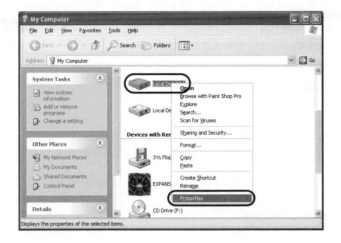

3. A Properties box opens for the disk. Click the Tools tab.

4. Click Check Now.

5. The Check Disk dialog box appears. Mark either or both of the check boxes as desired:

Automatically fix file system errors If you mark this, Check Disk will fix any problems it finds, rather than prompt you about each one. Beginners should mark this; advanced users who are curious about what errors are found should not.

Scan for and attempt recovery of bad sectors   If you mark this, Check Disk will do both a logical and a physical test. Because a physical test takes a long time (an hour or more in some cases) and physical errors are less common, most people turn this option on only occasionally (once every few months or so).

6. Click Start to begin the check.

> **WARNING**   If you see a message that the disk can't be checked now because it requires exclusive access, click Yes to schedule a check the next time you start your PC. Then restart (Start ➢ Turn Off Computer ➢ Restart).

7. If you didn't mark the Automatically Fix File System Errors check box, and if any errors are discovered during the check, a box will appear, asking whether you want to fix them. Click Yes to fix each error.

8. When the check is complete, an information box appears, letting you know. Click OK to close it.

Defragmenting Your Hard Disk

The storage system on a hard disk is not physically sequential. Files are stored in any available physical area, and the file allocation table keeps track of where each piece of each file resides. Then, when Windows calls for a file, it looks up in the FAT the location of the file, or the locations of pieces of the file, and puts the pieces together in memory.

When you initially write a file to disk, it is stored in one contiguous mass; but as you edit the file, the file can become fragmented. For example, suppose you have a hard disk that already has some data on it, and also some empty space. You write a new report, and its file takes up eight contiguous **clusters** on a disk, like this:

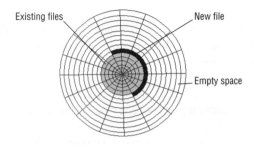

Existing files   New file

Empty space

You then copy some other data to the disk, so that there is no longer any empty space next to the original eight clusters:

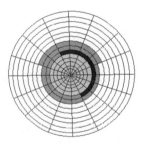

Then you edit your report, adding five clusters' worth of additional text. Where will it be stored? There is no room next to the original file on the disk, so the additional data is stored in some other empty area. Now the file is **fragmented**:

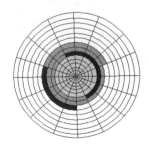

Cluster

A unit of organization on a hard disk. The disk is divided into sectors and clusters, each with a unique identifier in the file allocation table. For example, imagine a large wall of post office boxes, each with its own number. Each cluster is like a box, into which you can store data.

Fragmented

Not stored in a single, contiguous area.

389

As you can imagine, it takes longer to open a fragmented file than an unfragmented one, because the disk's read/write head must hop around on the disk, picking up the pieces of the file. That's why *defragmenting* a drive can improve its performance. Defragmenting a drive rearranges the files stored on it so that each file is stored in a single, contiguous area.

> **WARNING** Defragmenting takes a long time (an hour or more), so you might want to begin it before you go to bed or to go out for the evening and let the program run while you are away.

> **WARNING** Disable your screensaver and antivirus program before running the defragmenter, to minimize restarts due to disk changes.

To defragment a disk, do the following:

1. Choose Start ➣ All Programs ➣ Accessories ➣ System Tools ➣ Disk Defragmenter.

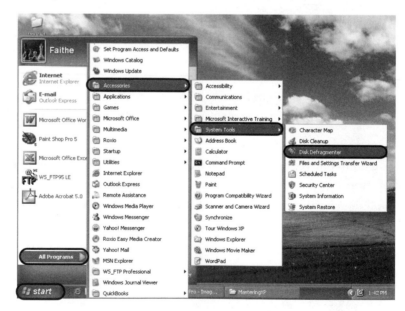

Or you can open the properties for the drive, as you did in the preceding section, and click Defragment Now on the Tools tab.

2. Select the drive you want to defragment. Then do one of the following:

⬥ Click Defragment to start defragmenting the drive now. Then skip to step 4.

⬥ Click Analyze to check how badly the drive needs to be defragmented.

3. If you chose Analyze in step 2, a dialog box appears momentarily with a recommendation. Do one of the following:

◆ Click Defragment if defragmenting is recommended.

◆ Click View Report if you are interested in the statistics. Then click Defragment or Close after examining them.

◆ Click Close to close the dialog box without defragmenting that drive. You can then return to step 2 to select another drive.

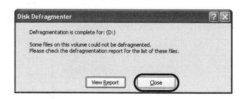

4. Wait for the drive to be defragmented. It can take hours, depending on the drive size, processor speed, and amount of free space left on the disk. When defragmentation is complete, a message appears; click Close.

WARNING You can continue to use your computer while it defragments, but usage may cause the defragmenter to restart frequently, increasing the overall time required.

Disk Defragmenter

Defragmentation is complete for: (D:)

Some files on this volume could not be defragmented.
Please check the defragmentation report for the list of these files.

View Report   Close

5. Return to step 2 to select another drive, or close Disk Defragmenter.

Cleaning Out Unwanted Files

Windows XP has two utilities for cleaning up your system. Disk Cleanup finds and deletes unnecessary files from your hard disk, freeing up overall disk space, and the Desktop Cleanup Wizard eliminates unused shortcut icons from your desktop. Let's look at each utility separately.

Deleting Files with Disk Cleanup

Disk Cleanup recommends certain files for deletion, to help you free up space on your hard disk. It might recommend, for example, that you empty your Recycle Bin, delete temporary Internet files, and delete some leftover **temporary files** from your word processing program.

There are two ways to start Disk Cleanup. The first way goes through the menu system:

1. Choose Start ➤ All Programs ➤ Accessories ➤ System Tools ➤ Disk Cleanup.

2. A dialog box appears, asking you to select the drive you want to clean up; do so and click OK.

Continue at step 3.

Temporary files

As a program operates, it sometimes creates temporary files, like scrap pieces of paper on which it jots down notes. When the program exits, these files are deleted automatically. However, if the program terminates abnormally, due to locking up or losing power, for example, the temporary files remain on your hard disk, taking up space.

The second way goes through My Computer:

1. Choose Start ➤ My Computer. Right-click the drive you want to clean up and then choose Properties.

2. In the Properties dialog box, click Disk Cleanup.

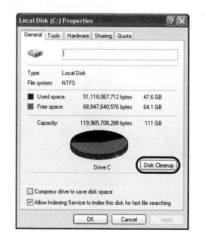

3. In the Disk Cleanup dialog box, a report appears for the chosen drive, showing what files Windows thinks can be safely deleted. Mark or clear the check box for each category of files that Windows presents.

For some file categories listed in the Disk Cleanup box, a View Files button appears. You can click it to see which files will be included in the deletion. Not all categories offer this.

4. After making your selections, click OK.

5. A warning box appears. Click Yes to confirm.

The files are deleted, and the Disk Cleanup dialog box closes.

Tidying Up with the Desktop Cleanup Wizard

Whereas Disk Cleanup actually frees up space on your drive, Desktop Cleanup doesn't delete anything. Instead, it takes icons on your desktop that are unused and moves them to a folder, reducing the clutter on your desktop.

Every 60 days, a reminder appears in your system tray prompting you to run Desktop Cleanup. If you see such a reminder, you can click it to run the program. Otherwise, do the following to start Desktop Cleanup:

1. Right-click the desktop and choose Properties.

How did those unused icons get on the desktop in the first place? Well, many programs that you install place icons for themselves there automatically. Also, at some point, you may have accidentally dragged icons from a file management window to the desktop.

2. Click the Desktop tab. Then click Customize Desktop.

3. On the General tab of the Desktop Items dialog box, click Clean Desktop Now.

4. The Desktop Cleanup Wizard starts. Click Next to continue.

5. On the Shortcuts screen, mark or clear the check boxes for each desktop shortcut. Next to each shortcut is the date on which it was last used; items that have never been used are marked by default. Then click Next.

6. A confirmation appears. Click Finish.

7. Close all open dialog boxes.

A new folder icon now appears on your desktop called Unused Desktop Shortcuts. It contains the removed icons. At any time, you can open this folder and drag one of the icons out to the desktop again.

21

Safeguarding and Troubleshooting

• •

You don't have to be an expert Windows user to encounter minor system problems. These days, simply reading an e-mail attachment or installing a new program can be enough to send a computer into a funk. In this chapter, you'll learn how to protect yourself from computer viruses and how to prevent new programs you install from wreaking havoc on your system. You'll also learn how to get help from a friend over a network or the Internet by using a brand-new feature in Windows XP called Remote Assistance.

Virus
A small, usually hidden program that damages a computer and/or replicates and spreads itself.

Protecting Your PC from Viruses

Windows XP doesn't include antivirus software. There is no built-in utility that identifies and removes **viruses**. However, Windows XP does have some security measures built into it that can help prevent a virus from taking hold of your PC. For example, Outlook Express usually detects an e-mail attachment containing a .vbs (Visual Basic Script) extension—a favorite distribution mechanism for virus creators—and blocks the script from running.

The virus protections are all turned on by default, so there is nothing special you need to do in order to enable virus protection. However, to make sure your PC remains free from viruses in the future, consider taking these steps:

❖ Purchase and install a full antivirus program such as McAfee VirusScan or Norton AntiVirus. You can get free trial versions at the vendors' Web sites (www.mcafee.com and www.symantec.com, respectively).

❖ Watch for the warning signs of virus infection: odd messages on your screen, decreased system performance, inability to access your hard drive, and missing data files. If you suspect a virus, run an antivirus program.

❖ Make sure you update Windows regularly, using either AutoUpdate or Windows Update, as you learned in Chapter 6. Often these updates will include security patches for Internet Explorer and/or Outlook Express.

❖ Don't open e-mail attachments from people you don't know. Even when an attachment comes from someone known to you, examine it carefully first. For example, look for a .vbs extension on an attachment. A file like *filename*.jpg.vbs is almost certainly a virus trying to look like a graphics file.

Saving Your Windows Configuration

The perfect time to think about system troubleshooting is when the PC is working well. Yes, you heard that right. When your PC is working exactly as it should, you can take a "snapshot" of the system. This snapshot includes a backup of critical Windows configuration files, such as the Registry. Then later, if you are having problems because the Registry has been damaged or you have installed a new program that has introduced errors, you can restore your system to the snapshot's configuration.

The feature that handles this functionality is called System Restore. It was also included with Windows ME. One of the best uses for System Restore is to back up your configuration right before you do something you aren't sure about, such as install a new, untested program on your PC.

Here's how to use System Restore to take a snapshot of your current configuration:

1. Choose Start ➢ All Programs ➢ Accessories ➢ System Tools ➢ System Restore.

2. In the Welcome box that appears, click Create a Restore Point and then click Next.

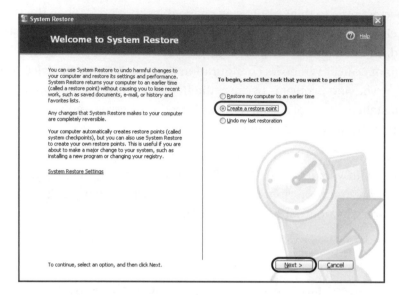

3. Type a description for the restore point. This can be anything that will help jog your memory. For example, if you are creating a restore point as a precaution before you install a certain new program, you might call it "Before Install." Then click Create.

TIP You don't need to include a date in the description because System Restore will automatically save today's date along with the description.

4. Click Close to exit System Restore.

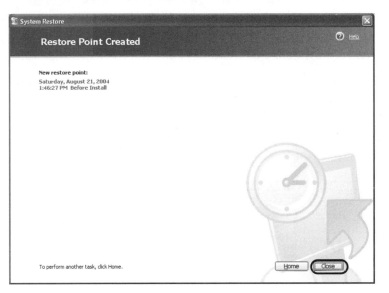

Restoring a Previous Windows Configuration

If your system is starting to have problems, such as error messages, inability to start normally, or lockups, and you just installed some new program or changed a system setting, you are probably wishing you had never done it! Fortunately, System Restore can help you go back in time, restoring your configuration files to the condition they were in before the unfortunate incident.

System Restore saves a **system checkpoint** every day automatically, so even if you haven't manually created a configuration snapshot (see the preceding section), you should still be able to back up to the previous day's configuration, at a minimum.

System checkpoint
A configuration snapshot taken automatically by the System Restore program.

When you go back to a previous configuration, you don't lose any data files, but Windows loses its recollection of any programs that were installed since that configuration snapshot was taken. Let's look at an example. Suppose you took a system snapshot this morning. Then you installed Microsoft Word and created a Word document. Then you installed a game that caused problems with your display. You decide to use System Restore to load the snapshot you took. After doing so, Word is no longer installed in Windows, but the Word document you created is still there. You can then reinstall Word.

To restore your system to an earlier configuration, do the following:

1. Close all open programs.

2. Choose Start ➢ All Programs ➢ Accessories ➢ System Tools ➢ System Restore.

3. Leave Restore My Computer to an Earlier Time selected, and click Next.

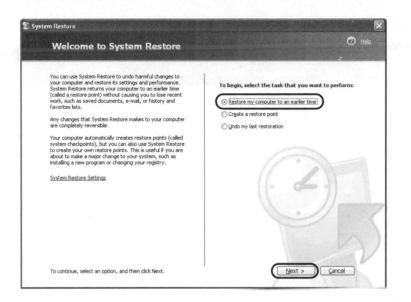

4. On the calendar that appears, click the date of the restore point you want to use. Dates containing restore points appear in boldface. Some dates have more than one restore point.

5. On the list to the right of the calendar, click the restore point you want. Then click Next.

6. A confirmation screen appears. Click Next.

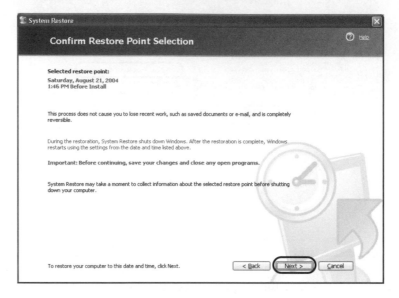

7. Your PC restarts itself. When Windows comes back up, a confirmation box appears. Click OK to close it.

Your system is now restored to the chosen configuration. If that solved your problem, great. If it introduced even more problems, you can always reverse the System Restore process. To do so, restart System Restore and choose Undo My Last Restoration.

Loading the Last Known Good Configuration

If you can't start Windows at all, you can't use System Restore to correct a problem. If that's your situation, you can use the *Last Known Good Configuration* feature of Windows startup to load the most recent backup copy of the Registry.

To start using the Last Known Good Configuration:

1. As your PC is starting, press the F8 key. The Windows Advanced Options Menu appears.

NOTE If you see the Windows XP Home Edition opening screen, you missed the window of opportunity. Try to press F8 as soon as possible after you see the video card and drive information on-screen.

2. Use the Up or Down arrow key to select Last Known Good Configuration. Then press Enter.

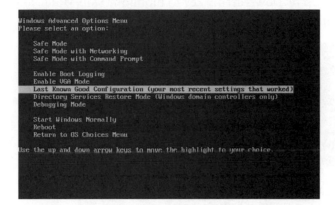

Your PC should start normally. Any system changes you made since the last time you started the PC are lost, so if you installed programs, for example, you will need to reinstall them. (Any data files you have created will still be there, however.)

Starting in Safe Mode

If a problem with your PC is preventing it from starting normally, and the Last Known Good Configuration hasn't solved the problem (see the preceding section), you might be able to solve it by starting up in Safe mode. Safe mode is a troubleshooting mode in which only a minimal set of drivers are loaded. You don't have access to your CD-ROM, modem, sound card, or any other nonessential components in Safe mode, and it uses a generic video driver rather than the one for your specific card. That's because one of those drivers might be causing the problem.

Starting up in Safe mode doesn't correct a problem by itself; it merely enables you to start the PC when you otherwise cannot. From there, you can remove a driver that might be causing a problem, adjust system settings, or do whatever is needed to fix the problem. (Beginners might need help from a Windows-savvy friend to do this.)

To start the PC in Safe mode:

1. As the computer is starting, press the F8 key. This opens the Windows Advanced Options Menu.

2. Press the Up or Down arrow key to highlight Safe Mode, and then press Enter.

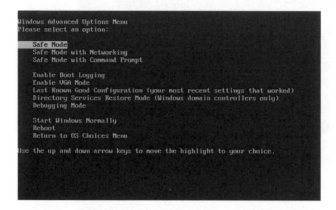

3. Depending on your system configuration, another screen might appear at this point, as shown here. Press Enter again to move past it.

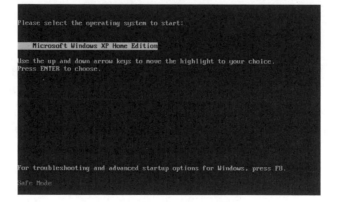

4. Wait for your PC to start. It might take a lot longer than normal because Safe mode doesn't use any memory management features. If you are prompted to log in, do so.

5. A message appears, explaining that Windows is running in Safe mode. Click Yes.

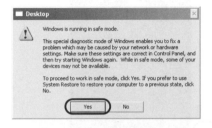

Safe mode uses no background pattern or picture, and the words *Safe Mode* appear in all four corners. This is so you will not forget that you are in Safe mode and will not try to work normally.

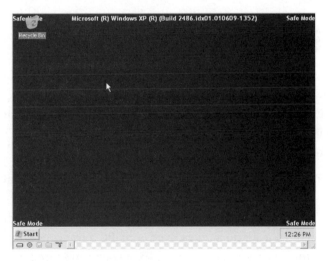

6. Take whatever steps are necessary to correct the problem that has prevented your PC from starting normally. For example, if the screen was garbled, reinstall the video driver. Consult the help system or work with a technical expert if needed.

7. Restart the PC by choosing Start ➤ Turn Off Computer.

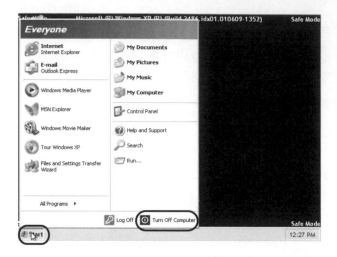

8. Choose Restart. Your PC restarts.

Requesting Remote Assistance

If you cannot figure out what's wrong with your computer, the Remote Assistance feature, new in Windows XP, can enable you to ask a friend or colleague to help. There's nothing new about getting help from others, but Remote Assistance allows them to take control of your PC across a network or the Internet, without actually being seated at your PC.

Here's how it works. You send a Remote Assistance request via e-mail to somebody else. Let's call that person "Expert." Expert responds to it, and a message appears on your PC asking permission for them to take control of your PC. If you assent to it, Expert takes over your PC's operation, and your screen appears on their screen in a window. Expert can then make any system adjustments needed to help you correct your problem.

Sending a Remote Assistance Request

To get help, send a request to someone who you think has the expertise to be able to help you. You can make contact by using either e-mail or Windows Messenger.

1. Choose Start ➤ Help and Support.

2. Click "Invite a friend to connect to your computer with Remote Assistance."

3. Click "Invite someone to help you."

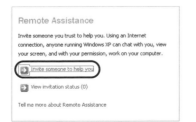

4. Do one of the following:

◆ To get help from a Windows Messenger contact, click the contact and then click "Invite this person."

If you see a message that the person is offline and it offers to send an e-mail invitation, click OK; or click Cancel and then enter the person's e-mail address in the Type an E-Mail Address box (shown in the second figure that follows).

◆ To invite someone—not necessarily a Windows Messenger contact—via e-mail, enter the e-mail address in the Type an E-Mail Address box and then click "Invite this person."

5. Enter your name in the From box if it doesn't already appear there. Enter text in the Message area that describes the problem you are having. Then click Continue.

Remote Assistance - E-mail an Invitation

Provide contact information

Instructions on how to use Remote Assistance are automatically attached to this invitation. Please type a personal message that includes the best way to contact you while the invitation is open, and a brief description of the computer problem.

From (the name you would like to appear on the invitation):

Faithe

Message:

Hi Sheldon, I am having some problems with my video driver. Can you help?

Continue >

6. Set an expiration duration for the invitation. This minimizes the chances of some unauthorized person finding the invitation and using it to gain access to your PC.

7. If you want to add a password to the invitation, type it in the Type Password box, and repeat it in the Confirm Password box. You must then let the recipient know in some other way what the password is. (You might telephone, for example.)

8. Click Send Invitation.

Remote Assistance - E-mail an Invitation

Set the invitation to expire

To lessen the chance that someone fraudulently gains access to your computer you can limit the time in which a recipient can accept a Remote Assistance invitation. Specify the duration that this invitation will remain open.

01 ⌄   Hours ⌄

☑ **Require the recipient to use a password**

For security reasons, it is strongly recommended that you set a password that the recipient must use to connect to your computer. Do not use your network or Windows logon password.

Type password: Confirm password:

●●●●●●   ●●●●●●

Important You must communicate the password to the recipient.

Send Invitation

If you chose to send an invitation via e-mail, a message appears, saying that the request has been sent successfully, and you are done.

> **WARNING** You might need to open your e-mail program and do a send/receive operation before the message will be sent.

> **NOTE** If you chose to send the request to an offline Windows Messenger recipient, a box appears, asking whether you would like to save the request as a file. Windows cannot automatically send the request for you in this case; you must save it as a file and then attach that file to an e-mail message.

What now? Wait for the recipient to respond. See the following section.

Responding to a Remote Assistance Request

So, what if you're on the other end of the equation—what if you're the expert? If someone sends you a Remote Assistance request, here's how to handle it:

1. Open the e-mail containing the request and then double-click the attachment.

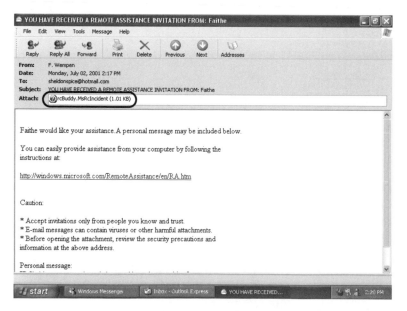

2. Click Open It and then click OK.

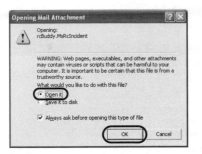

3. A Remote Assistance dialog box appears. Enter the password (if a password prompt appears) and then click Yes.

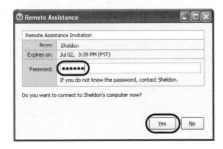

4. Wait for the person at the other end to authorize your connection to their PC by clicking Yes. On their screen, it looks like this:

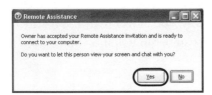

After the requester has authorized you, their PC's screen appears in your Remote Assistance window, like this:

Remote computer's screen

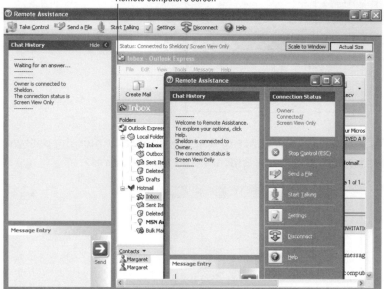

Chatting with Remote Assistance

On both screens, there is a Chat History pane while the two of you are connected. You can chat with the other person by typing your commands and clicking Send. Your contact can do the same. In this way, you can convey the nature of the problem you are having, so that the person can begin helping you troubleshoot it.

Taking Control of a Remote PC

Say you're the expert being asked for help, and you've used the Chat feature to determine what's wrong with the requester's PC. Now you're ready to take control of the PC to fix the problem:

1. In the Remote Assistance window, click Take Control .

At this point, a box appears on the other PC, asking whether it's okay that you take control. It looks like this:

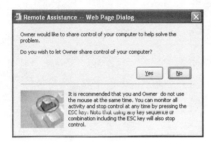

The other user must click Yes before you can take control.

2. Back on your PC, a confirmation box appears. Click OK.

3. Control the remote PC using the right-hand pane in the Remote Assistance window. You can use the Start menu, Control Panel, or any other tools needed; you have complete access.

> **TIP** Can't see the whole screen at once? You can use the scroll bars in the Remote Assistance window to move around, or click the Scale to Window button to force the display to fit in the pane, as shown here.

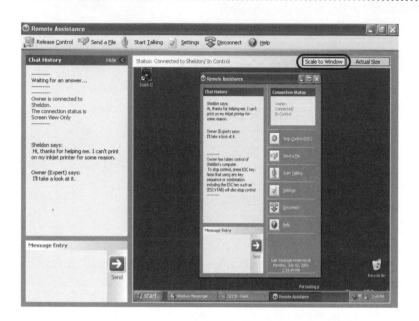

4. When you are ready to return control to the remote user, press the Esc key or click the Release Control button 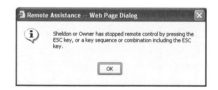.

5. A confirmation box appears. Click OK. (This box appears on both PCs; each user must click OK to clear it.)

6. When you are finished, close the Remote Assistance window.

Configuring Security Settings

If you have Service Pack 2 installed for Windows XP, you have access to a Security Center icon in Control Panel. From here, you can make sure your system is set up for the Windows Firewall, for automatic updates, and for virus protection.

Follow these steps to check your security settings:

1. Choose Start ➤ Control Panel.

2. Click Security Center. The Windows Security Center window opens.

3. If one of the three items is off, a Recommendations button appears below it. Click the Recommendations button.

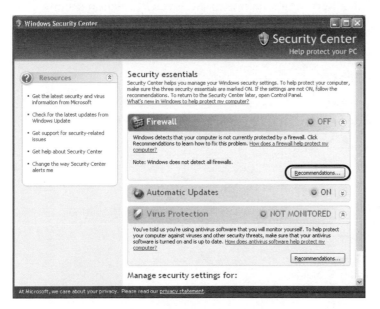

If the Firewall or Automatic Updates is off:

4. In the Recommendation window, click Enable Now.

5. A confirmation box appears; click Close.

6. Click OK.

If the Antivirus is off, it means that Windows cannot detect your antivirus program. If you have an antivirus program that Windows does not see, do the following:

7. Click Recommendations in the Virus Protection section.

8. Mark the I Have an Antivirus Program That I'll Monitor Myself check box.

9. Click OK.

10. Close the Security Center window when you are finished.

You can configure the Windows Firewall for each connection individually. To do this, open the Network Connections window (from Control Panel). Right-click the connection and choose Properties. On the Advanced tab, click Settings. This opens the Windows Firewall dialog box for that connection. Most of the settings there are fairly specialized, though, so you should not need to do this for most connection types.

22 Installing New Hardware

At some point, you might want to buy and install some new hardware—perhaps a better sound card, an additional hard drive, or a home networking kit. After following the directions to install the device physically, you must then set it up in Windows. Fortunately, Windows XP's Plug and Play feature is very good, and it almost always detects new devices flawlessly. In this chapter, you'll learn about Plug and Play and what to do if Windows does *not* detect your device automatically for some reason.

Hardware

A physical computer-based device, such as the keyboard, monitor, scanner, printer, and modem. The opposite of hardware is *software*, which is the computer's programs and which exists only as data bits.

USB

Stands for Universal Serial Bus. A hassle-free, high-speed interface found on most computers made in the last few years. USB requires Windows 95 OSR2, Windows 98, or higher.

Tips for Physically Installing New Hardware

When you buy a new piece of **hardware**, it probably comes with very good installation instructions, so follow those rather than trying to go on your own. Here are a few general tips, however:

❖ Many devices sold today, such as printers, scanners, mice, and keyboards, are available with a **USB** interface. If your computer has a USB port, look for USB devices. You can plug in new USB devices without turning off your computer, and Windows's Plug and Play works especially well with USB. (You must turn the computer off for all other types of installs and removals.)

❖ Before purchasing a device, check the Hardware Compatibility List (HCL) at the Microsoft Web site (www.microsoft.com/hcl) to make sure Windows XP will support the device. Most devices will work with Windows XP using manufacturer-supplied drivers, but if Windows XP directly supports a device, you won't have to use the Setup disk that came with the device to install a driver; Windows will configure it automatically.

❖ Look for the Windows XP logo on the boxes when shopping in stores. Only devices on the HCL can have this logo on their boxes. If you can't find a model you want that's XP-certified, look for one that's Windows 2000–compatible; most Windows 2000 drivers will also work in Windows XP. You can download a Windows XP driver from the manufacturer's Web site when they release one.

Device Detection with Plug and Play

When you plug in a new USB device for the first time, or when you turn on your PC after having installed some other type of new device, Windows will probably detect it automatically. A message will flash on-screen about locating the new device and installing the drivers for it, and then it'll be over. Blink, and you'll miss it. The new device is installed.

With some devices, a bubble will appear over the system tray, letting you know that the new device has been installed.

At that point, you can start using the new device! Yes, it's that simple. If it doesn't work, read the following section to figure out why.

Troubleshooting a Newly Installed Device

Let's say that you've plugged in your new device and turned on the PC, but nothing happens. Now what?

Does Windows Recognize the Device?

Maybe Windows was simply so good at installing the device that you didn't realize it was happening. So first, you should check to see whether Windows recognizes the device already. Here's how:

1. Try to use the device, according to the instructions that came with it. If it works, great. You're done.

Instead of step 2, you can choose System from Control Panel if you prefer.

2. If the device doesn't appear to be working, click Start; then right-click My Computer and choose Properties from the shortcut menu.

3. In the System Properties dialog box, click the Hardware tab and then click Device Manager.

4. In the Device Manager window, look for the device on the list. Click the plus sign next to a category to open it. If the device appears on the list, it is installed correctly, at least as far as Windows is concerned. If you can't find it, Windows hasn't seen it yet.

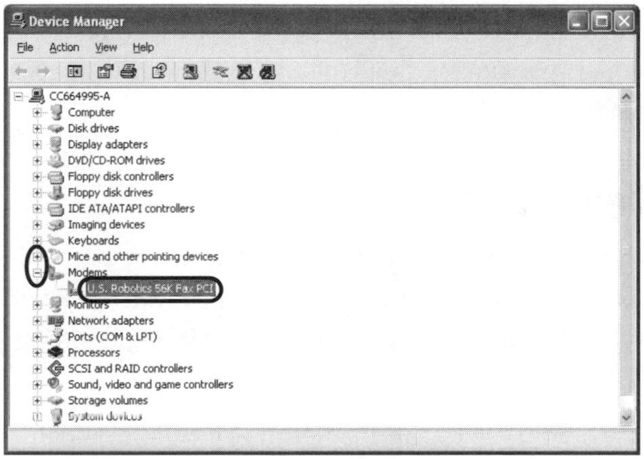

5. As a further check of the device, double-click it. A Properties box appears for it. The Device Status should read, "The device is working properly," as shown in the next figure.

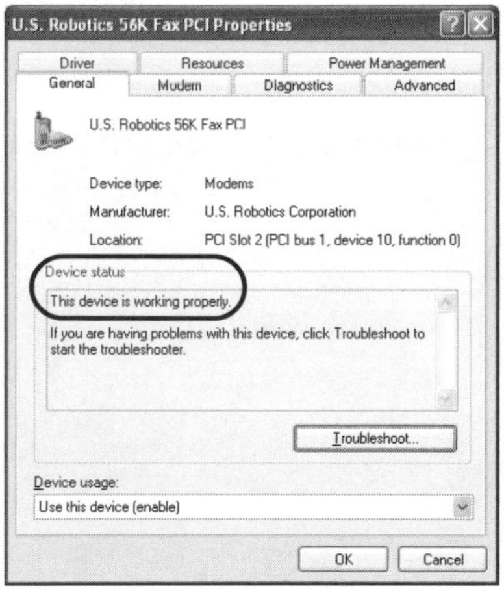

6. Do one of the following:

❖ If Windows reports that the device is working properly but in reality it doesn't work, click the Troubleshoot button and work through the prompts.

❖ If Windows reports that the drivers for the device aren't installed, run the Setup program that came with the device (probably on a CD-ROM).

If Windows Doesn't See the Device...

If the device doesn't appear in the Device Manager (see the preceding section), Windows has not been able to recognize it automatically. If it's a very old device, it might not be Plug and Play–compatible. Or it might simply not have been detected.

The first thing you should try is to run the Setup program that came with the device, on the CD-ROM or floppy. If you don't have a Setup disk, try downloading a Setup program from the device manufacturer's Web site. Only if both of those activities fail should you continue with the following steps.

To install drivers for a device that Windows doesn't automatically see, and that doesn't have a Setup program on disk, you can use the Add New Hardware Wizard:

1. Click Start; then right-click My Computer and choose Properties from the shortcut menu.

2. Click the Hardware tab and then click Add Hardware Wizard.

3. In the Add Hardware Wizard's Welcome screen, click Next.

Instead of steps 1 and 2, you can choose Add New Hardware from Control Panel if you prefer.

4. Follow the prompts to have Windows look for your new hardware and install drivers for it if possible. (The exact steps depend on what hardware it finds.)

Still No Luck?

If you continue to have problems with a piece of hardware, here are some additional suggestions:

- ❖ Restart the PC and then check the device again.

- ❖ Shut off the PC entirely, and also the device (if external). Wait 20 seconds or so and then turn both back on and try again.

◆ Check the physical connection of the device to your PC; make sure all plugs and circuit cards are firmly seated.

◆ Check the documentation that came with the device. Perhaps a special installation procedure is necessary. For example, some printers can be detected by Windows automatically, but in order for them to work correctly, you must also run the Setup program that came with them on disk.

◆ If the device appears in the Device Manager but reports a problem, try deleting it from there (select it and press Delete) and then restarting your PC. Windows will try to redetect the device at startup, and it might work correctly that time.

◆ Look in the documentation for a toll-free technical-support telephone number for the device's manufacturer. The people who staff the phones at these companies are experts in making their particular products work, and they can help you determine whether there is a physical defect with the device.

Index

Note to the reader: Throughout this index **boldfaced** page numbers indicate primary discussions of a topic. *Italicized* page numbers indicate illustrations.

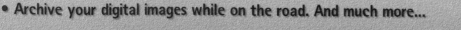